Exposed

Tragedy & Triumph in Mountain Climbing

Brad R. McQueen

With Melissa C. McQueen

BOWER HOUSE

DENVER

www.BowerHouseBooks.com

Designed by D.K. Luraas
Cover photography courtesy of Tim Brogan
Chapter icon by Todd McQueen

Printed in Canada

Library of Congress Control Number: 2015930777

Paperback ISBN: 978-1-55566-459-6

10 9 8 7 6 5 4 3

To my father and favorite climbing partner,
Rich McQueen

and to my amazing wife,
Melissa

Contents

Swiss Cheese and Mountaineering

In fields such as aviation, engineering, and health care, managers sometimes design controls and assess failures using something called the Swiss cheese model. The Swiss cheese model views processes, systems, and controls as being slices of Swiss cheese stacked on top of each other. The holes in the Swiss cheese represent weaknesses in that particular process, system, or control, such that something bad could happen. The idea is to make sure that the holes in the Swiss cheese never line up with each other, which would allow something bad to get through all of the various checks and balances and lead to a failure or accident. In aviation, this could be a plane crash. In engineering, it could be a bridge collapse. In healthcare, it could be a patient dying.

In the mountaineering world, there are many "slices of Swiss cheese" as well. Some things are within our control, such as wearing the proper clothing, having the proper equipment, the time we start a hike or climb, our selection of hiking companions (either human or canine), and our selection of our destination and route. Other things are outside of our control, including the weather, snow conditions, health conditions we may have, and other people climbing above or below us that day. Each of us makes a series of decisions and judgments about what we will need and whether our capabilities are appropriate for our route selection. We also make judgments about the weather and snow conditions based on forecasts and reports we read. We gauge the skill level of our climbing companions and others on the mountain. Assuming we get at least some of our decisions right and make judgments that prove to be true, the holes in the Swiss cheese won't line up and we can generally stay safe in the mountains.

But occasionally, the holes line up and something bad happens ...

CHAPTER 1

Nice Day for a Hike

I rolled over to look at my lovely wife of just over a year and said to her, "We can't fall asleep. If we do, we might not wake up." Then I proceeded to roll back over and close my eyes. I so desperately wanted to sleep—and I probably would have. My wife saved my life that night.

We learned afterward that it had gotten down to 10 degrees Fahrenheit where we lay at an elevation of over 11,500 feet that night of Sunday, May 20, 2001. It had been a beautiful late spring day down in Denver, Colorado, where we live. One of my co-workers shared with me his recollection of that day, "Oh, I remember that day well. I was at an outdoor wedding early in the day and had gotten sunburned. By late afternoon, I was shoveling snow!" According to examiner.com (in describing significant weather events over the years), it had been quite a weather day in Colorado:

> In 2001 ... damaging winds developed behind a vigorous cold front that moved south from Wyoming into metro Denver. High winds ... gusting to 58 mph at Denver International Airport. ... downed trees and power lines and kicked up blowing dust ... dirt ... and debris ... reducing the visibility to near zero at times. The poor visibility caused a multi-vehicle accident along U.S. Highway 85 north of Fort Lupton. Six people were treated for minor injuries. Several vehicles ... including semi-trailers ... were blown off I-70 east of Denver. About 32 thousand Xcel Energy customers in metro Denver were without electricity for up to 2 hours. At least a dozen incoming flights at Denver International Airport were diverted to other airports. All departing flights were grounded for at least an hour. At Southwest Plaza ... shoppers were evacuated as rocks holding a tarp on a portion of a roof under repair toppled into the mall. After the passage of the cold front ... temperatures plunged from

the lower 70s to the mid 30s in one hour as light snow developed. Heavy snow developed in the foothills during the evening.
Peak wind reports included 68 mph near Parker and 63 mph near
Sedalia. Snowfall totals included: 7 inches near Blackhawk ... at
Ken Caryl Ranch ... and near Sedalia; 6 inches in Coal Creek Canyon ... at Eldorado Springs ... and atop Lookout Mountain; 5 inches
at Chief Hosa ... in Louisville ... Rollinsville ... and Wheat Ridge; and
4 inches in Aurora ... Bailey ... Parker ... Castle Rock and near Mor-
rison. Low temperature of 31 degrees during the early morning of
the 21st equaled the record low for the date last set in 1931.

The rapidly changing weather was an inconvenience for people in Denver (and for people trying to land airplanes in Denver), but for us, it was life
threatening. My wife, Melissa, our one-year-old golden retriever, Malcolm,
and I had for weeks been planning (okay—Malcolm wasn't much help on the
planning) a late spring 14er hike (slang for climbing one of Colorado's fifty-
four peaks reaching 14,000 feet or more above sea level). We had originally
planned our hike for Monday, May 21, but saw in the weather forecast that
a late spring storm was predicted. We decided to move our hike up a day to
Sunday to be on the safe side. When we moved the hike from our planned
Monday outing to Sunday instead, my father, Rich, decided to join us as well.
We planned to climb 14,264-foot Mt. Evans, the behemoth that dominates
the view 36 miles from Denver to the west, from the Guanella Pass trailhead—a round trip hike of 9 miles with 3,100 feet of elevation gain.

By the age of twenty-seven, I had climbed sixteen of the fifty-four Colorado 14ers, including Mt. Evans once before and its southwestern neighbor, 14,060-foot Mt. Bierstadt, twice (once in the summer before traversing the "Sawtooth Ridge," a jagged Class 3 ridge connecting Mt. Evans and
Mt. Bierstadt, and once on Valentine's Day of 1999 in my first winter 14er
ascent). My dad, then fifty, had climbed eight of the 14ers with me, including
a winter ascent of 14,265-foot Quandary Peak three days after Christmas in
1999. Melissa, also twenty-seven, had three 14er summits under her belt—
Mt. Massive, Mt. Yale, and Mt. Sherman (with Malcolm the dog joining us
on Sherman). So ... we weren't rookies, but we still had *a lot* to learn about
the mountains.

We were excited to get outside and begin the summer with a nice hike.
Melissa had just wrapped up her final exams in her Master's program the
week before and we had the whole summer ahead of us now. We opted for a
sunrise start on the morning of May 20. The theory behind such an early start
is to give yourself time to climb the difficult upper sections of a mountain in

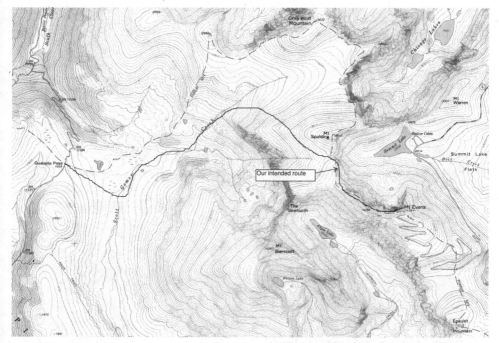

Mt. Evans, Mt. Bierstadt, and Mt. Spalding from Guanella Pass with our planned route shown.

the daylight with enough time to safely descend before dark. On some longer approaches or more difficult climbs, climbers use "alpine starts," which begin hours before sunrise or even in the middle of the night. Mt. Evans isn't a technically difficult mountain, nor is a nine-mile round trip hike particularly long, so we were merely getting a sunrise start to live by the golden rule of climbing 14ers in Colorado—be off the summit by noon to avoid the dangerous afternoon thunderstorms, which tend to move across Colorado's mountains from the west almost daily.

The approach to the summit of Mt. Evans from the Guanella Pass trailhead initially follows the standard approach for climbing Mt. Bierstadt. That means crossing an area known as "the willows"—an area burned into the memory of anyone who has climbed Mt. Bierstadt. Hundreds of Coloradans every summer weekend set out to climb Mt. Bierstadt, many trying to reach their first 14er summit. Many have an initially pleasant surprise when they begin "climbing" their first 14er and find the trail sloping slightly downhill out of the parking lot for the first mile. They must be thinking in that first mile, "This isn't so hard! I can do this all day long!" But what goes down must eventually come back up when it comes to climbing mountains …

Melissa, Malcolm, and I ready to begin.

The willows are really a massive swamp where Mt. Bierstadt and Mt. Evans drain their western slopes every year. The trail weaves through the willows and alternates fairly evenly between mud and wooden boardwalks that have been installed over the years. After descending that first mile from Guanella Pass, the route to Mt. Evans takes you to the northeast just before crossing a creek that marks the bottom of the willows. This was our route on May 20—across the pattern of spring snow and still frozen mud of the trail through the willows and into the broad drainage north of the Sawtooth Ridge.

The morning was crisp, clear, and characteristically calm with no wind. High above us, the massive Sawtooth Ridge dominated our view to the east and blocked out the early morning sun. We were all dressed in layers for warmth and were moving along pretty well that morning. Given that this was our first hike of the season, we were taking it slow and steady, stopping for snacks and water periodically as we worked our way up the drainage. At about 13,200 feet, I made the initial mistake that began the slow deterioration from our nice day hike into an overnight adventure that would nearly cost us our lives (and did cost Melissa dearly).

The Guanella Pass route up Mt. Evans gets very little use and with the winter snows still stubbornly clinging to the mountainside, there was no obvious trail for us to follow. It was also still a week before Memorial Day, the commonly accepted start of summer in the Rockies, so we were the only hikers on our route that morning. At 13,200 feet, the route to Mt. Evans contours southeast across the slopes of 13,842-foot Mt. Spalding. Unfortunately, rather than traversing to the right, I continued to lead us straight uphill toward Mt. Spalding's summit.

Slowly and steadily we continued up the rounded west shoulder and reached Mt. Spalding's summit around 10:00 a.m. Mt. Spalding is itself a worthy destination as one of Colorado's "Centennial Thirteeners" (meaning the group of peaks from 13,800 to 13,999 feet, and when added to the fifty-four peaks over 14,000 feet, get you to the tallest 113 peaks in Colorado). We could have called it a day at that point after having the traditional summit snack. But I'm a fairly driven person once I've set a goal—we had set out to climb Mt. Evans, it was still early in the day with the weather still nice, and we were all feeling good, so we continued on.

And then I made a second mistake—this one a *very big one.*

Melissa, my dad Rich, and Malcolm on the "trail."

CHAPTER 2

A Road!

We had another chance to get down that day even though we had missed the 13,200-foot traverse to the right toward the northwest ridge of Mt. Evans. From the summit of Mt. Spalding, we could have descended 250 vertical feet south from Mt. Spalding's summit to a saddle, then climbed 400 vertical feet onto the northwest ridge of Mt. Evans, putting us back on route with just under a mile to go to reach Mt. Evans' summit.

I still can't quite get my head around this—I was clearly not thinking properly at 13,800 feet that day—but I proceeded to lead us down the *east* ridge of Mt. Spalding. I distinctly remember that I was looking across to the east at a mountain that I was sure was Mt. Evans. I thought, "Wow, that's a bigger loss of elevation than I was expecting here," but down we went nonetheless. I now know that I was looking across to the east at Mt. Warren, some 500 feet below us at 13,307 feet. How I looked at a mountain 500 feet shorter than the one we were standing on and thought it was Mt. Evans, I just don't know.

Descending Spalding's east ridge would have actually been kind of fun under different circumstances. It was rugged and rocky in many places, but with solid hand- and footholds. Yes, it would have been fun indeed were it not for Malcolm, the eighty pound golden retriever, needing some guidance and coaxing to negotiate some of the steeper places. It was nothing that we or the dog couldn't handle—it just took some time (a precious commodity we would run out of later in the day).

As we descended the ridge, the lake far below us on the right hand side was getting larger. We saw that there was a road that went right by the lake and we thought that was odd. We continued down to the saddle by the lake and began climbing Mt. Warren (which I was convinced was Mt. Evans). We had not yet gone far along the ridge toward Mt. Warren when a glint of light high above us caught Melissa's eye as she turned to gauge our progress. She pointed to something high up on the ridge to the south of us and said,

Mt. Spalding and our descent route to Summit Lake.

"What's that?" My dad and I both looked up and were horrified when we realized what it was—the Mt. Evans observatory on the summit of the mountain we were supposed to be climbing. We had just descended 1,000 vertical feet and then climbed another 100 vertical feet in the wrong direction. We now found ourselves above the Summit Lake trailhead and the Mt. Evans road. We hurriedly changed directions and descended back down to the road.

The summit of Mt. Evans as seen from Summit Lake.

The Mt. Evans road is the highest paved road in North America and is a popular tourist attraction in Colorado since it provides access to within a hundred feet of the summit of a 14,000-foot mountain by car. The road is opened each year around Memorial Day and generally stays open until Labor Day. Opening the road is no small task; snowdrifts that can be 10 feet tall form across the road every winter. It was a week before Memorial Day in 2001 when we found ourselves standing beside the road, and it was not yet opened. We were all alone up there and had our first sense of fear. Melissa did notice an emergency phone by the side of the road and we briefly considered calling for help, but decided that it was still reasonably early in the day with the weather appearing to be holding just fine.

Melissa and Malcolm on the Mt. Evans road.

Once it sunk in where we were, we had a brief strategy session. We were 4.5 miles from our car and had two choices—we could climb back up the 1,000 feet to the top of Mt. Spalding and head down from there or we could climb 1,400 feet to the top of Mt. Evans and head down from there. Either way, we had to climb to get back to our car. We were a little concerned about Malcolm's ability to climb back up Mt. Spalding since he had struggled a bit on the way down. We decided we might as well climb Mt. Evans since we had to climb either way and we thought, let's just follow the road at this point—we know it takes us to the top and it will be easier to walk on the road.

So off we headed up the Mt. Evans road, feeling cautiously optimistic since we finally knew exactly where we were and had a solid plan to get back to our car. The time was around 11:00 a.m., so we thought we still had plenty of time. None of us had ever driven up the Mt. Evans road, however, and we failed to appreciate that we were at mile 23 of a road that runs 28 miles to the summit. In hindsight, it makes perfect sense that a road built for cars will have a much more gradual slope than a hiking trail. After traversing southeast across from Summit Lake for over a mile, the road then transitions into a series of fourteen significant switchbacks in the final 4 miles as it weaves its way up the more gentle southeast slope to the summit.

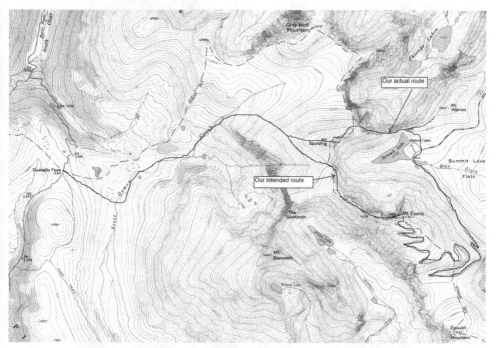

Our actual ascent route to the summit of Mt. Evans.

As we hiked the 5 miles up the road to the summit, we were beginning to fatigue and our sense of concern was building. Even the dog was asking for breaks more often! Finally, at 3:00 p.m. with 9.5 miles of hiking under our belts, we reached the summit of Mt. Evans. There is a saying that mountains should be climbed in thirds. This means using one-third of your energy on the ascent, one-third on the descent, and saving one-third in reserve just in case something bad happens. When we reached the summit of Mt. Evans that day, we were relieved, but also exhausted, having used easily two-thirds to three-quarters of our energy just to get to the top. It was a little scary to realize that we were only halfway done with the hike.

Exhausted on the summit of Mt. Evans.

CHAPTER 3

Descent

When bad weather moves into Colorado, it usually comes from the west across the Rockies. On summer weekends, many a climber can be seen looking to the west to determine if the current weather is likely to be soon replaced by lightning, rain, or hail. When we finally got to the summit that afternoon, we had our first glimpse back to the west in several hours. We didn't like what we saw, either to the west or to the north (both of which had been obscured for the last couple of hours by the Mt. Evans massif).

Bad weather moving in above Mt. Spalding.

The sky to the north and west had turned dark and the storm was moving in, once again proving that weather forecasting in Colorado is far from an exact science (this was the storm that was supposed to arrive the following day—the reason we had moved our trip from Monday to Sunday). We knew we needed to get down and we were racing against both the storm and the clock at this point. After a short rest and one of the least fulfilling summit snacks I've ever had, we set off across Evans' west ridge, back toward Guanella Pass, our car, and safety. It's funny how obvious the trail is when looking down on it from above—"How could we have missed such an obvious trail?" we wondered.

The west ridge is about a mile long and consists of large broken slabs and talus. The trail generally consists of picking the best path across, between and over the slabs. In that mile on the ridge, you only lose about 300 feet of elevation (compared to what I usually think of as about an average of 1,000 vertical feet per mile when climbing in the Colorado Rockies). Normally a more gradual slope would be a nice change, especially for tired knees that take the brunt of a normal descent. Today, however, we needed to get down—*quickly*.

Malcolm the dog didn't understand that the weather was moving in toward us, but he did understand that he was pretty tired. He was trying his best to keep up with us two-legged folk (not generally an issue for our four-legged friends), but he was having difficulty moving from block to block across the ridge. We were not about to leave our beloved dog behind (although at least my dad and I remember having thoughts of leaving the dog behind before quickly dismissing them), so my dad used his MacGyver-like mind to come up with a solution. He was carrying a cheap poncho in his daypack (similar to the heavy-duty plastic bag that Disney sold me for $18 when it began to rain at Disney World one year, except without the mouse ears). He took out his knife and sliced the poncho in two. When the dog came to places he could not negotiate, Dad and I put poncho strips underneath the dog, one in front and one in back, and used them to lift our eighty-pound friend between the slabs. Again, it was terrain we could negotiate—the problem was that it just took time.

As we climbed across the final quarter mile of the west ridge, the clouds turned black and the snow started. Malcolm and I started to pull away from Melissa and my dad, having to wait for them on occasion. Thankfully, there was no lightning that afternoon as we were still at 13,800 feet, thousands of vertical feet above the nearest trees. The rocks became wet and slippery as we made our way off the ridge back toward the drainage we had climbed early that morning. The vast majority of accidents in the mountains happen on the way down. It is somewhat counterintuitive at first—downhill should be the easy part, right? It is true that gravity is on your side on the way down, but several other things are working against you including fatigue, extended time at altitude, and a natural sense of relief upon reaching the summit that causes you to drop your guard. We were fortunate to get off of the west ridge and its now slippery rocks without anyone slipping and twisting an ankle or knee, but we still had a long way to go.

The snow starts as we descend Mt. Evans' west ridge.

And we did let our guard down. We all felt a huge sense of relief when we were off the ridge and back on Mt. Spalding's gentle west shoulder. We genuinely thought that the worst was behind us and even stopped to sit down and have a snack break (a shortage of food and water was not our issue—we had brought plenty). That morning, we had been walking on top of the snow because it was still frozen from the night before, but now the snow was softer from melting in the sun all day. Punching through a layer of snow on top into softer snow below is something known as "post-holing" and it is one of the most exhausting experiences that hikers can have. The windblown surface layer of snow is crusty and teases you into thinking it will hold you—right up to the point where you fully weight that leg. Then the top layer collapses and down you go into the deeper, softer snow below.

We were post-holing through snow easily up to our knees and beyond. The dog and I were moving much faster than Melissa and Dad. Each time I stopped to wait for them, Malcolm was trying to dig a nest in the snow to go to sleep. I remember thinking this was odd and being more than a little bit concerned that the dog was ready to dig a hole, crawl in, and call it a day. I actually took my fleece vest off and put it on Malcolm to try to keep him warm. When he and Melissa caught up, Dad suggested that it might be best if we dug a cave in the snow and settled in as it was snowing harder and harder. Melissa recalls that her initial reaction was that he was joking; she still thought we would get off the mountain that day. At my urging, she and Dad tried to pick up their pace, but they were so tired that they started stumbling and falling, which slowed down their pace even more. I was becoming frustrated.

I continued to coax them (at times not so gently) that we *had* to keep moving. It was 5:30 p.m. now and we had only another two hours of daylight. Deep down, we all knew that we needed to move down as quickly as we could, but we couldn't get our bodies to cooperate. It was slow going. Through the falling snow, we could see the faint outline of some trees below us that marked the transition back into the willows. We kept telling ourselves that if we could just get back down to the trees, we would be okay.

When we reached the trees at the bottom of the drainage, we were relieved—but it proved to be short-lived. We found what looked like an obvious trail, so we thought we were home free. All we had to do was follow the trail down through the trees and across the valley of willows to the car. We started talking about a pizza place we were going to go to for dinner and Melissa kept saying that she was going to go get a manicure and pedicure the next day to reward herself. I actually commented about how beautiful it was with the snow coming down through the trees.

With the clock at 7:00 p.m. now, it had been snowing steadily for three hours with several inches of accumulation. We knew that my white Subaru Outback was parked no more than a mile and a half away at the Guanella Pass trailhead. The only thing standing between us and the car was the famous Bierstadt willows. Unfortunately, that obvious trail that we were on through the trees simply vanished, replaced by the vast expanse of willows. We felt our sense of optimism replaced by sheer dread. The main Mt. Bierstadt trail was south of us at this point, so we headed in that general direction.

The willows are a terrible place to be without a trail. They are extremely dense shrubs and are 4 to 6 feet tall in this area. You can pick your way through them for a while and even convince yourself that you have found a trail—especially when the ground is snow covered as it was that afternoon. But the willows love to shatter dreams. I am convinced that all "trails" through the willows lead to one thing—water. The whole area is a swamp after all!

Our experience in the willows that evening was *extremely* frustrating.

Our car—and safety—was so, so close and we simply couldn't find our way out. On most any other mountain, you could literally crawl the last half-mile back to your car if you had to, even in the dark, but not through these dreadful willows. The dog and I were in the lead as we sought a way out of this treacherous place. I found a promising looking clearing and was able to walk across the top of the snow. The dog and I stopped again to wait for Melissa and my dad. Dad was following in my footsteps and was thus quite surprised when the snow he was walking across gave out. He yelled to us that he was in the creek. He found himself up to his waist in *very* chilly water that was running beneath the recently collapsed spring snow bridge. He was able to climb back out of the hole, but being drenched from the waist down added another challenge to our day hike gone wrong. As he pulled himself out, Melissa dropped to her hands and knees in an attempt to better distribute her weight and started to crawl across a few feet from where my dad had tried to cross. But her efforts were only partially successful and her feet eventually punched through the snow and into the creek. Since she was crawling, she was able to pull her feet out quickly, but the water had filled her boots, soaking her socks.

I must have weakened the snow bridge just enough with my weight (I outweigh my father by about ten pounds and Melissa by sixty-five pounds). Now we were really in trouble—it was a near whiteout, we were cold, tired, and lost, and two of the three of us were wet—not a good combination.

We continued floundering around looking for a way out of the willows until 8:30 that night. Every break in the willows that we tried led to either more willows or more water. It was almost dark now, none of us had a headlamp with us, and the realization that we were not going home today hit us like a punch to the stomach. We were scared. Even if we had carried cell phones (which we hadn't in 2001), they would not have worked because most places in the backcountry still have no service. From high on a ridge you might get service, but down in a valley, you are generally out of luck.

Our focus turned toward staying as dry as we possibly could during the night, which meant trying to climb out of the swamp we were in. At one point, the snow let up enough that we could see a patch of good-sized pine trees not far away up on a slight hill. We thought the trees could provide us some shelter and surely the slight hill they were on meant drier ground. We quickly made the decision as a group that this was where we would hunker down for the night, and began fighting our way through the last willows that stood between us and our makeshift 11,500-foot camping spot for the night.

As we climbed the small hill to the clump of trees, I felt some relief and the peace of mind that comes from making decisions. When you are making decisions, even tough decisions with a lack of clarity as to the outcome,

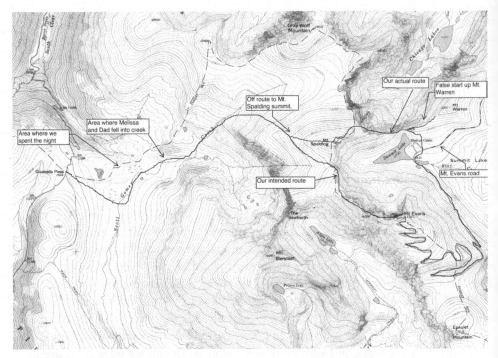

Locations of our missteps.

it feels as if you are somehow more in control of your situation. I had no idea how the decision to bivouac (a term for improvised and/or unplanned camping—"bivy" for short) for the night would play out, but I think we all knew that getting more and more wet trying to get out of the willows in the dark was not going to end well. Once we had made the decision to bivy, our next concern was to maximize our warmth during the coming night.

Our first attempt at nighttime warmth was naturally trying to make a fire. I had wandered the aisles at REI enough times by now without anything specific on my shopping list that I had all sorts of cool stuff in my pack, including storm-proof matches and an emergency strobe-light beacon. Matches!!! Perfect!!! I had sort of missed the part about needing something to light with my storm-proof matches, however. The matches lit just as advertised, but the little bit of tinder we could gather up nearby was soaking wet from all the snow, and it would not light despite our best efforts. We finally resorted to pulling the money out of our wallets, figuring it was our best chance of getting a small fire going that might dry out some pine needles and things. Unfortunately, even our money was too damp to light on fire. We were out of luck in the warmth department. I turned on the emergency strobe-light beacon and hung it from a branch on a tree. One thing my mother wisely insisted on when I first started hiking was that I always tell someone where I was going and when I could be expected back. We had told my mother of our plans and knew that she would make the call to search and rescue if needed. We hoped the strobe-light beacon might help them find us that night. On a clear night it might have, but tonight was a whiteout.

My dad was getting very cold in his wet cotton jeans, themselves a no-no in the mountains since cotton doesn't dry out nearly as quickly as synthetic materials. As the temperature continued to drop, his pants were literally freezing and we knew that he needed to get out of them. One good decision that I had made on this train-wreck of a day was throwing an extra polypropylene long underwear bottom into my fanny pack. Melissa had wisely brought a spare pair of wool socks in hers. This little bit of spare clothing would likely be the difference between life and death for my father that night.

I recalled from some sixth-grade outdoor education trip a few tidbits about hypothermia and I knew that we were prime candidates for it right now. Hypothermia is basically a condition where the body is unable to maintain that magical 98.6-degree temperature that we've been told since childhood was "normal." Our bodies have to produce heat to counteract being outside in the cold weather. Walking, hiking, or climbing helps generate that heat. When we stop moving, we stop generating as much heat to counteract the cold. Wet clothing is a big drain on heat from our bodies, so one of those sixth-grade things that came to mind was—when in danger of hypothermia, get out of wet clothing. This made good sense to us in our exhausted state, so we focused on getting my dad out of his wet clothes. He took off his boots, then his wet jeans and replaced them with my spare long underwear bottoms. His socks were soaking wet, too, so he removed those and put on Melissa's spare dry wool socks. Putting his boots back on at that point was a daunting task with cold fingers, so he opted to go without.

By the time my dad was in warmer, dry clothes, Malcolm the dog had dug himself that burrow he had been longing for since the upper slopes of Mt. Spalding, and had curled up and gone to sleep. He even had the nerve to snore.

Not too long after, Melissa realized that her boots and wet socks were freezing to her feet. Applying the same logic of "get wet clothes off," we decided to take Melissa's boots off. Her bootlaces were frozen and wouldn't untie, so we would have to cut them off. Dad handed me his knife and I cut the laces. Just as we suspected, her socks were soaked. Now we had a problem. We had brought one extra pair of socks and those were already in use. Time for another big mistake. "Get wet clothes off" had become my new life purpose and the socks came off. We thought the best option would be for her to put her feet up my shirt to keep them warm. We tried that for a while, but she was too tired to hold them there. Plus, this was letting cold air up my shirt and causing me to get much colder. We put her wool ski-cap over her feet and tucked them between my legs. Her gloves were also frozen, but she found a quick solution for that. She took them off, pulled her arms in her jacket and tucked her hands in her armpits. This made any movement very difficult.

Now that we weren't moving anymore, I began to realize how cold my feet were. With my thinking distorted by hypothermia, I looked at my boots and saw that they were also quite wet from tromping through the snow all day and reentering the always damp willows. I tried to take off my boots, too, but the laces were frozen and wouldn't budge. I could have cut them off, but they were brand new laces from a recent REI walkabout and I'm a pretty cheap guy—it seemed a shame to cut them. So I kept my boots on and got ready for the longest night of my life.

It was at this point that I rolled over and imparted my last piece of sixth-grade hypothermia wisdom—"We can't fall asleep. If we do, we might not wake up." Then I rolled over and closed my eyes.

CHAPTER 4

How Did We Get Here?

Lying on the ground that night, I asked myself over and over again—How can this be happening? How did we get here?

Growing up in Colorado, I didn't give the mountains a whole lot of thought—they were just always there. My parents taught me directions as a kid by teaching me that the mountains were always west. To this day, my father still hates downtown Denver because he can't see the mountains to figure out which direction is which. Both Melissa's and my family spent plenty of time in the mountains when we were kids. My grandfather had a cabin on a trout-fishing lake near Kenosha Pass. We spent a few long weekends up there fishing every summer and even got to go up a few times in the winter for snowmobiling. I learned very early in life that the mountains were a special place with immense natural beauty. We also took family camping trips every summer, which generally involved biblical rains and leaky tents, but with quality family time.

One of our family camping trips took us through Glenwood Springs, where I did the first hike that I can remember—Hanging Lake. My parents now fondly recall (as opposed to the panic they felt at the time) me sprinting off ahead of them on the 1.2-mile hike up 1,000 vertical feet to the beautiful lake and waterfall that awaited at the top. They stopped each person coming downhill and asked them whether they had seen a young boy heading up and felt relieved when each person said, "Oh yes, we saw him a few minutes ago—quite a little mountain goat you've got!"

I started putting my "mountain goat" skills to work for real after I graduated from college, beginning with basic hikes in the Lost Creek Wilderness and other areas of the Front Range of the Colorado Rockies. I soon found myself flipping through my guidebooks, scanning the difficulty ratings of the hikes, quickly dismissing anything with an "easy" or "medium" rating. One day, a hike of Missouri Gulch (rated at "difficult") caught my eye because it said that if you continued up to the end of the trail, you could climb one of Colorado's 14,000-foot mountains.

As fate would have it, in the summer of 1998, I caught a viral strain of conjunctivitis (or by its common name—"pink eye"). Bacterial pink eye is easy to treat with drops and is gone within a day or two, but I had a viral strain requiring steroid drops and the sheer passage of time to heal. My father kindly (but as it turns out unwisely) volunteered to drive me to an early doctor's appointment. I naturally thanked him for his kindness by passing along this highly contagious virus to him so that he, too, could enjoy it. Afterward, we were pretty well quarantined together to prevent others from getting this nasty viral strain. After a week, our symptoms were nearly gone, but the doctors weren't ready to release us back to our normal lives just yet, so Dad and I decided we might as well go for a hike. I showed him the Missouri Gulch hike in my guidebook and off we went.

By the time I was twenty-four years old and three years out of college, Dad and I honestly hadn't spent all that much time together. He was in the Air Force and stationed in Abilene, Texas, when I was born, so he traveled a ton when I was a baby. Dad was honorably discharged from the Air Force when I was two, but then started working two jobs back in Denver, where he and my mom were both from, to keep food on the table and a roof over our heads. In 1982, my dad fell from an icy roof trying to investigate a claim for the insurance company he worked for, landing on and crushing his heel and ankle in the twenty-foot fall. A morphine drip helped to manage the pain, but the damage was done. His ankle had to be fused, rendering it motionless. In 1984, he was diagnosed with cancer and was undergoing chemotherapy because it had spread to other parts of his body. His motto was "Stay Alive in '85" after my mom told him that he was not allowed to die and leave her alone with two teenage boys. As a kid of eight or ten years old at the time, I knew that these things were going on and recognized that I was spending far more time than normal with my grandparents, but I can honestly say that I had no appreciation for how hard that time in my parents' life must have been for them.

By the time he was through the cancer and could afford to give up the second job, I was a teenager and didn't think either of my parents knew anything about anything. Soon I was in college and working as a bank teller, slowly realizing that my parents were pretty darn good people. I remember finally coming to this realization sometime toward the end of my accounting degree at Metropolitan State College of Denver; I told my dad I wanted to be more helpful around the house by starting to mow the lawn and things like that. He graciously thanked me, but told me that I was busier than he was at the moment and asked me to keep focusing on my studies. After college, I started working at a large public accounting firm, Arthur Andersen, doing financial statement audits and working quite a bit myself. The viral pink eye in 1998 was one of the first real breaks I had from work after three long busy seasons in the world of public accounting. I was anxious to get outside and spend some quality time with my dad.

Like Mt. Bierstadt, the Missouri Gulch trail begins with a short downhill stretch as a cruel early confidence builder. After crossing a bridge over a creek, one's confidence quickly wanes as the trail begins to climb steeply up the hill in switchback after switchback after switchback … these relentless switchbacks are as memorable to hikers on this trail as the willows are to those who climb Mt. Bierstadt from Guanella Pass. We took breaks periodically as we worked our way up into Missouri Gulch, usually for my father to lie down in the meadow to carefully photograph one of the many beautiful alpine flowers. These were the days before digital cameras, so my father had to carefully set up each shot—he had *only* brought six rolls of film after all—a mere 150 or so exposures! He used every one of them that day.

Soon the trees were below us as we reached the upper portion of Missouri Gulch, and we took the left-hand fork in the trail that led to Mt. Belford, a 14,197-foot peak in the Sawatch Range of the Rockies. Neither of us

Dad setting off up Missouri Gulch toward Mt. Belford.

had ever been up to this elevation before. We had heard it was a bit harder to breathe as you climbed and quickly validated this with our own huffing and puffing. But up we went, slowly and surely. At around 2:00 p.m. on Wednesday, July 15, 1998, we finally reached the rocky summit area of our first 14,000-foot mountain. It was absolutely amazing! Being up so high, we had a 360-degree view of the surrounding mountains, with ribbons of early summer snow still clinging to the steep slopes and deep ravines. The lower valleys were a vivid green and we felt as if we could see forever! This "summit feeling" was now definitely in our blood.

We knew that there were a lot of 14,000-foot mountains in Colorado, but that was about the extent of our knowledge. We celebrated our success all the way down the mountain, our arms growing tired from patting each other and ourselves on the back, and told ourselves that Mt. Belford *must* be one of the

Me high up on Mt. Belford's slopes.

most difficult of all the Colorado mountains. We weren't cleared to go back to work until the following Monday, so I still had a couple more days off to recover from the pink eye. That next morning, I rushed to a bookstore to try to find a book about Colorado's 14ers in order to validate our feeling that we had just climbed the hardest one. I located Gerry Roach's excellent book, *Colorado's Fourteeners—From Hikes to Climbs*, and anxiously flipped the pages to locate Mt. Belford. I was *crushed* as I read his description of the Belford Group of 14ers—"The high, gentle mass of Belford and Oxford requires little more than a sturdy pair of legs, while more rugged

Missouri offers a choice of technical routes." Gentle mass? Nothing more than
a sturdy pair of legs? You must be kidding! That mountain ate us alive!

Despite my disappointment, I bought the book (the now seventeen-year-
old copy sitting in front of me as I type this morning is tattered, worn, and
filled with notes from over the years) and phoned my dad to break the news
to him that there were tougher mountains out there after all. He had already
done some homework of his own and learned from some friends that we
hadn't actually done the "easiest" 14er either. Apparently Grays Peak and
Torreys Peak, standing side by side about an hour west of Denver, were the
ones you were supposed to climb first. It didn't take us long to agree that we
should climb those on the upcoming Saturday, just three days after our Mt.
Belford climb. My dad went to work on
my mother, Susie, explaining to her that
it would be a shame for any Colorado native to not experience the view from the
top of one of Colorado's highest peaks.
My mother hates heights, but reluctantly
agreed to join us for this outing on Saturday. My mom's only condition to my father was that he hike with her, no matter
how slow she might be; he agreed (I was
not a party to the agreement, however).

Saturday arrived and up we went,
driving up the rough but passable road
to the Stevens Gulch trailhead. Back in
1998, climbing 14ers was not as popular as it is now and we were able to get
a parking spot at the trailhead (nearly
impossible on a summer weekend now).
Off we went as a trio, my mother wearing the soon-to-be famous "orange hat,"
which was a large-brimmed canvas sun-
hat only slightly less orange than the jer-
seys worn at home by the Denver Broncos. The only thing missing was a cord to
be placed under the chin to prevent the
massive hat from invoking its sail-like
properties in high wind. It was quite a
hat and proved memorable to everyone
on the trail that day.

My mom and I starting up the
Grays Peak trail.

The trail is wide and well worn as it climbs up into the alpine meadow below these twin peaks. It didn't take me long to realize why my mother had set forth her condition of my father staying with her no matter how slow she was—it turned out she was quite slow. Patience is not something I am particularly known for today and I assure you I have learned to be *much* more patient in the last seventeen years. In 1998, this slow pace was driving me crazy, so I left my hiking partner from Wednesday behind with the woman in the orange hat (not to be confused with the man in the yellow hat who accompanies Curious George). We agreed I'd meet back up with them later on the mountain, or at the very least, back at the car after the hike.

I was intrigued by the other people on the trail that day. There were people like me in their twenties, older people like my parents, a few families with kids, and *really* old people that could have been my grandparents. Mostly I focused on the young women in their twenties, though (I did not meet Melissa until Labor Day weekend 1998, so I was still an eligible bachelor), talking to a few as I passed by. The trail up 14,270-foot Grays Peak switchbacks up through some far less-famous willows, then flattens out for a stretch while rounding the corner below 13,164-foot Kelso Mountain before climbing again up into the basin below 14,267-foot Torreys Peak. From the basin, the trail gets steeper as it climbs south onto Grays' broad shoulder. The fragile alpine tundra through which the trail weaves eventually gives way to dirt and rock as the trail switches back up the face of Grays.

I reached the top more easily this time and again felt that rush of joy that comes from achieving a goal and being able to take in the picturesque view from the summit. I had a snack on the summit and waited to see if my parents might be close behind me. After fifteen or twenty minutes, my patience quotient was again at capacity, so I joined another group that was setting off down toward the saddle between Grays and Torreys. The descent down the northwest ridge of Grays to the 13,707-foot saddle is straightforward. From the saddle, the trail heads up the south slopes of Torreys, with an occasional switchback to regain the roughly 600 vertical feet necessary to reach the much smaller summit area of Torreys Peak. After climbing Torreys Peak and logging my third 14er in three days, I headed down the standard trail back toward the car.

As I descended from the saddle back across the face of Grays, I checked all of the uphill climbers for orange hats—none. That meant that my parents were either above me on the upper flanks of the Grays trail or they had turned back and were already waiting for me at the car. I hoped it was the former, but I hustled down the trail just in case it was the latter. There was no sign of the woman in the orange hat in the trailhead parking lot, so I took off my hiking boots, donned my more comfortable sandals, and began to wait. And I waited. Then I waited some more. Hours were passing. I began to survey the other hikers who were returning to the trailhead, "Did you happen to see a woman in an orange hat up there?" The answers were coming back nearly identical, "Oh yes! We were on the summit of Grays with them. They are heading down, but they are moving *very slowly.*" I was glad to hear that Mom and Dad had reached the summit, but I was also anxious to go home.

At one point I got bored enough that I started back up the trail in my sandals. It was mid-afternoon by now and I got many disapproving looks from well-intentioned climbers returning from the summit. (The same look I have given to others who, in my opinion, are starting up a mountain too late in the day—remember the golden rule, off the summit by noon—or do not have the proper attire—sandals??? Come on!) With each disapproving look, I inquired as to the woman in the orange hat and the disapproving looks softened as the now friendly people updated me on my mother's slow but steady progress down the mountain. Finally, my parents reached the trailhead after summiting Grays Peak (they did not go over to Torreys as I had) and my mother declared that she would never do that again! It had been a nine and a half hour roundtrip hike just to and from the summit of Grays Peak versus a pretty standard summer roundtrip time for *both* peaks of six to seven hours.

My mom on the summit of Grays Peak, her first and only 14er.

It is not commonly known, but there are three types of fun. There are things that are fun while you're doing them. There are things that are fun when they're over. And there are things that are not fun at all. My father and I were finding that hiking 14ers was fun while we were doing it. My mother looks back now and says she is glad she climbed a 14er, but she has kept her word that she will never do it again. For her, it was fun when it was over.

I was now cured from the conjunctivitis, but I had caught a fever … summit fever. Three weeks later, I was back for more 14er fun. I decided to do another mountain in the Front Range called Mt. Bierstadt, and depending on how it looked, possibly go across something called the "Sawtooth" ridge that led over to Mt. Evans. The combination was rated as "Class 3." Most of Colorado's high peaks are rated as Class 1 or Class 2, meaning the trail is well worn and reasonably easy to follow. Climbs can be rated as Class 3 for a variety of reasons, but generally Class 3 involves using both your hands and feet to scramble up steeper rocks that might also have some exposure or fall potential. Class 4 climbing enters the arena of "technical climbing" where there are a handful of moves that are difficult and exposed. Class 5 (and beyond, using a decimal system 5.1, 5.2, etc.) is technical rock climbing that generally involves the use of ropes, placement of equipment called protection, or using existing bolts in the rock in the case of sport climbing.

The solo climb up Mt. Bierstadt was uneventful, and on the summit I met another solo climber who had parked on the Mt. Evans road, descended, and then climbed Bierstadt's rugged east ridge. He planned to go across the Sawtooth, then climb Mt. Evans and return to his car a bit farther down the road. I told him I was also thinking about doing the Sawtooth over to Mt. Evans, but that I had never done any Class 3 climbing before. I asked if it was okay if I tagged along with him across the Sawtooth and he agreed. I quite enjoyed the Class 3 scrambling across the ridge and learned about route finding through the use of small piles of rocks called "cairns" that mark the way. The Sawtooth has significant exposure once you cross over to the west side and many climbers have met their demise over the years trying to cross it when it is wet or after having gotten off route. Thankfully, it was a clear, warm August day and the ridge was dry.

After negotiating the Sawtooth, we moved onto easier ground and began the mile-long traverse across Evans' high west ridge to the summit. I must admit that I was very sad when my new friend bid me farewell and walked down the road a short distance to his car. The thought briefly crossed my mind of asking him for a ride down the 28-mile Mt. Evans road and up to Georgetown and on to the summit of Guanella Pass 13 miles out of town.

Wisely, I decided we weren't that good of friends just yet and I didn't ask (he might still be laughing if I had!).

Instead, I set off alone back to the west toward my car on Guanella Pass. I descended down the same drainage below Mt. Spalding that I would later climb with Melissa and my dad on that fateful day in May 2001. When I got to the bottom, I got my first real taste of those willows, fighting my way through them to get back to the main Mt. Bierstadt trail. Frustrated by all of the dead ends I encountered, I eventually resorted to wading the creek just to get out of them! It was the first time I learned firsthand that water that was snow not long before is *cold* water. I eventually found my way out of the creek, out of the willows, and back onto the main trail. I was wet, muddy, scratched, and bloody when I popped out on the main trail, much to the surprise of a few Bierstadt hikers, but I was happy to have two more 14ers under my belt, including my first solo climb and my first Class 3 experience.

The following weekend, I climbed another peak with a group of friends—this time La Plata Peak at 14,336 feet and my peak count was at six. My future wife picked me up in a bar three weeks later over Labor Day weekend and I hung up my hiking boots for the year. I'm so happy my attempt at dancing didn't scare her off. Instead, she just said, "Okay, if I'm going to continue to be attracted to you, we can't dance anymore. Let's go outside and talk." Good call.

In February 1999, a colleague at work who had done almost all of the 14ers asked me if I wanted to accompany him up Mt. Bierstadt on snowshoes on Valentine's Day. I don't think he had any romantic intentions, but I made sure he knew that I had to be back in time for a date that night with my girlfriend all the same. He loaned me a pair of snowshoes and across the Bierstadt willows we went over the snow. We stashed the snowshoes on the shoulder and continued on to the summit for my first winter 14er summit—it was even more beautiful than in the summer, looking out across countless miles of snow-covered peaks. Melissa and I had a lovely Valentine's Day dinner that evening and I was already thinking of how cool it would be if she would climb a mountain with me that summer of 1999.

For Melissa, the mountains meant family time and skiing. Her grandparents had a condo in beautiful Snowmass, Colorado, where they would frequently gather. It was crowded when all of her aunts and uncles and cousins were there, but they enjoyed the time together nonetheless. She hadn't done much hiking or camping, but was young, fit, and willing to give it a try for me. We chose the Fourth of July 1999 as the date for our first hike. I studied my Roach guidebook, trying to find a good mountain for us to try. We settled on Mt. Massive, the second highest peak in the state at 14,421 feet. I gave Melissa the choice of which route she wanted to follow—the 13.4-mile, 4,400 vertical foot standard/easiest route or the 6.2-mile, 3,950 vertical foot route that is shorter, but much steeper. Before I had even finished my sentence, she chose the shorter route.

That Independence Day morning we drove up the dirt road, past the trailhead for the standard/easier route and continued up for another mile and a half to the trailhead for the shorter, steeper trail. It was a nice summer day and we both wore shorts for the hike. I carried my usual daypack, which was just a small fanny pack, and we started up the steep trail. A lot of subtleties and romantic opportunities in life escape men in general and me for certain; Melissa was very tuned into these things, however. We had now been dating seriously for ten months (far past my prior record time of ten *weeks*) and we had talked about marriage. We had looked at engagement rings in recent weeks so that I would have some idea of her taste.

Melissa was hiking very well that day and seemed especially motivated to reach the summit of her first 14,000-foot mountain. I was taking it more casually, offering to take breaks more often and generally trying to make sure it was a pleasant day for us. During one of those breaks, I set my daypack down on a rock beside me and it began to tumble down the hill. The slope was steep, but it wasn't *that* steep, so I didn't think much of it—the pack wouldn't go more than a few feet down the hill. Melissa didn't share my casual view of my pack falling down the hill. She lunged for it, desperate to stop it from falling. I assured her it wouldn't have gone far, but thanked her for her effort. It had not occurred to me that she thought there was something very important in that pack.

Onward and upward we went toward the summit, at one point kicking steps up a gentle snowfield for a few hundred feet. It was this snowfield that taught us the important lesson of snow's reflective power coupled with the sun's intense rays at higher elevations. The backs of our legs, including the knee joints, got terribly sunburned that day—one of the more painful sunburns I've ever had. We reached the summit tired, but happy, and sat down to have a snack. Melissa looked at me expectantly as I rummaged through my daypack looking for an apple. I thought it was odd that she was still so excited and looking for more. We were on the summit, having achieved our goal—what else was there? Her mood gradually deteriorated as we finished our snack and looked to the west to see how the weather was looking. She then announced that the trail we had ascended was too steep and there was no way she was going back down that way. I was surprised, but tried to take it in stride.

Melissa and I on Mt. Massive's summit.

She seemed pretty upset, so I agreed that we could descend the standard route. So much for only having 3.1 miles to go—we now had 6.7 miles down to the standard trailhead, plus another 1.5 miles up the dirt road to get back to my car! The skies were turning dark with a thunderstorm moving in from the west, so we followed another group's lead and slid down a short snowfield on our rear ends to get off of the summit a bit more quickly. When we reached the standard trailhead a few hours later, Melissa had blisters on the bottom of both heels and she still seemed pretty upset with me for some reason. She told me that she would wait there for me and I should go up and get the car and come back to get her. She also "offered" to keep the water with her while I went. I hung my head, still not sure what I had done wrong, and went to get the car. At least I didn't have to worry about the extra weight of the last water bottle!

The car ride was a bit tense and after much probing as to why she was so upset, it came out that she had been sure I was going to propose on the summit. What a great idea! I just wish I had thought of it—but it had never occurred to me even though I had already put in the order for an engagement ring. Oh well. Luckily, she still said yes a few weeks later when I asked her to be my wife after the ring was done.

I climbed five more 14ers that year, including my second winter ascent, this time of Quandary Peak with my dad a few days after Christmas. Melissa was busy making wedding plans to prepare for our May 2000 wedding. After the wedding and honeymoon at the Pink Beach Club in Bermuda, we got a cute little golden retriever puppy and named him Malcolm. Melissa mentioned shortly after we were married that she had been thinking about going to graduate school to get a Master's degree in education so she could begin a teaching career. I have always had a thing for teachers and quickly agreed it was a great idea. I started hiking 14ers again after our wedding, getting five additional summits under my belt (with Melissa joining me on two of those, Malcolm on one). We were a happy newlywed couple, joyfully entertaining friends and family frequently at our new house. Life was good.

Melissa, Malcolm, and I on the summit of Mt. Sherman during the summer of 2000.

My dad and I also climbed a Class 3 route on Torreys Peak called Kelso Ridge during the summer of 2000. The route branches off from the main Grays and Torreys trail at about 12,500 feet, and then ascends the rugged ridge in between neighboring Kelso Mountain and Torreys Peak. There are four main areas that require Class 3 moves, including a short knife ridge at over 14,000 feet. This route has become my favorite over the years; I currently have fifty-one summits of Torreys Peak via Kelso Ridge to my credit. During August of 2000, Dad and I got our first taste of defeat on a mountain with a resounding dismissal due to inclement weather from one of Colorado's best-known mountains, 14,255-foot Longs Peak in Rocky Mountain National Park. Things went fine up to the famous Keyhole, but the sky was black on the west side and bad weather was clearly moving in.

Over the Christmas holidays in 2000, Melissa decided she wanted to try snowshoeing, so we bought a new pair of snowshoes for her and bought Malcolm a doggie backpack. We thought we would hike up from the Interstate to the summer trailhead for Grays and Torreys—about 6.5 miles round trip. We were having a nice hike that day up the snow-covered road, through the pine and aspen forest when Melissa asked to take a break about two-thirds of the way up to the summer trailhead. As we wrapped up the break, she said that she was getting tired and thought we ought to turn back. I proceeded to give an impassioned speech about the importance of finishing what you start in life, much to my wife's chagrin. I insisted that we continue the rest of the way up to the summer trailhead since that is what we set out to do. I don't think Melissa spoke to me for the rest of the day. The spot on that road where my speech occurred has now been fondly named by Melissa as "Inspiration Point." I've become slightly wiser as I've aged and I now steer clear of speeches like that, especially speeches addressed to my lovely wife. Survival and a happy marriage are well worth holding my tongue from time to time.

The year 2001 started out uneventfully for us on the mountain front. Melissa was working diligently on her graduate degree in elementary education and I was frantically working another public accounting busy season as a certified public accountant, often approaching eighty hours per week. I was up for a big promotion to audit manager that year, so work was a huge priority for me. We were both looking forward to the spring of 2001 when we could get back up to the mountains together for more hiking and time together.

CHAPTER 5

Morning

But here we were now, in a sea of snow, in freezing temperatures, and lying on the ground in our little clump of trees on a small hill somewhere above 11,500 feet. Getting through the night was miserable. As it got dark, the reality of our situation set in. It would be nine hours until the first light appeared on the horizon and we were cold, wet, and tired. My father's lower half was in just a thin pair of long underwear and socks—no boots. Melissa was barefoot, her feet wrapped in her wool hat and sandwiched between my legs as best we could.

People have asked us many questions over the years about that night—some of them great questions (like "Why didn't you put her feet underneath the dog?") and others somewhat comical, my favorite of which is "Why didn't you cut the dog open like a Tauntaun and put Melissa inside it like Han Solo did with Luke Skywalker in *The Empire Strikes Back*"? Unfortunately, REI doesn't sell light sabers, and while Malcolm was certainly not petite, his eighty-pound frame wasn't going to be quite big enough to get Melissa inside. Putting Melissa's bare feet underneath the dog would have been a wonderful idea, I'll admit; however, in a hypothermic trance, logical thinking and problem solving goes out the window pretty quickly and it never occurred to us. We did use the dog as a pillow for our heads though, keeping them off the frozen ground.

Hypothermia's physical effects come on slowly and with subtlety. As your body temperature begins to drop, natural defense mechanisms kick in, the most common of which is shivering. Most of us associate shivering with cold and view it as a negative (how often have you heard the phrase "I'm so cold that I can't stop shivering"?). It is exactly *because* you are cold that your body normally turns on the shivering reflex. Somewhere deep in our brains, there is recognition that we are getting cold and that getting cold is not a good thing. So out goes a transmission from brain to muscle—MOVE!!!!

QUICKLY!!! The muscles start to spasm, resulting in a common shiver. That muscle spasm also results in something else—heat. This is the body's natural attempt to warm itself back into that comfortable range of 98- to 100-degrees Fahrenheit. When you are suffering from hypothermia, however, that little brain transmission ordering the muscles to move either gets lost or doesn't occur at all. Even within the brain, transmissions are getting lost, so thinking becomes foggy.

One of the worst signs for someone suffering from hypothermia is when they *stop* shivering. That is the time when the body gives up its natural defenses and ceases trying to warm itself. Concurrently, blood vessels in your hands and feet constrict, limiting the blood flow to the extremities in an attempt to maintain an adequate temperature on the vital organs for as long as possible. As circulation to the extremities decreases, the tissue begins to freeze and we suffer frostbite.

I have not had another experience as near to death as I did that night, and I hope to not have one until it is really time to go. I do not know how close any of us came to succumbing, but what I can tell you is that for me personally, dying of hypothermia would have been a very peaceful way to go. There are numerous tales of mountaineers on Mt. Everest stripping off all of their clothes shortly before they succumbed to death from exposure. There are similar stories about hunters or arctic explorers. Once you stop shivering, it is quite an odd feeling—you actually feel warmer. Toward the end of a hypothermic death, people have reported feeling as if they were burning up in their clothes. They remove their hats, gloves, coats, shirts, pants, boots, and socks because they feel so hot. This of course accelerates their ultimate demise, but the point is that at this stage, you *think* you are quite warm and comfortable, so you remove your clothing, peacefully go to sleep, and simply don't ever wake up.

We maintained our wits for as long as we could that night. At one point, Melissa asked us if we thought we would be on the news and if we thought we would have to go to the hospital. I'm pretty sure my dad and I just grunted, not wanting to think about it. After I reminded Melissa and Dad that we were at risk of hypothermia and could not let ourselves go to sleep (then proceeded to close my eyes), Melissa took over. I wish Melissa took all of my husbandly suggestions with this level of passion and commitment! She was going to single-handedly keep us awake and alive that night. We used to call our son the "Quizmaster" when he was four years old because of his incessant questions about everything in life around him. In hindsight, I know where he got that skill—from his mother.

To keep us awake, Melissa started with the easy stuff, quizzing us about our birthdates, anniversaries, addresses, social security numbers, home phone numbers from when we were little kids, etc.—anything to keep us talking, thinking, awake, and alive. Next, she resorted to trying to get my poor father to remember what gift he had given to my mother on each of their twenty-nine wedding anniversaries to date. That didn't go very well, so she quickly turned her sights on me and began rattling off random numbers and asking me what accounting standard corresponded to that number and asking me to explain some of the key provisions of each. Now if I started spouting off accounting pronouncements here and telling you about them, you would be asleep in about two minutes (see the irony?), but for me this was very exciting to have my spouse suddenly so interested in my work! Malcolm the dog was of course unable to participate in the accounting standards quiz-a-thon, but he did his part to keep the rest of us awake with his loud snoring throughout the night.

At one point during the early stages of the night, Melissa thought she saw the beam of a flashlight shining against a nearby tree. She started yelling, but soon it became evident that there was no one there. A couple of times she thought she heard people out there over the howling of the unrelenting wind and again started yelling. We don't know whether the wind reached the same 58-mile-per-hour gusts in the mountains as those registered at Denver International Airport, but we would be surprised if they didn't. All night long, the wind blew through our little clump of trees, taunting us and adding insult to injury. To this day, Melissa has flashbacks to that night anytime she is outside in more than a gentle breeze.

Melissa also recalls hearing snoring frequently during the night and telling my dad to wake up because she was convinced it was him. Each time, it was the dog. At some point during the night, we came to accept that no one was coming to look for us until morning. The hours passed by slowly. Melissa could tell that her feet were frozen although they were not causing her any pain. She described it as more of a tingling sensation. During the night, she kept bouncing her legs to keep the circulation moving. At one point, she recalls her feet hitting each other and making a noise like the sound an ice cube tray makes when you crack it or two frozen chicken breasts bumping against each other. That sound would haunt her memory for years to come. She could also feel the "freeze" moving up from her feet and into her legs.

So where was the cavalry to rescue us? Had my mom not called the authorities to report us missing? We couldn't be sure. My mom had a very rough afternoon down in Denver dealing with weather-related issues. My sister-in-law Monica was due to fly into town from Phoenix on Sunday afternoon for a press check for one of her marketing clients. My mom had agreed to pick her

Our last photo the day of the accident—the view from our little clump of trees.

up at the airport at 3:00 p.m.; we all planned to have dinner together around 6:00 p.m. that evening. As Mom drove to Denver International Airport that afternoon, the weather was moving in. She recalls seeing the sky darken and the snow start to fall. When she checked the monitor to see if Monica's flight had landed, it simply showed "delayed." So she waited at the airport, continuing to watch the ever-worsening weather outside and continuing to read the word "delayed" on the flight status screen. She occasionally called her home phone number to see if Melissa, my dad, and I had made it back yet—there was never an answer. Feeling helpless as the hours continued to pass with no word on when my sister-in-law's flight would arrive, she called my brother Todd in Phoenix to see if he had heard from his wife.

Monica had just phoned Todd and told him that, due to inclement weather, her flight had been diverted to Colorado Springs (as one of the "more than a dozen" noted by examiner.com) to the much smaller airport, about 60 miles south of Denver. She was in the process of renting a car to drive the 60 miles to Denver, through the whiteout and over the top of treacherous Monument Hill, a very nasty place to be in a snowstorm. Phoenicians are not particularly known for their winter driving skills on snowy roads, but Monica eventually made it to a Subway near my parents' house in Lakewood, a western Denver suburb at the edge of the foothills, where she agreed to wait for my mom. Meanwhile, Mom was fighting through the snow and slick roads trying to return home from the airport on the very northeast edge of Denver. When the two of them finally pulled up to the house around 9:00 p.m. that night, they found it dark and quiet. Mom went to look at the answering machine, thinking surely we would have at least called and left a message by now, updating her on our status, but the light was not blinking and there were no messages. She was terribly worried about us. At about 9:15 p.m. she made the phone call to 911 to report us missing. She was put on hold before she could even say why she was calling, and then she got disconnected. Frustrated, she tried again.

She told the officers that we had intended to climb Mt. Evans and had not returned. The officer asked her from which side we were climbing Mt. Evans. We either hadn't told her or she couldn't remember. The problem was that the two main trailheads for Mt. Evans were in two different counties and the dispatcher needed to know which sheriff to notify. During the several phone calls with various sheriff's dispatchers and search and rescue team leaders, my mom felt somewhat comforted that people were being mobilized to find us and help us. The dispatchers also tried their best to ease her fears. The officers offered to send a car up to each of the two trailheads that evening.

The Guanella Pass trailhead parking lot where our car was parked is not a particularly big place. I would estimate that no more than forty cars could have fit there at once. That might sound like a lot, but picture driving your car slowly up one aisle of your local Target parking lot. Your job is to identify whether or not there is *any* other vehicle in that aisle. You'd probably like your chances, right? The dispatched officer braved the whiteout conditions and did just that through the Guanella Pass trailhead parking area that evening. Unfortunately, he came to the incorrect conclusion that our car was not there. Imagine for a moment how bad the weather would have to be with you driving up that Target parking lot aisle for you to drive within ten feet of another vehicle and conclude that there were no cars in the lot! Those are the conditions we were lying on the ground in, one of us barefoot and another in just long underwear and socks.

The officers who had done the parking lot inspections reported back to their supervisors who then telephoned my mother several hours after the first 911 call. "Good news" they said, "the car is not in either parking lot. That means they made it off the mountain and merely slid off the road into a ditch. As long as no one was seriously injured when they went off the road, we at least know that they have shelter from the weather. We can't really do anything else until morning when it's light, but don't worry—they'll be warm enough in the car for the night," he told my mom. She recalls being angry with us because we either hadn't told her from which side of the mountain we planned to climb, or if we had, she couldn't remember. She didn't want to be angry with us though, because what if one of us was hurt badly? What if we weren't in the car and really were out in the snow? Her anger reminded her of when my brother and I were teenagers and were late coming home. During those teenage years, she thought, "They better be in a hospital somewhere— or I'm going to kill them when they get home!" But on this night, she recalls that she couldn't even think that. She was worried that we *needed to be in a hospital* somewhere, but instead thought we might be out in the snow. She continued to wonder, "Where are they?" but then caught herself, not wanting to try to picture where we were. It was truly agonizing, wondering where her husband, son, and daughter-in-law were, and in what condition.

The hardest part of that night for her was the four or five hours after the officers said there was nothing else they could do until morning. Knowing that no one was actively trying to assist us during those late-night/early-morning hours was really tough on Mom. My mom's sister and her husband came over to keep her and Monica company. They all talked, asked themselves "What if ..." questions, ran through "If only ..." scenarios in which we might be okay. They also prayed a lot. They tried to rest, but they couldn't. They were scared and worried—it is tough to get any rest when you are fretting. Monica recalls that they did whatever they could to pass the time—including baking cookies sometime after midnight—to keep their minds from wandering to the possibilities of what might have happened to us. They did not want to confront those possibilities. My mom has since told me that she has no desire to ever be the mom on TV saying, "Well, at least he died doing what he loved."

Back on the mountain, Dad, Melissa, and I finally saw the valley start to lighten and the sun shining on one of the mountain faces to the west. From that point, time seemed to stand still. All night we had been telling ourselves that search and rescue would come at dawn, so when they weren't there right when the sun came up, Melissa started to despair.

I had another big decision on my hands now that it was dawn—and it was a tough choice. I don't remember at what point the previous day I had last urinated, but it was time to do it now. I lay there, acutely aware of how badly I needed to go for what seemed an hour. I knew that I should stand up and get it over with, but my feet were numb and it seemed a gargantuan task to stand up. I thought about trying to pee while lying horizontally on my side, but I wasn't sure that would work either. Then the thought occurred to me that I didn't have to go anywhere or do anything—I could just go. This seemed a viable option and was frankly the leading contender until I played it out one step further in my head, past the point of the nice warming liquid draining into my groin and leg areas. "It might feel good for thirty seconds, but then I'll be wetter and colder" I thought. After wrestling with the issue for as long as I could and not coming up with any great solutions, I begrudgingly decided to try to stand up. I remember thinking, "Be careful now—you can't feel your feet, so don't roll your ankle or do something stupid." Once I was upright, I took a few steps away from our improvised campsite and unzipped my pants and began to urinate. What a relief! It went on and on and on, much like when Austin Powers, the fictitious British spy, emerges from his frozen slumber to resume his decades-old fight against Dr. Evil. Evacuation complete!

I looked around to try to get a sense of where we were in relation to the trailhead. All around, I saw a frozen swamp covered in six inches of fresh, wet snow that had fallen the previous afternoon and evening. Under different circumstances, it would have been quite beautiful. Then something caught my eye—a glint of light. I couldn't believe it! The early morning sun was reflecting off a car at the trailhead. I practically ran the few steps back to where Melissa and Dad were and told them the exciting news, "I can see the trailhead and there's a car there!!!" I told them that it didn't look like it was that far and asked them whether they thought they could walk out with me. My father just groaned and Melissa told me her feet were frozen solid and there was no way she could walk. It was at this time when she got the first look at her feet. Apparently, the hat had fallen off of them at some point, so she realized she was barefoot. Mostly her feet were pure white, but other parts were black and blue. She knew then that it was really serious.

I told them that I would go get help. We had two walkie-talkies with us, so I left one with them and set off toward the trailhead with the other. Malcolm made no attempt to follow me as he was quite content still sleeping soundly in his burrow.

Back down in Denver, Mom and Monica had the TV news on very early Monday morning and heard a news report that we were missing. Fortunately, they were spared much more waiting and received a phone call from the leader of the Alpine Rescue Team. He informed Mom that they had checked the parking lot at the Guanella Pass trailhead again that morning, and it turned out that our White Subaru Outback was there—and we weren't in it. Monica called her boss and her client and told them what was going on. She unfortunately wasn't going to be at the press check for which she had flown in the day before—family emergencies come first.

It had been cold enough during the night (about 10 degrees Fahrenheit) that the swamp and various layers of snow below the fresh powder had again frozen. With the trailhead slightly uphill from where we were, I was able to fight my way through the willows in a straight line. Soon I came to a clearing, and thankful to be out of the willows for a few minutes, I continued my straight line toward the car across the snow. I did not realize until afterward that I was crossing a frozen lake—luckily the ice held my weight.

At this point, someone started yelling to me from the car through a megaphone. "Are you the party of three that we are looking for?" he yelled. "If yes, wave your arms over your head." I frantically waved my arms over my head. "Is everyone in your party alive? If yes, wave your arms over your head." Again, frantic arm waving over my head. "Please confirm—*no one* in your party requires medical attention. If correct that no one needs medical attention, wave your arms over your head." I panicked and thought he was going to drive away. I waved my arms down low as if I was signaling an incomplete pass in the NFL. Then I began to run toward him (not an easy thing to do in six inches of fresh snow with frozen feet). Luckily he didn't leave.

He waited for me at the trailhead and I saw that it was a sheriff's vehicle with a uniformed Clear Creek County sheriff inside. He told me to get into the nice warm Blazer and I jumped at the chance. Only twenty minutes had passed since I had left the others. The sheriff was communicating with the Alpine Rescue Team leader who was still on the phone with my mother. The officer asked me how Melissa and my father were doing and I told him that they were cold, but okay. He told me that members of the Alpine Rescue Team were en route and that the Flight for Life helicopter was on standby.

He asked whether they would be able to walk out on their own. I told him I had a radio and that I would radio to them. I pressed the talk button and told them that I was at the trailhead with the sheriff, and that it was only about a twenty-minute walk. "Can you follow my tracks and walk out or do you need to wait for assistance?" I asked. They discussed it for a few seconds and came back with, "We don't think we can stand up or walk. Please send help." The sheriff informed my mom that we had been located and were all alive; they would update her once they knew where they were taking us. During the initial conversations my mom had with the sheriff, there was never any mention of Malcolm the dog, which was leading my family back home in Denver to the conclusion that the dog must have had a problem and died or forced us to abandon him.

Not long after, three or four members of the highly trained volunteer Alpine Rescue Team arrived with sleeping bags and ran over to the sheriff's vehicle to be briefed. My tracks were visible across the fresh snow, leaving them with little doubt of finding the others by following my tracks. Off they went to help, as this amazing group so often does. I radioed to Melissa and she heard the words she had been waiting for, "They are on their way to you now." When the rescuers arrived, they saw an odd sight—my father's jeans were standing up, leaning against a tree, frozen solid. (This was odd enough that the same shot was broadcast on the TV news that morning during the story of our rescue.) They radioed back to us when they had Melissa and my dad in sleeping bags. Additional members of the Alpine Rescue Team arrived a few minutes later, this time with stretchers. Because of Dad's age, they were very concerned that he may have suffered a heart attack. He recalls how nice the heating pads felt in the sleeping bag with him. I heard the rescue leader radio the sheriff and tell him to bring in the chopper to evacuate my dad.

Melissa's recall of the rescuers' arrival:

Soon I could hear them, so I started yelling again. As they burst into our area I finally started to cry. Our poor dog, who was awake by then, started barking at them and trying to protect us. I convinced Malcolm they were okay, and he showered them with kisses. Immediately, they zipped Rich and me into sleeping bags they had brought with them. They also gave us water from their canteens as ours was frozen. While we waited for the helicopter, they formed a game plan. They decided they would put me on the helicopter first and fly me to the road (the helicopter is only equipped to carry one adult patient and two care providers in addition to the pilot). There was an ambulance there with Brad in it, which could take both of us to the hospital. Then they would fly back and pick up Rich and fly him straight to the hospital in Denver. They were really worried about Rich's hypothermia, so they decided it would be best to get him to the hospital the fastest.

Once the helicopter arrived on the mountain, three of the rescuers picked up my sleeping bag to carry me to it. I could only see out of a small gap in the bag around my face. Every now and then, one of them would look down to talk to me. The helicopter ride was very fast, and soon I was in the ambulance with Brad.

In the ambulance, they unzipped the bag to put heating pads on my chest, but I could not stop shivering. The EMT said that he was not going to put them on my feet because he didn't want them to thaw before we got to the hospital. He also immediately started a saline IV to help me get hydrated. He finally told me he didn't want to get my hopes up, because my feet looked pretty bad. At this point, I was so relieved to be rescued, that I didn't get that upset. I even managed while going downhill at around 80 miles-per-hour to relax enough that I started to fall asleep, but the EMT quickly put an end to that. He said that I needed to be coherent when I got to the hospital, so I couldn't sleep yet.

As I was sitting next to the sheriff who was quarterbacking the rescue effort, I decided to take my boots off to see how my feet looked. When I got my socks off, I noticed that my pinkie toes on both feet were grayish blue. I said something like, "Huh, that's not good" and he looked over to see them. He told me an ambulance would be here any minute and that when it arrived, I would be going down with Melissa to get checked out at the hospital. Before it arrived, I saw the yellow and orange Flight for Life helicopter coming in and looking for a place to land close to Dad. Things were happening very fast now all around me—the ambulance arrived in the parking lot, the rescuers unloaded Melissa from the helicopter and the sheriff told me to go get into the ambulance. I got into the rear of the ambulance first and was thrilled to see Melissa again when they loaded her up. The EMTs told me to just stay out of the way for a few minutes while they got her settled in and checked her vital signs.

One thing I thought very odd was that they were trying to get Melissa warm again—except for her frozen bare feet. I asked why they were not putting the same electric warming blankets on her feet as they were the rest of her body and the EMTs explained to me that the thawing process was extremely painful and that it would be done at the hospital under close supervision. With that, the ambulance headed down the snow-covered steep, windy road leading back down to Georgetown and Interstate 70. That wild ride down the hill on the snowy road in the back of the ambulance was certainly the most nauseating part of this ordeal.

One phase of the story had ended and the long recovery process was about to begin.

Search for hikers successful

A family of three were hiking on Guanella Pass on Sunday when the snow storm blew in

By Summer Parsons
Staff Writer

Three hikers were found Monday morning after spending a cold, snowy night in the wilderness on Guanella Pass.

The three suffered some frostbite and hypothermia and were taken to a Denver hospital for treatment.

Brad McQueen, 27, his wife, Melissa, 25, and his father, Richard, 50, went hiking on Guanella Pass Sunday morning. An afternoon snowstorm, complete with whiteout conditions, disoriented the trio and forced them to spend the night in the wilderness.

Richard's wife reported her family missing to the Clear Creek County Sheriff's Office Sunday around 11 p.m.

Eighteen members of the Alpine Search and Rescue Team started up Guanella Pass around 7 a.m. Monday. Park County Search and Rescue Team assisted with the rescue efforts.

Clear Creek County Deputy Steve Gremillion spotted Brad walking along the road about a half mile from a parking lot near the top of the pass.

All three were taken to Exempla St. Joseph Hospital in Denver. Richard was airlifted to Denver by Flight for Life, Brad was able to walk off of the pass, and Melissa was taken by ambulance.

Officials said the McQueens were lucky.

"You should never go hiking in a field in the high country without being prepared for drastic changes in the weather and the possibility of having to spend the night," said Clear Creek County Sheriff Don Krueger.

Richard and Brad were released from the hospital Tuesday morning and Melissa was listed in fair condition.

CHAPTER 6

Reunited

Frostbite is a lot like a burn, with stages similar to first, second, and third degree burns. The most common form is frost nip (first degree frostbite), which forms when exposed skin is subjected to the elements for too long. A small patch of skin turns white, frequently on the tip of the nose or on the cheek. Once the exposure period is over, it will tingle slightly as it warms. Over the next few days, the patch will turn reddish and then probably peel off, much like a sunburned area. There is no permanent damage to the underlying tissue. Superficial frostbite is second degree frostbite and typically involves slightly larger areas. The area will often turn slightly black and blue like a bruise. The freezing is deeper into the tissue and blisters generally form as the body tries to isolate the damaged surface tissue from the unharmed tissue underneath.

The final phase is deep frostbite (third and fourth degrees) in which the tissue below the skin freezes solid. Water is the primary ingredient in our bodies, comprising some 57 percent of our body weight. When the water in our bodies freezes, it forms sharp crystals of ice that cut blood vessels, nerves, tendons, and muscles, inflicting permanent damage on the area. Deep frostbite is one of the most painful injuries and frequently leads to amputation of the affected areas. Melissa's bare feet had frozen solid during the night, sustaining deep frostbite. My father and I got off easy; I had only sustained frost nip on my pinkie toes and my dad had sustained superficial frostbite on the backs of his heels.

Monday morning, my mom and sister-in-law, with the help of my aunt and uncle who had stayed up through the night with them, were in high gear coordinating efforts with the sheriff's office, rescue personnel, and medical personnel. Other coordination efforts going on at the time included getting Malcolm back to Denver (he walked out with the rescuers and ended up spending the night in nearby Idaho Springs with the emergency dispatcher who had talked with my mom). On Tuesday, my mom's cousin Mike (who has a heart the size of Texas and would do anything for family) and my grandfather volunteered to drive to the trailhead together, retrieve my car, then proceed to Idaho Springs to get the dog.

Melissa and I were taken by ambulance to Exempla Lutheran Medical Center in Wheat Ridge, where the excellent medical staff began the process of thawing Melissa's feet. Monica and my aunt and uncle met us there. The nurses inserted an IV into Melissa's arm to liberally administer pain medicine as the excruciatingly painful thawing process began. Overwhelmed by the emotion of seeing Monica and being safe in the hospital, Melissa started to cry. She asked Monica, "How bad are my toes?" then sobbing, "I don't want to lose my toes." Monica left that to the doctors. Feeling somewhat helpless, but yet honored to be there and able to help, Monica recalls that she just sat with Melissa and brushed her hair for a long time. Melissa recalls:

> Immediately after arriving at the hospital, a team of nurses swooped down on me and began to cut off my clothes. They also started a new IV in the other arm. I was comforted because Brad was in the bed next to me where I could see him. They put a hot air blanket over me and soon I began to warm up. But, as my body warmed up, my feet began to thaw and a pain a hundred times worse than I could have imagined began. I was begging for painkillers and several times sent Monica to find out where they were. It felt like forever, but I was later told that it was actually only a couple of minutes.
>
> Finally, they started a morphine drip and the pain gradually subsided. While I was lying there, I noticed that a TV at the end of the room had a picture of our car on it. It was an odd sensation to lie there, numbed by the morphine, and watch a news story about our rescue. My next visitor, coincidentally, was the hospital's press person. She said that she was going to tell the press that Brad was in good condition, and I was in stable. She explained that I was downgraded because of the condition of my feet.

It was difficult to come to grips with the fact that Melissa was clearly in worse shape than I was. The doctors carefully monitored Melissa's dorsalis pedis, the artery that runs in the middle of the top of the foot. You can feel your pulse in your foot by placing a finger on this artery and that is exactly what the doctors were hoping to feel—a pulse. The doctors were hopeful, but not yet convinced, that Melissa would get to keep her feet (toes were another story). Melissa's toes by this point were turning a deep purple, and reddish blisters were beginning to form at the base of each of her toes on the top of her feet as well as on the tips of the toes themselves—about seven blisters on *each* foot. Melissa also had a silver dollar-sized blister forming on the inside of her right lower leg, about three inches above her ankle. On the bright side, she had had a stubborn wart on the inside of her right heel that appeared to have been thoroughly frozen at last.

I was able to walk from the ambulance into the hospital and was given a quick medical exam. My pinkie toes had already returned to their normal color, with a slight tingle all that was left of my frost nip. They still wanted to keep an eye on me for a while, though. I was feeling well enough that I was sitting up in bed drinking water. When Melissa asked if she could have some water, she was told that she could not, because her stomach had to be empty in case she needed emergency surgery. It was coming up on noon Monday and I was starving, having had only a few handfuls of nuts since the previous afternoon. Melissa's appetite was also coming back and she, too, was anxious for something to satisfy her hunger. I requested a Big-Mac and fries from my aunt and uncle who volunteered to make a food run; Melissa's eyes lit up at the idea. Her hopes were quickly dashed, however, by the medical staff telling her that they had not yet ruled out surgery to remove her feet in the near term and that until they were sure they didn't have to amputate immediately, lunch would have to wait. When the food arrived, I ate my Big-Mac as quickly as I could while Melissa glared at me with jealousy.

The pulse came back strong in each of Melissa's feet along with normal coloring down to the start of the blisters at the base of her toes. We felt a huge sense of relief when the doctors came in and informed us that they no longer believed there was a possibility of needing to amputate either of her feet that day. They also said that she was deemed stable enough for transfer to Exempla St. Joseph Hospital, our primary care facility.

Once at St. Joseph, Melissa and I were taken up to a room on the eighth floor. She recalls being so excited because they were going to let us be roommates! My mom showed up to check on us, and she was the beginning of a steady stream of visitors. Monica had gone to call some people that Melissa and I needed to notify. The wheels were also in motion to notify Melissa's parents, but this was no small task as they were vacationing in Italy.

My mom reached Melissa's aunt and she was able to reach Melissa's parents. They called our room immediately. Melissa assured them that she was fine, and there was no reason to rush home. Since they were due back to the states in just a few days and knew that Melissa was in good hands at the hospital, they opted to keep their original return travel itinerary. For Melissa, the rest of the day was a blur as the morphine really started to kick in and the fatigue of hiking over a dozen miles and not sleeping for thirty-plus hours caught up with her. Eventually she and I were alone in the room and could sleep. Unfortunately, the doctors were changing the bandages on her feet every four hours, so she had to wake up multiple times during the night.

Meanwhile, my father had been loaded into the Flight for Life helicopter and was en route to the University of Colorado Hospital. My father recalls that the emergency medical personnel working on him in the helicopter kept coming back to a singular question, "Sir, are you *sure* you are not having chest pains?" "They wanted to crack open my chest right there in the helicopter!" he recalls thinking. At altitude, your fingers frequently swell up and my dad's silver wedding ring was beginning to cut off the circulation to his left ring finger. The doctors decided to cut off the wedding ring to prevent damage to that finger.

Dad had not had a heart attack thankfully, and after spending a few hours wrapped in a similar warming blanket and a thorough exam at University Hospital, they were ready to move him to Exempla St. Joseph Hospital to join Melissa and me. Monica recalls that my dad's and my eyes were both terribly red and bloodshot that day. They did not have a room for my dad though, so he had to stay downstairs in the emergency room. Dad had suffered superficial frostbite on his feet as well. For him, the damage occurred on the backs of his heels, which lay on the frozen ground throughout the night with just a pair of socks between his heels and the snow. His heels were bright red as though they had been sunburned and giant blisters formed across the entire two-inch width of his heel, rising up about an inch toward his Achilles tendons. That was the extent of his physical injury though; he and I were released from the hospital on Tuesday morning after being kept overnight for observation.

On Tuesday afternoon, Melissa started hydrotherapy. They submerged her feet in a warm bath where jets stimulated them for fifteen minutes each day. As soon as they put her feet in the water, she would become nauseated and vomit. This was the only time she got

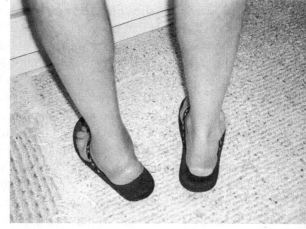

The blisters on Dad's heels from his frostbite.

out of her bed those first few days. She had lots of visitors, but mostly she just wanted to sleep. Melissa would spend the next ten days at St. Joseph Hospital (although she says the time went by quickly) where we began to learn about the long, slow recovery from severe frostbite. Her treatment was focused on two primary objectives: 1) managing the excruciating pain that she was feeling, and 2) preventing infections on her deeply wounded feet. To relieve the pressure, each new blister that formed was pierced with a sterile needle and drained. Once the skin covering the blister had died, the doctors ever so carefully cut it off. Deep, dark scabs began to form at the base of her toes where the blisters had been removed.

The treatment for her still purple, red, and white waxy toes consisted of gently applying pure aloe to them with medical swabs. Severe frostbite is a rare injury for the otherwise young and healthy, so Melissa's room was a popular teaching and research spot at the hospital, with young residents being paraded through her room constantly to see what severe frostbite looked like in real life and to discuss treatment protocols. Most cases of frostbite occur in the homeless population or among elderly diabetics, and such treatment is either never sought or is part of a much larger, more complicated medical plan. The doctors were quite candid with Melissa and the rest of the family that there was a good chance that at least some of her toes would need to be amputated. The doctors were also not in any hurry to give up on them and proceed to surgery as long as nothing got infected. So we waited and they managed Melissa's level of pain.

My father and I were each struggling through pain of our own—but of an entirely different type. Survivor's guilt is a common phenomenon experienced by people who have survived an event where others perished. Frequent causes are car crashes, plane crashes, and other similar accidents. In our case, we were fortunate that none of us lost our lives, but it was still extremely difficult for us to watch Melissa suffering amid crippling pain with badly damaged feet, amputation an acute possibility. Since Dad and I were discharged from the hospital with very minor injuries by comparison and were able to walk under our own power, we felt immense guilt. My father felt the added burden of initially not going on this hike, then spending the night wearing Melissa's spare dry socks while she ended up barefoot. I tried to console him as did Melissa, reminding him that we had dealt with the most pressing needs first—getting him out of his wet jeans, boots, and socks and into dry long underwear and socks. When we put the spare socks on his feet, we didn't yet know that Melissa might need them (and certainly didn't even remotely envision that she would end up barefoot for the night).

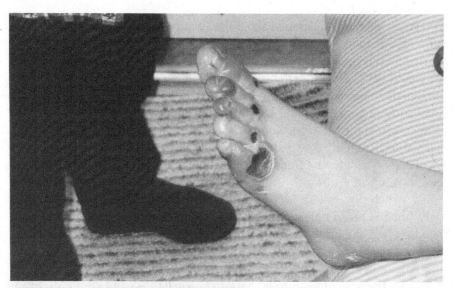

Melissa's feet shortly after being discharged from the hospital.

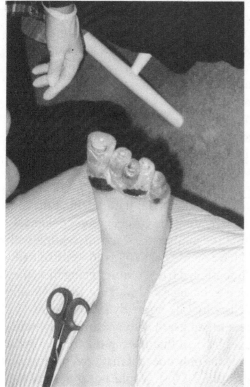

Dad was taking it pretty hard, blaming himself for slowing us down and needing Melissa's spare socks. He honestly believed that the whole thing would not have happened had he not been with us. Toward the end of the summer, after receiving an $11,000 bill for his helicopter ride off the mountain, he suggested with no element of jest that we sue him for damages and he was convinced that he would be found liable, with the insurance company agreeing to pay out damages under his umbrella policy. Melissa and I both resoundingly refused to sue him, insisting that this was just an unfortunate accident in which we shared fault equally.

When we were questioned about the decision to take her boots and socks off, I explained my simple sixth-grade logic of "get wet clothes off." What we learned (which makes good sense now with a non-hypothermic mind) is that we would have been far better off to leave Melissa's boots and socks on, even though they were wet. She was wearing high quality leather hiking boots and wool socks. The boots would have provided enough of a shell layer from the elements to allow Melissa's blood flow to naturally warm the water that had been absorbed in the socks. This would have been the best decision, followed by placing her bare feet underneath the dog, with the light saber Tauntaun plan coming in a distant third. Both Dad and I wished like crazy that we could switch places with Melissa or change our decisions along the way. If only I hadn't taken her boots and socks off. Dad thought, "If only I hadn't handed Brad the knife to cut the boot laces." But we couldn't trade places with her and we couldn't undo what we had done.

For some strange reason, a burning desire that I had in those first few days after the accident was to go back to Guanella Pass and climb Mt. Evans again via the proper route on the way up to prove that I could find the trail on the way down. I felt somehow that if I redid it, I would wake up and this would all just be a dream. My mother talked me out of this and assured me that the outcome would be the same—my wife would still be lying in her hospital bed with badly frostbitten feet—and that my time and energy was better spent keeping her company in the hospital. I knew she was right, but I still felt an urge to go take refuge and grieve in the mountains.

Melissa's life in the hospital became more routine with each day, still with parades of doctors coming in daily to view her feet and trim off any new blisters or skin that had died since the previous day. Her room was filled with flowers and balloons from family and friends, but she had a bit of trouble even seeing them. The medical staff had crafted a miniature tent at the foot of her bed, with a three-foot high arch holding the covers up off of her badly damaged feet. We began researching toe amputations and discussing with the doctors what impact this would have on Melissa's ability to walk. Initially, old wives tales surfaced from well-intentioned friends announcing that "they had heard" that pinkie toes were vital to balance and walking, or that losing any toes would make it hard for Melissa to walk normally ever again.

As we began to replace what people had heard with research and discussions with qualified professionals, we learned that the big toe (or the "great toe" as the doctors called it) was really the only one that mattered too terribly much in walking. And even the great toe, if lost, would not prevent walking—really the ball of the foot is the key part. To prevent Melissa's muscles from further atrophy, the medical staff added daily physical therapy, but she still could not walk.

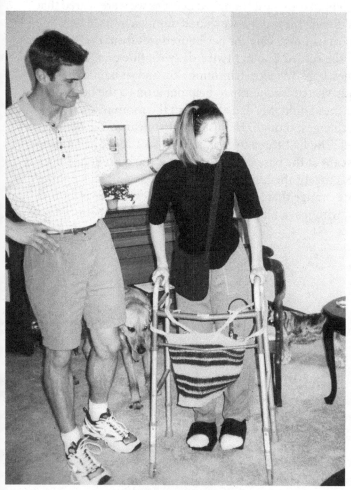

Melissa back at home with her walker.

Finally, after ten days in the hospital, Melissa was ready to go home. She recalls being very nervous when it finally came time for her to go home, but she knew that her beloved cat, Boulder, would enjoy spending extra time with her. It was also comforting that her parents were now home from their trip; her mom did most of the heavy lifting that summer when I had to go back to work. Melissa's feet were still swollen, and the blisters kept coming. She didn't know what she was going to do when she got home. "I knew I wouldn't be able to take care of myself," she recalls. Her feet were heavily bandaged, as had become the routine. First, a thick layer of aloe was applied to her toes, then sterile Vaseline strips were placed over the blisters, whose open wounds were still healing, and finally a thick wrap of gauze engulfed each of her feet. She still couldn't walk very far, even with her fancy new black shoes, so she had a wheel chair for getting around longer distances (including from the hospital room to the car).

Back at home in our eight hundred square-foot West Highlands bunga-low, Melissa claimed the living room couch as her new home during the day. At night, she initially slept in our guest room bed because we were scared that I would bump her feet during the night if we shared our queen-sized bed. She would require months of in-home care for her injured feet from the Visiting Nurse Association, so she settled into her twice-daily routine of a nurse cut-ting off the old bandages, applying aloe, trimming skin and re-bandaging her feet. Family and friends visited frequently to help out around the house and to support us however they could. My dad always left the room when it came time for the bandage changes, though. He just couldn't bear to see Melissa's painfully damaged feet. The first three toes on her left foot remained a deep purple color and the scabs at the base of the toes where the blisters had been were deep and dark. Strangely, the last two toes (the pinkie and its neighbor to the right) were more orange than purple. All of the toes on her right foot looked gray and waxy, with just a bit of purple strewn here and there.

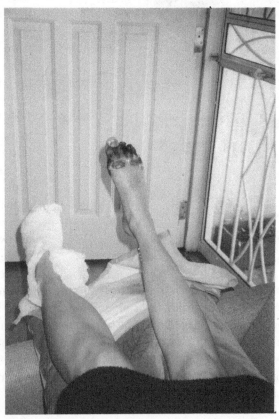

Melissa's badly damaged feet.

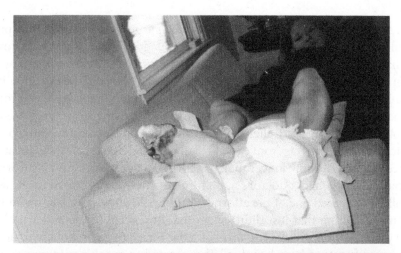

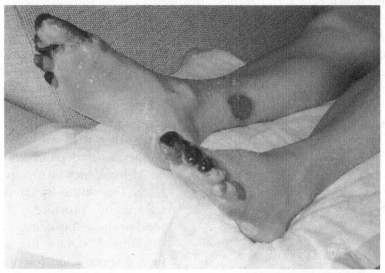

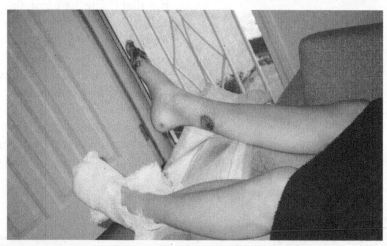

Adding insult to injury, a week after Melissa got home from the hospital, Boulder the cat suffered from kidney failure and we had to put him down. Melissa would have been crushed anyway to lose her cat, but with all of the pain she was already in, this loss just seemed as if someone was sticking it to her. I was back at work full time now and was struggling to balance professional demands on my time with wanting and needing to support Melissa through this. My largest client was involved in a major acquisition, so this delicate balance was far from easy. I recall one conference call I was on at the office that was running longer than its scheduled time; I was growing worried because Melissa had a doctor's appointment where I was due to meet her. I finally interrupted one of the attorneys on the call who was going on and on about something that just didn't seem that important to me and said, "I'm sorry, but I'm going to have to drop off now. I need to go find out whether or not my wife gets to keep her toes." That seemed to put things in perspective for everyone on the call and they agreed that our call was finally over.

Melissa recalls that in the early days, I didn't want to talk at all about the accident unless it related to specific medical care decisions. She wanted and needed to tell me how she was feeling, but I was still struggling with guilt and didn't want to discuss my own feelings. Instead, we just stared at each other and reassured each other that we would get through this (we were determined that it would make us stronger) and everything would be okay.

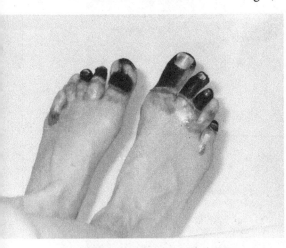

Melissa's feet shortly before her first amputation surgery.

As the weeks slowly went by, the permanently damaged tissue on Melissa's toes turned to solid black. The whitish toenail on her right big toe provided a strange window into the damaged tissue beneath, almost like a gray frosted window looking out into the night. She had lost the toenail from her left big toe, so that toe had an odd concave shape to it on the top. Her doctor, Dr. Mangione, had Melissa come in weekly so he could inspect the progress and help decide the next steps—still they were in no hurry to amputate as long as no infections were present. It was becoming clearer to all of us, though, which toes were going to live and which ones were not.

Melissa's recall from that summer:

My parents got back the night before they released me from the
hospital. This helped to calm my fears some. My last day in the
hospital, they got a walker for me and had me practice walking. I
had been outfitted with a special pair of shoes. My toes were clearly
the worst, so the shoes were designed to ensure that I did not use
my toes to walk and that they weren't touched. They had a two-inch
platform sole that tilted me back slightly and my toes hung out the
end. I had to walk as flat footed as possible. I was also given the instructions that I was only to walk the bare minimum necessary (e.g.
to the bathroom) and I was to keep my feet elevated.

I soon began to realize how much my life was going to change,
at least in the short term. Before the accident, I had been planning
on taking three classes at the University of Colorado at Denver for
my Master's over the summer. I dropped all but one of them. I was
very optimistic and really thought I would be back on my feet in no
time, so I didn't see the point in dropping all of my classes.

The first few weeks I was basically helpless. I couldn't even
carry a glass of water from the kitchen to the living room because
of the walker. Brad was very helpful at night, but he had to return
to work, so I needed help during the day. My mom, Brad's mom,
and my cousin, Amanda, spent a lot of time with me during this
period. They drove me to school and to the doctors and made my
meals for me. Many of our friends were also helpful and brought
over meals to us. That was tremendously valuable.

Somehow I managed to keep a fairly positive outlook. (It might
have been all of the pain medication I was on.) However, I was starting to get frustrated because no one understood what I was going
through. The pain had been tolerable in the hospital once they had
started my morphine drip. It dispensed the medication at regular
intervals and I also had a button I could press for an extra drip if
the pain was too bad. When they sent me home, the doctors put me
on Vicodin to handle the pain. The Vicodin, at best, took the edge
off the pain.

I cannot even begin to describe the level of pain I was in. The
doctors explained to Brad at one point that frostbite and burns
are two of the most painful injuries. From my experience, including walking on a broken foot for a day before going to the doctor
and two caesarian sections, this was an entirely different level of

unrelenting pain. The pain was isolating. Thankfully, my nurse listened to me and noticed that my blood pressure was rising because of the pain. The doctors put me on Dilaudid, an opioid related to morphine, and it brought some relief. Dilaudid is so powerful that when Brad would pick it up from the pharmacy, there were special procedures including doing a pill count in front of him so he could confirm the number of pills he received with his signature. I was just happy that the pills made me feel better. Brad had other concerns, however. He would frequently ask my nurses and doctors if we needed to worry about me becoming addicted. They assured him that every bit of the pill was going to pain management and he didn't need to worry. Thankfully they were right and I basically went cold turkey with no problems within a week of my first surgery.

The pain was not the only part of the recovery that had me feeling isolated. I did not know anyone who had had severe frostbite and was longing to connect with someone who could understand what I was going through. My mother-in-law was really helpful and got on the Internet to locate someone. Eventually she e-mailed the American Alpine Club and asked if they knew of anyone. They replied that there were two men here in Colorado who had lost fingers and toes to frostbite who were willing to talk to me.

It took me awhile to get my courage up, but finally I called the first name on the list, climber and author Ed Webster. I got his answering machine and started to leave a message when he picked up. He told me he had been waiting for my call. We talked for over an hour about what I was going through and what his experience was like. The more we talked, the better I felt. It was so reassuring to talk to someone who had been through everything I was experiencing. Brad later told me that he felt that my spirits really jumped after that call.

Melissa's positive attitude, ability to tolerate the intense pain, and her mental toughness were amazing to watch. The fall semester for Melissa was due to start toward the end of August and she was determined to continue to pursue her Master's degree. She used the wheel chair to get around the Auraria Campus in downtown Denver and even took the light rail over to my office after class one day, bringing with her a tub of popcorn for an afternoon surprise. She was seeing a wonderful counselor named Todd, who was also a student at the University of Colorado at Denver. Seeing Melissa, he got quite a bit more "real world" experience than he was bargaining for as he did his "student counseling" on campus each week. I'm sure Todd has become an outstanding professional counselor—he was off to a great start while still in school. Each and every day, Melissa was finding more and more mental toughness, determined not to let this accident become the defining event of her life. On September 1, 2001, one of Melissa's good friends from college got married and we attended the wedding in the mountains. Melissa was determined to have a normal life and insisted that we dance to one of her favorite songs at the wedding. I accidentally kicked one of her bandaged feet, and yet again, Melissa said maybe we shouldn't dance anymore.

Melissa's body had pretty well done what it could do to heal. Where her body had given up on the toes, the tissue began to close up underneath the dead exterior. It was strange to look at—the tips of her toes were black, hard to the touch, and clearly dead. Where the dead, black tissue met the living, vibrant, pink tissue, there was a slight detachment and indentation, almost as if the dead tissue was a helmet placed on top of a nub of pink tissue underneath. The black tips were becoming more and more detached from the living tissue underneath and could be wiggled slightly, back and forth, like a loose tooth. While taking a bath one day, Melissa was inspecting one of the black tips. She had the distinct sensation that this "tooth" was about ready to come out and she was horrified at the thought! There was no way she wanted to be walking around the house one day on her toeless platform shoes and have one of her toes fall off right there onto the floor! She told her doctors that it was time; she was ready for surgery.

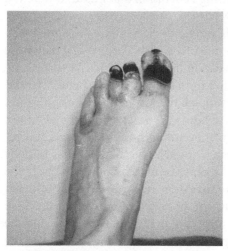

Melissa's left foot just before surgery with the tips of the middle toes becoming like loose teeth.

Four out of the five toes on her right foot were dead all the way to the base, with the only living toe being the pinkie's neighbor to the left. On her left foot, the pinkie and its neighboring toe were going to make it. The tips of the next two toes were dead and her left big toe was badly damaged, but we were still hopeful that she might keep at least part of it. We thought it was odd that the second to last toe on each foot had survived (and had been the only toe to survive on the right foot). We thought perhaps there was a correlation between this and the old belief that there was a vein in the left ring finger that went straight to the heart (the reason many of us wear our wedding rings on that finger—it signifies proximity and direct linkage to the heart). In reality, all parts of our bodies are connected directly to our hearts (we need blood everywhere).

Although the penultimate toe on her right foot had lived, Dr. Mangione recommended amputating it. Having one small toe on a foot with no protection on either side of it was just asking for numerous breaks and dislocations going forward. Melissa agreed and had her first of what would be four surgeries done. This first surgery in early September removed all five toes from her right foot and the tips of the two middle toes on her left foot. He also did some investigative diagnostics on the depth of the wound on her left big toe. Because they were going to be working on both feet, and doing so much work, she and her doctor decided it would be best if she checked into the hospital overnight. When she woke up from surgery, she felt terrible from the anesthesia and had earned herself a new nickname. When she was coming to, she tried to attack the anesthesiologist, so the nurses were calling her "WWF" after the old World Wrestling Federation that I used to watch as a kid.

After the surgery, Melissa's friends and family were there to comfort her. Eventually they all left, since all she wanted to do was sleep. While they were gone, Dr. Mangione dropped in to check on her. He told Melissa something that her family had agreed not to tell her until she was feeling better. He told her that the wound on her left big toe went all the way to the bone and would not heal. He had not amputated that toe during surgery since they had not discussed that option beforehand, but they would have to go back and remove it. This was going to leave Melissa with just two toes. She was initially quite upset at this news, but grew to accept it within a couple of days. She recovered from surgery quickly and returned one week later to have the left big toe partially amputated. Somehow the bottom of the toe had lived, so the doctor proposed that the second surgery should consist of removing the dead tissue from the top of the left big toe, then taking living tissue from the bottom and folding it up and over the top so that she could keep about a half a toe there (with the old bottom becoming the new top).

Melissa was truly sad to lose her toes. She looked at her feet constantly and mourned the loss. What was worse, though, was the phantom pain and phantom itching that started not long after surgery. Imagine having the insatiable urge to itch your big toe only to remember that it isn't there anymore. That realization, unfortunately, didn't make the itch go away. It was the same with the phantom pain—a very strange feeling all around as Melissa recalls—pain coming from a part of your body that no longer exists. She recalls this being extremely frustrating.

By now, she was pretty well used to walking without the use of her toes, having had months of practice, so once the incisions healed, she began to walk without the assistance of the toeless platform shoes, which she had decorated with flower stickers of varying shapes and colors. She got a bigger test than she bargained for at the end of September, though, just ten days after the second sur-

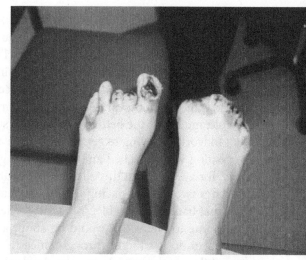

Melissa's feet after the first amputation surgery.

gery. Another of Melissa's college friends was getting married, with this wedding occurring on September 29, 2001, on Nantucket Island, off the coast of Massachusetts. A lot had happened in the world since the last time we had flown on an airplane.

Nineteen days earlier, on September 10, 2001, I had left for a business trip to Seattle to work on an audit for my largest client. My co-workers and I grabbed dinner after work at a brewpub and watched into the third quarter of the Monday Night Football game between our Denver Broncos and the New York Giants. I distinctly remember Ed McCaffrey catching a pass over the middle then taking a vicious hit that visibly broke his leg on national TV. Ouch. After dinner, we had been invited to go out on a boat on Lake Washington with a friend. It was a great night and I'll admit that we consumed a fair amount of wine as we took in the beautiful views. We took a taxi back to the hotel in downtown Seattle and I settled in to bed, thankful that I could sleep in a bit tomorrow since I didn't need to be at my client just a few blocks away until 8:30 a.m. (Sleeping in for me is quite a bit different than for most people—my normal alarm time is between 4:00 and 4:30 a.m.)

Much to my chagrin, my phone rang at about 5:50 a.m. PDT, waking me before my planned 7:30 wake-up time. It was Melissa telling that something was going on in New York and I should turn on the TV. I told her I'd catch it later and hung up and went back to sleep. She called back moments later, more persistently telling me to turn on my TV, which I reluctantly did. I watched as the initial news coverage of the first plane hitting the World Trade Center in New York City unfolded, and then just like millions of people around the world, I watched live as the second airplane hit the other tower. Needless to say, I didn't go to my client's that day. But I couldn't give my wife a big hug either and tell her it was going to be okay since she was in Denver and I was a thousand miles away in Seattle. We watched the news together for most of the day, talking on our phones as long as my cell battery would last. One of my colleagues had the better frequent flier status with United Airlines, so he went to work on trying to get us booked on a flight back to Denver. Nothing. Everything was cancelled and no one was going anywhere in the "Friendly Skies" for a while until this all got sorted out.

After two days of pacing the city of Seattle, we found a rental car company that had cars available, so my two colleagues and I rented a car to drive back home to Denver. It would be about a twenty-two-hour drive, but we decided to do it straight through since there were three of us—one could rest, while one drove and one kept the driver company. We finally got home on September 14, 2001, and I gave Melissa the big hug that she had needed for three days. Given everything we had been through since May 20, both of our emotions were running pretty high and it was good to be together again.

The new reality of air travel was still in its infancy two weeks later when we were due to fly to Providence, Rhode Island, where we would catch a puddle jumper to Nantucket. We left a little bit earlier than we otherwise would have and found Denver International Airport to be a sea of people, all of whom were on our side of the security checkpoint, trying to get to the gates to board their flights. As everyone has now experienced, security lines since September 11, 2001, take a lot longer to get through than they used to. Shoes, belts, and laptops are removed. Liquids and gels over three ounces are no longer allowed aboard aircraft. All of these precautions designed to keep us safer took a lot more time however, and we anxiously checked our watches as we moved at a snail's pace toward the x-ray machines. We made it through security about forty minutes before our flight was scheduled to depart, so it was going to be tight. Melissa announced with tears in her eyes that we were NOT missing this flight and her friend's wedding in Nantucket. She began to run through the concourse when the train doors opened in the atrium. I was doing my best to keep up with my lovely wife, running on her newly toeless feet. We got to our gate just in time, boarded our flight, and made it to Nantucket for the wedding.

By the third surgery the following March, some ten months after the accident, Melissa was pals with Dr. Mangione and had opted for a mere ankle block to deaden her foot while he worked on removing some bone spurs from the middle of her right foot that were putting pressure on the incision area. While he worked his little whirring saw that sounded like a drill at the dentist's office, he and Melissa played the trivia game on the radio in the background! This was one tough woman. Melissa finally had her fourth and final surgery to remove a bit more tissue from beneath her right big toe in an area where her incision continued to split open regularly like badly cracked hands in the cold, dry Colorado winter. Much to Melissa's chagrin, however, that wart on her heel was coming back. She was outraged! How could someone lose eight toes to frostbite and fail to kill one silly wart! Thankfully, someone told us of the miracle of apple cider vinegar to kill warts, so Melissa attacked and killed that wart with a vengeance (it has never returned).

With the medical aspects of the accident on the mountain now behind us, we continued to fight the mental battles and move forward with life.

CHAPTER 7

Life Goes On

Part of my grieving and acceptance process involved getting back outside to have time to think and time to talk about my feelings of guilt with my dad and other hiking partners. When I could sneak away from work and when Melissa didn't have doctor's appointments, I would go climb. I think the lingering feeling of so desperately wanting a "redo" kept driving my desire to go back into the mountains. I climbed six 14ers during the rest of 2001 with a new friend named Mark Golden. He accompanied me on my first 14er outing after our accident, a late-June Kelso Ridge climb. Mark was a great hiking partner, as he was willing to listen to me when I needed him to that summer, but he was also willing to share his excitement with me about this new series of movies that were coming out called *The Lord of the Rings*, based on the books by J.R.R. Tolkien. One day on Pikes Peak, almost the entire time up the mountain was consumed with Mark telling me all of the amazing things in this story, like the different kinds of beings, the growing force of evil, the trees that could walk and talk, etc. Oh my, he was excited! I had not yet read these books, which have become a favorite series for both me and my son.

It was a tough fall for Melissa for sure. She still had a lot of physical and mental healing to do. Melissa's friends questioned why she was letting me continue to hike while she recovered. At a fall 2001 happy hour, one of my co-workers cornered her and told her that I was a terrible husband for continuing to hike after I had gotten her into this mess. She went on to tell Melissa how weak she was being for letting me get away with this. Melissa vehemently defended me to this co-worker and anyone else who looked to use the accident as a wedge between us. It meant the world to me that she defended me during this time because I was still struggling so much with my survivor's guilt. Melissa was determined that the accident was going to make us stronger as a couple, not the other way around. She also steadfastly defended my dad and his need for our spare clothing that night long before we

Dad, Mark Golden, and I on Mt. Belford's summit in August 2001.

knew Melissa's feet were in trouble. She knew how much my dad wished he could trade places with her now and she tried her best to let everyone know that she believed we all shared fault equally for what had happened.

She recalls growing tired of people telling her to keep a positive attitude any time that she got a little bit down. She was doing her best to stay positive through all of this, but she needed it to be okay to have a bad day every now and then, and she needed to be able to talk to me about it—not for me to solve anything, just for me to listen and hear her.

Over Christmas of 2001, I somehow convinced Melissa that we should go back up to the Guanella Pass trailhead to snowshoe around in the area of the accident, thinking it would help her mental healing process (with the added bonus of it feeling like a "redo" for me). It might have helped both of us, except that I took us on the wrong trail right from the start and we were soon wallowing around through the willows on our snowshoes. Being back in this place and again feeling cold and lost made the accident coming roaring back into Melissa's memory. She cried. I felt terrible. We retraced our footsteps through the snow back to our car and went home in silence. So much for my burning desire to return to the scene of the accident and prove that I could do this the right way.

I returned to the site yet again just a little over a month later. My father and I set off to climb Mt. Bierstadt on February 10, 2002, our first time back to the area together since the accident. He and I climbed the standard route up Bierstadt with another climbing friend of mine, Ryan Gosney. Everything was so beautiful and peaceful, covered in a blanket of winter snow. As we climbed up the shoulder of Mt. Bierstadt, we kept turning around and looking down into the willows, trying our best to retrace our route from the previous May to determine which clump of trees had been our makeshift camp. But everything looked the same and we couldn't be sure where we had ended up that night.

I continued to take refuge in the mountains, climbing twenty-five of the 14,000-foot mountains during 2002, with sixteen of them being new to me and the other nine being ones I had previously climbed. I was beginning to think about setting a goal of climbing all fifty-four, but I was nervous about the Class 4 difficulty of a handful of them. The year 2002 was also the start of a tough time in my professional life, when Arthur Andersen suddenly collapsed due to the Enron scandal. I decided to leave public accounting rather than join the rest of my colleagues when they merged with another large CPA firm's Denver office. Instead, I joined a public company as director of accounting, but quickly found that I missed the fast pace of working with a number of clients on their most pressing financial needs. My hours were significantly less than at Arthur Andersen, however, so I poured my energy into climbing that summer. Melissa noticed that I wasn't working nearly as much also, and despite my frequent climbing outings, she told me that I needed to quit pacing around the house so much at night. She told me to find another hobby, so I began the application process to attend the University of Denver's MBA program beginning in the fall of 2003.

In May of 2002, Ryan Gosney and I traveled south to attempt three new peaks including one of Colorado's most difficult peaks, Little Bear, which is nestled into a group of three 14ers just southeast of the Great Sand Dunes National Park. Little Bear is rated as a Class 4 peak, so Ryan and I took my rope, our crampons, and we set off. We lugged huge backpacks up the trail from the valley floor to our planned camp at Lake Como, which sits beautifully at the base of the three peaks. This would be my first time ever on Class 4 terrain, so I was quite nervous, but grateful to have an experienced friend leading the way.

We decided to tackle 14,037-foot Little Bear first, being the hardest of the three. After climbing an initial 700 feet to the crest of Little Bear's west ridge, we traversed along the south side of the ridge toward the peak's face. The crux of the route is an area called the "Hourglass" or "Bowling Alley," a smooth, polished gully climbing steeply up 150 feet. Sadly, many climbers have lost their lives here. It was May 17 and we expected to find snow still firmly tucked in the deep gully, making our ascent slightly easier and safer with our crampons versus climbing the smooth rocks. Unfortunately, it had been a very light snow year the previous winter and all we found in the gully was a stream of ice and water in the center.

We tied into the rope with figure-eight follow-through knots and Ryan competently led the way, straddling the ice in the center, eventually reaching a solid belay stance. He put me on belay and I followed his lead up the pitch. Once out of the gully, we continued up the broad bowl that leads to Little Bear's summit ridge and tiny high point. The bowl is technically much easier, but you must be cautious, for any loose rock that is kicked down will end up rolling through the steep Hourglass/Bowling Alley gully, with the potential to injure or kill someone below you on the ascent. We had not seen anyone else coming up behind us, but we still used great care not to accidentally kick any rocks down.

We reached the summit uneventfully and saw from the summit log that we were the first ones up the peak since the previous September. Descending back down the Hourglass was much harder than climbing it (as is virtually always the case), so Ryan belayed me from above as I descended first. Thankfully I never slipped and tested the rope or Ryan's belay stance, and I was soon down at the base. Ryan then expertly down climbed the pitch and we were back at camp in no time, ready to tackle 14,345-foot Blanca Peak and its 14,042-foot neighbor, Ellingwood Point, the following day. After summiting both peaks, we quickly packed up our camp and descended in a torrential downpour.

Two weeks later, Ryan would lead us up my first steep snow climb, Dead Dog Couloir on Torreys Peak, where he taught me about crampon and ice

My dad near the top of Dead Dog Couloir in 2006.

axe use and where I first heard the phrase "this is a no fall zone." I was loving the knowledge and experience I was gaining and actually starting to enjoy some of the more difficult climbing that would be required to complete all of Colorado's 14ers.

In June of 2002, I again traveled south to the Sangre de Christo range of the Rockies with my eyes set on another new peak, to be my thirty-second unique summit out of the fifty-four—Mt. Lindsey. To my great joy, Melissa and Malcolm wanted to join me on this trip. Melissa's incisions were healed and she wanted to start getting outside and hiking again. She didn't want to climb the mountain with me, but wanted to come camp out and hike a ways up the trail. I definitely felt less guilty going on another climb since Melissa was joining me this time. The approach to Mt. Lindsey is one of the prettiest of all the 14er approaches in my opinion. The trail leads through an alpine meadow with wildflowers as far as the eye can see, with Blanca's sheer north face dramatically dominating the view to the south. We hiked together through that alpine meadow, then Melissa and Malcolm decided to stop while I climbed Lindsey's upper slopes. It was a wonderful trip for both of us, and Melissa realized that she didn't necessarily have to climb all the way to the summit to still get outside and enjoy the mountains.

In July of 2002, my dad and I climbed the "S Ridge" route up Snowmass Mountain and returned to my car only to find that it had a flat tire. It was almost as much of an adventure trying to get the car out on the four-wheel drive road with a small spare tire as it had been to climb the mountain. The

Great Sand Dunes National Park visible from Crestone Peak's summit with Blanca and Little Bear in the background.

following month, Melissa, Malcolm, and I packed into South Colony Lakes, at the foot of two of the most difficult of Colorado's 14ers, Crestone Peak and Crestone Needle. Mark Golden would join us there a day later. These spectacular jagged peaks that stand watch over the Great Sand Dunes from the north were initially viewed as unclimbable by early explorers due to the steep rock faces. Upon closer inspection though, the knobby conglomerate rock is actually quite solid and provides ample hand- and footholds to make these peaks difficult, but doable.

Across the small valley to the north of the Crestones lies another 14er called Humboldt Peak, which is an easy Class 2 trail hike all the way to the summit. Melissa had said that she wanted to climb another 14er, even if it was her last one ever, just because she was determined not to let our Mt. Evans accident be the last 14er summit on which she stood. We thought Humboldt would be a great peak for her to try, so on August 15, 2002, we set out for the summit with Malcolm the dog. Malcolm unfortunately petered out about two-thirds of the way up the trail, so we were going to have to split up. Melissa went for the summit first while I impatiently waited with Malcolm. I checked in often with her via walkie-talkie and grew frustrated when she was having trouble finding her way up the ridge to the summit. At last, she reached the summit, her first since the accident in May 2001. Melissa recalls:

> I sat alone on the summit that day and cried. I had proven that I could summit a 14er again, but was this what I wanted? Malcolm was injured down on the trail and Brad kept radioing to me that I needed to speed up. I'm not sure what I had expected from summiting another 14er, perhaps lights shining down from the heavens and an epiphany about where to go now with everything that had happened since the accident. I desperately sought direction for my future in the outdoors. The experience could not have been further from what I was searching for. I did have some joy about the view and my successful summit, but it did not fill the hole that I still had in my spirit.
>
> Heading back down, the trail was so obvious, as it had been going down Evans that day, that it was almost comical. It did not take long to make my way back down to Brad and Malcolm, and off Brad scampered to the summit. I was partially vindicated when Brad radioed back to me that the trail was indeed harder than he had thought it would be.
>
> As Brad practically ran up the mountain (I've often contemplated how he can "walk" so quickly, and decided it must be the

length of his legs) I tried to start down with Malcolm. He would go at most a couple of steps and I could tell he was just doing that out of his love for me. I noticed that the paw that he was favoring appeared to be swelling up. When we returned home two days later, Malcolm was able to hike out with his swollen foot wrapped, but we took him straight to the vet. Looking back, I don't know why we didn't hike out right away to have him examined. I think that it was because he seemed to feel fine except the paw and we were hopeful that if he rested it for a couple of days it would improve. In the end he was fine. The vet's best guess was that he had been bitten by something.

The bright spot of the trip for me ended up being my time alone in camp while Brad and Mark were climbing the Crestones. Sitting in peace with nature was what my soul craved. There is a beauty in the simplicity of nature. Things either must get done, like filtering drinking water and setting up camp, or they are not necessary. All of the noise and demands of civilization just fall away. As I sat on the boulder we would call "breakfast rock" that day, a herd of mountain goats came through the camp. One actually jumped up onto the boulder and looked at me for a moment before continuing on his journey. It was a very spiritual moment and I decided that I did want to get back out there. I just wasn't sure if it would be climbing mountains or as "base camp manager."

The view from the summit of Humboldt to the south is spectacular, with Crestone Needle's steep sharp mass on the left hand side, Crestone Peak's jagged tooth-like face on the right hand side, and an amazingly jagged ridge connecting the two. Melissa returned to me and Malcolm, then it was my turn to make a run for the summit, which I did as quickly as I could since it was getting into the afternoon. I topped out, then descended to Melissa and Malcolm. Malcolm wasn't budging though. I tried carrying him, but that wasn't going to be the answer. We ended up having to coax him all the way back to our camp, as he seemed to have injured his paw somehow. Mark had arrived and found our camp while we had been out, so all three of us enjoyed dinner together that night.

The next day, Melissa acted as "base camp manager" while Mark Golden and I set off to make an attempt on the Crestones. We planned to climb up toward Humboldt, then traverse west and south across the ridge to a large high plateau called the "Bear's Playground," then ascend Crestone Peak's northwest couloir. Mark and I climbed the steep couloir, carefully picking

Crestone Needle from Crestone Peak's summit (note the two people on the summit).

our way up the route to keep the difficulty at Class 3 and eventually reached the summit of 14,294-foot Crestone Peak shortly after I inadvertently kicked a rock down that nearly hit Mark. We looked to the west, saw clear weather and radioed Melissa that we were going to attempt the famous traverse from Crestone Peak to Crestone Needle, across that jagged ridge.

The Peak to Needle traverse actually drops several hundred feet below the jagged ridge crest on the southern side of the ridge. The route finding is very tricky as you traverse from west to east across the conglomerate rock. After several hours of carefully picking our way and just before we reached the steep southwest face of Crestone Needle, we climbed back up to the ridge crest via a narrow gully. Standing in this tiny spot on the crest of the ridge, I learned what exposure really is! We could look straight down to Upper South Colony Lake to the north and down toward Cottonwood Lake to the south. The next pitch was the crux of the entire climb and involved climbing east up a 100-foot Class 4 stretch of knobby conglomerate rock right on the ridge crest. This is the kind of pitch that can get the best of you if you stand there too long looking at it and thinking about it. To avoid getting paralyzed by fear, we started to climb and found plenty of hand- and footholds. Falling was simply not an option here on this airy face.

Soon I saw an eyebolt drilled deep into the rock and I knew we were at the top of the pitch looking at the rappel anchor. I was elated as I topped out and walked the few short feet to the summit of Crestone Needle. After radioing Melissa to update her on our progress, we descended down the southeast face of Crestone Needle, down to Broken Hand Pass and back down to our camp at Lower South Colony Lake. What a day! Melissa made us a delicious dinner and we packed out the next morning.

Melissa felt great about going on the trip, getting her first 14er summit since the accident and being such an integral part of Mark's and my success doing the challenging Peak to Needle traverse. Those two mountains, still two of my favorites in Colorado, were 14er numbers forty and forty-one out of fifty-four. A few weeks later, I climbed the remote but easy San Luis Peak with my dad and another friend whose wife and Melissa accompanied us up to timberline. With San Luis done, I had just twelve left.

Despite his reservations that perhaps it was still too soon after the accident for us to go, my dad and I had signed up for our first big glaciated peak climb, so we trained hard that fall to be ready. Melissa assured me that it was okay to go and that it was important for my dad and I to spend this quality time together. In late October 2002, Dad and I climbed 14,110-foot Pikes Peak from the Crags Campground, an 11.4-mile, 4,100 vertical foot climb (a challenge even during the summer months). That afternoon as we approached the summit, we found wintery conditions, with wind and blowing snow fighting us for each step. This time we had brought the appropriate clothing and gear, so the foul weather was just a nuisance for us. The unique thing about Pikes Peak is that you can reach the summit in any of three different ways: via hiking, as we were; via car along the Pikes Peak Highway to the summit; or via the cog railway. The two latter options are very popular with tourists, as you would expect. By the time we arrived at the summit early that afternoon, we had our full body armor on—hats, balaclavas, gloves, heavy coats, goggles, etc. Neither of us had much skin showing when we decided we'd step inside the restaurant and gift shop that sits atop the summit.

We grabbed a booth in the restaurant and treated ourselves to a cup of hot cocoa to warm up. We recognized that we had nearly 6 miles to go on our return journey and agreed not to linger long on the summit. As we walked out of restaurant at the summit, we passed a woman who had stepped outside to have a cigarette. She looked at us as if we had three heads, and with a donut in one hand and her cigarette in the other, asked us incredulously, "Did you *walk* here??" Dad was in a sassy mood for some reason and replied, "Yes. Yes we did. You should try it sometime." I don't think she quite caught Dad's sarcasm as we headed down the trail, chuckling at her shocked expression.

We descended down the trail, the weather only marginally improving, to a point where the trail is right along the side of the road. We heard a descending car slow down behind us, so we turned to look. The license plate read Louisiana. The two guys in the car gawked at us for a moment before getting up the courage to ask in a southern drawl, "Can we please take your picture?" We lightheartedly agreed that it might seem a bit silly to be walking when there was a road right there, but told them they could certainly take our picture to show their friends back home—the freaks who walked all the way to the top of a mountain when there was a perfectly good road. Every time I return to the summit of Pikes Peak, I think about the lady with the donut and cigarette and the two guys from Louisiana, and have a good laugh.

I was learning a lot about my dad as we climbed together—his amazing sense of humor, his strong sense of responsibility (both for my safety in the mountains, but also his genuine concern for how Melissa was doing and how we were doing as a young married couple). I was frankly a bit surprised at how physically strong Dad was during our training climbs, but I was even more impressed by his mental toughness and perseverance. He mentored me extensively during this time toward being a good husband and we were truly becoming friends, confiding in each other frequently. We each still wished that we could trade places with Melissa, but we knew we simply couldn't.

Melissa recalls:

Many times since the accident I have had to deal with people who felt that we were not responding to the accident as they thought we should. A frequent question was why I kept "letting" Brad go back out on hikes, "leaving me alone." It's funny, but it never occurred to me to tell him not to go. I know that hiking and the outdoors are a deep-rooted part of him. If I asked Brad to stop hiking, I would be asking him to be someone else. I did not want him to be someone else. I also recognized how important these outings were to Brad's healing process. Brad and I have always lived very busy lives with our careers, continuing educational forays, and family. The outdoors has been our place to seek solace and time to reflect and process. These outings, especially those with his dad, were as important to his recovery as my work with my counselor was to mine. Additionally, having grown up an only child of two working parents, I have always enjoyed time alone when I can find it. I have a deep need to be alone with no demands upon me. His trips were therapeutic for both of us.

We wrapped up 2002 with Dad and I traveling to central Mexico to attempt to climb North America's third highest peak, el Pico de Orizaba, at 18,491 feet—far higher than I had ever been. Orizaba is a long-dormant volcano that is viewed as being a good glaciated peak to climb first while testing your body at higher elevations, as it is much warmer and more forgiving than Denali in Alaska and Mt. Logan in Canada, North America's two tallest mountains. We joined a trip being put together by a guide out of Boulder, Colorado, and prepared to spend our Thanksgiving high on Orizaba's slopes.

Due to a couple of last minute cancellations, we ended up being the only two clients on the week-long trip. We flew into Mexico City and stayed the night in a hotel after touring parts of this massive city (the largest in the western hemisphere). The next morning we went to the bus terminal, which rivals many of the nicest airports in the United States, and boarded a bus to Puebla first, then another to a small town at the base of the mountain called Tlachichuca (pronounced la-chi-chu-kah). A local surgeon there named Senior Reyes runs a mountaineering compound with food that is absolutely delicious. As we were milling about outside on the afternoon of our arrival, we talked to some climbers who had just come down off of Orizaba. We learned that earlier that day, a climber had crashed into the rocks at the bottom of the glacier, requiring a helicopter evacuation, after having tried to glissade down with no ice axe. He had broken his pelvis among other injuries and was really quite lucky to be alive. We were sobered by hearing this and looked up at the upper mountain and the snow-white glacier on its side, hoping that we would be able to safely climb it. Eventually we moved inside and after a wonderful dinner, we stayed the night in a common area with bunk beds.

The next morning we loaded our gear into a four-wheel drive vehicle and drove to about 11,000 feet, where we set up our first camp to begin acclimatizing for the higher elevations ahead. The acclimatization process is one of the most important aspects of climbing taller mountains. As you move higher, there is less atmospheric pressure, so your circulatory system has to work harder to get the level of oxygen needed to power the muscles. Gradually, your body produces more red blood cells to assist in getting the oxygen distributed and your respiratory rate increases. Some in the climbing community believe that drinking water is one of the best things you can do to help your body acclimatize more quickly, and our guide instructed us at our 11,000-foot camp to drink triple the amount of water we normally would.

Ordinarily I drink quite a bit of water—usually 2.5 liters a day from a Nalgene bottle that accompanies me almost everywhere I go, much like Charlie Brown's friend Linus's blanket. Triple 2.5 liters a day would be 7.5 liters, and being the obedient client, I started pounding water all afternoon at camp. We got our first glimpse of what was to come with our guide when he berated me for drinking too much, telling me that I was going to drink all the water he had brought and we'd have none left for the upper mountain. I tried to explain to him that I was just trying to follow his instructions of tripling my normal intake. When he inquired how much I normally drank and I told him 2.5 liters per day, he told me that was plenty and not to drink extra after all.

We broke camp the next morning to move higher up the mountain. Our guide sent Dad and me off up the road on foot with small daypacks containing just some snacks and water to give us an acclimatization hike while he accompanied the rest of our gear in the four-wheel drive vehicle. Our destination was a camp at 14,000 feet where we would spend another night to continue to let our bodies get used to the altitude. There is a hut at this camp, but it can be quite noisy and isn't the cleanest place in the world, so we opted to set up our tents a quarter mile lower, off to the side of the trail. Dad and I were sharing my small two-man tent while our guide spread out in a three-man tent that we would all share higher up the mountain. Dad and I are both six foot-four and fairly skinny. When you see a label on a tent that says "Two man," what it really means is that you can get two adults into the tent if you really have to, but you are going to fill every square inch of that small space. That can actually be a nice thing on cold nights at higher elevations with the tight quarters being warmed considerably. Much to our dismay, however, we spent a lot more time in that tent at 14,000 feet than we had planned.

It started raining mid-afternoon that first day at 14,000 feet. And it rained, and it rained. Our guide heated water and brought it over at dinner time for us to make our food. It was Thanksgiving Day and I had brought a dehydrated turkey tetrazzini meal to celebrate. This was not how I was used to spending my Thanksgivings—stuck in a two-man tent, eating dehydrated turkey tetrazzini for dinner with the rain pounding down outside. Not wanting to leave the tent and get drenched, we used our pee bottles when we needed to go. Dad and I tried to stay positive and passed the time until bed playing gin rummy in our cramped little tent. It continued to rain throughout the night with the water gradually overwhelming the seams of the tent, dampening our sleeping bags and clothes inside. The itinerary called for us to move up to our high camp at almost 16,000 feet just below the glacier the next afternoon to prepare for our summit climb. The weather was putting our summit attempt obviously in question.

It finally stopped raining at 4:00 in the afternoon, after more than twenty-four hours straight of heavy rain. The intense high altitude sun came out and our guide quickly yelled to us to get our wet stuff out of the tent and spread it out on the nearby rocks so that it could dry. It was astonishing just how fast everything dried in that hot afternoon sun. Within an hour, we were packed up with our dry sleeping bags and climbing up to our high camp. I closely watched my watch altimeter, anxiously waiting to cross over my previous high point at 14,400 feet, which happened not far above camp. As we climbed higher, the trail became narrower and all of the vegetation disappeared, replaced by volcanic rocks as far as the eye could see. We reached high camp at the foot of the glacier at dusk and quickly set up the three-man tent that we would all share for a few hours before our midnight alpine start for the summit climb.

We ate a quick dinner, and then turned in early, hoping for a few hours of sleep before it was time to go. We were very excited and nervous about the upcoming summit climb, so Dad and I had a hard time sleeping. Our guide was used to the routine and was soon asleep. Around 10:00 or 11:00 p.m., we heard rustling outside the tent. Our guide jumped up and unzipped the tent, finding tiny alpine mice trying to get into his food bag that was outside the tent. He began yelling at the tiny creatures and throwing rocks to try to scare them away, which we found slightly humorous. In what seemed like only minutes after things settled back down again, the alarms went off and it was time to get up and get moving.

We dressed in our warm layers and donned our plastic insulated double boots for the first time on the trip. Since we would almost immediately leave the rocks and start up the glacier, we also needed to put on our crampons. I had worn mine a few times before on snow climbs in Colorado, but this was a first for my dad. He was struggling to get the toe bail to fit into the groove across the front of his boot to secure the crampon before snapping the rear buckle above the heel plate. I tried to assist, but my hands were cold and I wasn't having much luck either.

Our guide asked what was taking so long and my dad said he was having trouble. "They went on just fine at REI," Dad said. That really set our guide off and we caught a glimpse at what we have to assume was an earlier career in the marines as a drill sergeant. He began yelling and screaming at us and asking why we had wasted so much time in our tent in the rain playing cards when we should have been checking our gear. He was dropping expletives like crazy while mumbling to himself, "… they fit fine at REI, huh? Well that doesn't do us a #*!% bit of good up here, now does it!!!!" All of the points he was making were fair as I look back on it now. We should have been checking our gear in our downtime and had this been offered as a suggestion to us, given that it was our first ever climb like this with a guide, we would have gladly done so. We simply hadn't thought of it and were now paying the price. The guide grabbed a rock and began banging away on the toe bail on the front of Dad's crampons trying to bend them to fit. Finally, the crampons were on and despite feeling belittled, we followed our guide onto the glacier.

As we tied into the rope, we were instructed on something that would become my dad's new favorite hiking term—"expedition pace," meaning that we were going to be moving slowly and steadily as we climbed, stopping for breaks only about once an hour. To sustain our upward movement for a full hour at this altitude, we would need to slow our pace significantly and use a technique called the "rest step," in which your back leg locks after each step to put the vast majority of your body weight on the skeletal system, saving the muscles from fatigue. This was a game changer for us as I was used to climbing mountains with Dad much as a dog would—running up ahead as fast as I could until I was out of breath, turning around and trotting back down to where Dad was, checking in with him and repeating the cycle again and again. From now on, whenever I took off quickly up the trail, I would hear Dad saying, "Whoa junior!!!! Expedition pace!!!!"

We climbed steadily up the glacier during the night, deliberately rolling our ankles (a challenge for Dad with his fused ankle) to get all of our crampon points firmly attached to the hard glacial snow as the terrain got steeper and steeper. We had nearly reached the crater rim of this huge volcano by

Climbing up Orizaba's glacier just after sunrise.

sunrise. When the sun began to rise in the east, we saw the spectacular cone-shaped shadow of the mountain dominating the valley to the west. When we reached the crater rim soon thereafter, we got our first ever look down into the inside of a volcano. There was very little snow inside the crater, but rather, it was a wasteland of rotten, crumbling sulfuric rock, complete with that strong sulfuric rotten-egg smell. We traversed along the rim of the crater to the highest point and high-fived each other. It was Saturday, November 30, my Dad's fifty-second birthday and I finally got to give him his birthday present, which I was carrying in my pack, hoping we would get to the summit—a two pack of Hostess cupcakes to serve as his birthday cake. He offered to share, but my stomach was a little upset as the effects of the altitude were taking their toll on me.

By mid-morning, we were going back across the crater rim to begin our nearly 2,500-foot descent of the steep glacier. As we descended, I remember getting to the point of boiling, still wearing my hard shell jacket that I had put on to keep warm on the summit. I asked our guide if we could stop so I could strip off a layer and he went ballistic again. He told me that I couldn't, then yelled to my dad, "Brad's not with us anymore! He must be getting hypothermic since he wants to strip off all of his clothes!" I tried to explain that I really was just hot, but it was no use. I wasn't permitted to take off my hard shell until we got off the glacier nearly 2,500 feet below. I have since learned the importance of knowing your body and the temperature at which you are comfortable hiking. A future guide shared with me a wonderful guideline that I use every time I go up now, which is to start the ascent or descent just a little on the cold side since you will quickly warm up and be at the perfect temperature once you start moving. If you are comfortable or even worse, a little warm, before you start walking, you are going to be miserable, soon baking yourself!

Orizaba was a great bonding experience for Dad and me, but our first experience with a guide left a lot to be desired.

Orizaba's shadow on the valley floor.

Dad's fifty-second "birthday cake" on the summit of Orizaba.

CHAPTER 8

The Quest Continues

I went back to Mt. Bierstadt in January 2003, climbing through the willows that had claimed Melissa's toes, and reached the summit for the fifth time. At the end of May that year, I organized a trip up to Aspen to make my first attempt on the famous picturesque Maroon Bells via the steep snow Bell Cord couloir that ascends the west face between South Maroon Peak and its neighbor to the north (which is really nothing more than a high point on a rugged ridge, despite looking like two separate mountains in the common photos seen from Maroon Lake). My spirits were pretty down due to my continued feelings of guilt, the unplanned change in jobs and where my career was headed at this point, so I was anxious to take solace in the mountains and enjoy some challenging terrain that summer before beginning my MBA program in the fall. It was definitely the first time I actually *looked forward* to the more difficult Class 3 and 4 terrain.

My father and Ryan Gosney joined me for this attempt on the Bell Cord, which turned out to be quite futile. Starting around 3:00 a.m., we encountered deep snow on the approach hike to the base of the couloir and made very slow progress once in the couloir. When doing snow climbs, avalanche danger increases considerably by mid-morning as the sun warms up the snow that had been frozen during the cold night before. By our targeted summit time at 8:00 a.m., we had only climbed to around 13,000 feet, leaving us with about 1,200 feet to go before the summit (after which we obviously had to descend). The three of us made the wise decision to turn around and try again another day—the mountain would still be there.

Two weeks later, my parents joined Melissa and me on a trek into South Colony Lakes, at the foot of the Crestone Peaks that I had climbed the year before. This had clearly been a much snowier winter and it became obvious that my father and I were not going to be able to ascend either of the Crestones without crampons and ice axes. Instead, we set off to try to climb another new peak, 14,165-foot Kit Carson, which is just northwest of the Crestones and is accessible from the South Colony Lakes area. The conditions were much easier as we traversed across the broad ridge in between Humboldt Peak and Kit Carson. We eventually reached the 13,980-foot high point on the ridge known as "Kat Carson." From here, the route descends 250 feet of Class 3 rock to a saddle, then climbs to the summit of Kit Carson. Unfortunately, a storm was brewing to the west and we decided we'd better turn back before the weather moved in. That was the wise choice of course, but I seemed to be stuck at forty-two of the fifty-four Colorado 14ers, having been dismissed by the Maroon Bells and Kit Carson in back-to-back attempts. Oh well, I thought—it's better to be alive and try another day than push a bad situation.

In July of 2003, Dad and I were back for more, this time traveling to the southwest corner of the state near Durango to attempt a group of three peaks known as the "Wilderness Peaks" because of the difficulty of access. We had a wonderful time of it, though. First, you board the famous Durango-Silverton narrow gauge railroad in downtown Durango. A few tourists give you strange looks when they see the massive backpacks that climbers load onto the train. After chugging along up the narrow canyon for an hour or two, the train stops at a place called "Needleton," which consists of nothing more than a bridge across the Animas River. Again, you get strange looks as you stand up from your seat and depart the train with the crowd of tourists believing that you surely must be confused ... "The train stops in Silverton where there are restaurants and shops—there is nothing in between" they must be thinking. As you pull your backpacks out of the luggage car on the train and throw them on, people continue to stare at you out the windows as the train continues its journey north.

Across the bridge and into the wilderness we went, not knowing exactly when we would return to this place called Needleton to board the train for our return trip. We lugged our heavy packs up into Chicago Basin where we set up our camp in the beautiful high alpine meadow, which many mountain goats call home. The next morning, we set out for the first of the three 14ers that surround the upper basin, 14,083-foot Mt. Eolus, named for the Greek god of the winds, Aeolus. Thankfully, the mountain wasn't true to its name and we had a delightfully calm day, reaching the summit without any issues. When we returned to camp, I was anxious to take off my hiking boots and put on my leather sandals, which I had left under the vestibule of our tent. Much to my dismay, a mountain goat had already found them and chewed the leather beyond recognition in an attempt to extract the salt that goats so crave. Bummer!

The next day we ascended into the upper basin again, this time veering to

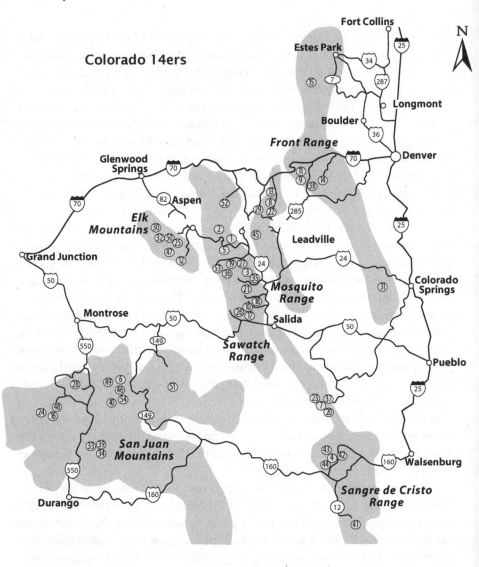

Colorado 14ers

1. Mount Elbert	14,433	11. Torreys Peak	14,267
2. Mount Massive	14,421	12. Castle Peak	14,265
3. Mount Harvard	14,420	13. Quandary Peak	14,265
4. Blanca Peak	14,345	14. Mount Evans	14,264
5. La Plata Peak	14,336	15. Longs Peak	14,255
6. Uncompahgre Peak	14,309	16. Mount Wilson	14,246
7. Crestone Peak	14,294	17. Mount Shavano	14,229
8. Mount Lincoln	14,286	18. Mount Princeton	14,197
9. Grays Peak	14,270	19. Mount Belford	14,197
10. Mount Antero	14,269	20. Crestone Needle	14,197

21. Mount Yale	14,196	38. Mount Bierstadt	14,060
22. Mount Bross	14,172	39. Sunlight Peak	14,059
23. Kit Carson Peak	14,165	40. Handies Peak	14,048
24. El Diente Peak	14,159	41. Culebra Peak	14,047
25. Maroon Peak	14,156	42. Mount Lindsey	14,042
26. Tabeguache Peak	14,155	43. Ellingwood Peak	14,042
27. Mount Oxford	14,153	44. Little Bear Peak	14,037
28. Mount Sneffels	14,150	45. Mount Sherman	14,036
29. Mount Democrat	14,148	46. Redcloud Peak	14,034
30. Capitol Peak	14,130	47. Pyramid Peak	14,018
31. Pikes Peak	14,110	48. Wilson Peak	14,017
32. Snowmass Mountain	14,092	49. Wetterhorn Peak	14,017
33. Mount Eolus	14,083	50. North Maroon Peak	14,014
34. Windom Peak	14,082	51. San Luis Peak	14,014
35. Mount Columbia	14,073	52. Mount of the Holy Cross	14,005
36. Missouri Mountain	14,067	53. Huron Peak	14,003
37. Humboldt Peak	14,064	54. Sunshine Peak	14,001

---

the north toward 14,059-foot Sunlight Peak. We climbed up the steep broken rock ledges to reach Sunlight's famous Class 4 crux move—a step across an exposed gap, then being forced to pull yourself up onto the rounded summit block. This is the only mountain I've climbed where the only part of me to touch the summit was my chest as I hugged that final rock, staring 2,000 feet down the northwest face on the other side. After Dad gave the true summit his version of a bear hug, we settled to eat our snack at a less exposed spot just below.

For some strange reason, Dad decided to see whether he could still get his wedding ring off his altitude-swollen fingers—the same wedding ring that had been cut from his hand at the hospital after coming off Mt. Evans, which he had taken in and had repaired. This small task became a mission for him—one that he was determined to see through. He finally succeeded in prying the ring from his finger, and it flew up into the air. He tried to catch it but failed. Clink, clink, clink (softer), clink (softer) was all we heard as the ring fell down deeper and deeper into the mound of loose rocks just below the summit. The ring was hopelessly lost. First my leather sandals and now Dad's wedding ring! This wasn't going very well. Dad told me many years later that when he passes away someday, he wants to be cremated and have his ashes spread on the summit of a 14er. I've assured him that I'll take his ashes back to Sunlight Peak and sprinkle them down on that same spot just below the summit so that he can be with his wedding ring again.

We planned to do both Sunlight and the final peak, 14,082-foot Windom Peak, the same day, so we descended to about 13,100 feet and then traversed

Dad cautiously hugging the summit of Sunlight Peak, where his wedding ring still resides.

east to the base of Windom. As we climbed Windom, the Greek god of wind from neighboring Eolus had awakened and it was quite breezy. We quickly topped out on Windom, and then retraced our steps back down to our camp for another night before packing out the next day.

If we thought that we had gotten strange looks from the tourists on the train on the way *into* the wilderness, we quickly learned that those were nothing compared to the looks we got coming *out* of the wilderness! The passengers were confused as to who these dirty, smelly people were that wanted to board the train at this little river crossing in the middle of nowhere. Were they Old West bandits? Were they lost? Were they drifters? The conductor understandably requested that we take seats in one of the "open air" cars for the return trip to civilization, not wanting us to disturb the other passengers with our stench in the cars that didn't have any airflow. It didn't matter to us—we felt great and I had logged off peaks forty-three, forty-four, and forty-five toward that magical number of fifty-four.

From Durango, we decided to take the rugged route north and into the town of Telluride to attempt one more peak before we returned home to Denver. Two days after climbing Sunlight and Windom, we began our ascent of 14,150-foot Mt. Sneffels via the Class 3 southwest ridge route. Mt. Sneffels is a magnificent, rocky peak that dominates the view to the south from the town of Montrose and is often photographed in the fall, with early snowfall providing a white blanket on the upper mountain, while the aspen trees on the lower slopes dramatically change into their splendid oranges, reds, and yellows. We thoroughly enjoyed this scramble up the steep but solid ridge, having to retrace our steps just once after getting slightly off route. We reached the summit in fine weather, logging off my forty-sixth unique 14er, and descended down the easier south slopes route and returned to Denver. It had been a great trip, but I was anxious to see Melissa again. I thanked her for being so understanding of my time away.

Three weeks later, a friend at work, Chad, told me he would really like to join me for a 14er climb one day. I quickly agreed and convinced him to accompany me on my second attempt of Kit Carson, this time from the west side from Willow Lake. Chad's wife and Melissa joined us as well for the short hike by headlamp in the dark into our camp, but didn't plan to attempt the summit climb with us. Instead, they slept in and did a short hike up to the lake after breakfast. Chad decided he had had enough when we reached the summit of a neighboring high point on the ridge called Challenger Point at 14,081 feet, itself above 14,000 feet, but standing too close to Kit Carson with not enough of a drop between them to be included on the most commonly accepted list of fifty-four. I was in great hiking shape by this time of the summer, so I scampered off alone from Challenger Point, quickly climbed the final Class 3 blocks up to Kit Carson's summit, and returned to descend from Challenger Point with Chad. But it had taken us quite a while to round-trip the hike, and we returned to camp finding angry and concerned wives. Melissa recalls this being the first of three times that I have put her in a position of needing to talk another significant other off the ledge, assuring each of them that we were okay and there was no need to call search and rescue just yet. Despite Melissa's success in this discussion (and that we really were okay), it was still a long, quiet drive back to Denver.

I was now at forty-seven peaks, with just seven to go: Capitol Peak, South Maroon, North Maroon, Pyramid Peak, Culebra Peak, Mt. Wilson, and El Diente. Six of the seven (all but Culebra) were viewed to be tough peaks, with several rated among the most difficult of all. But summer was ending and my MBA program was starting, so they would have to wait until the summer of 2004.

CHAPTER 9

Tragedy Strikes

I worked hard in my MBA program during the fall, winter, and spring quarters of 2003–2004. I was really enjoying the program and had gotten all A's so far (I had plenty of spare time given my reduced weekly workloads in private industry). I had high hopes for the summer of 2004, having requested a week of vacation at the end of August and reserved a condo in Aspen with plans to try to climb my four remaining peaks in the difficult Elk Range—the Maroon Bells, Capitol, and Pyramid. I wanted to be in great shape by the time I went to Aspen, so I climbed Mt. Bierstadt again in April and yet again in early June. I logged off two more ascents of Torreys Peak, both via Kelso Ridge, one on June 9 with my friend Chad and one on June 27 with my dad. On Monday afternoon, June 28, I got the phone call at work.

An executive assistant that I knew from my friend and climbing partner Mark Golden's work was on the other end of the phone. She was crying. "Brad" she said, "I have some very bad news. Mark Golden died Saturday in a fall from Snowmass Mountain" (a 14er in the Elk Range). I felt as if I had just been punched in the stomach. I couldn't breathe and I suddenly felt faint. I just couldn't believe what I was hearing.

I had been sitting in this exact spot at my desk the previous Thursday when Mark had called me to ask for advice on the route he was planning to climb on Saturday, the "S Ridge" from Snowmass Mountain's south side (so named for its curving shape). Mark was training for a climb of Kilimanjaro later that summer and had big plans to climb some new 14ers in Colorado prior to leaving for Africa. Mark knew that I had done the route a few years before and also knew that this was not the standard/easiest route up Snowmass. The description of this route is not overly robust in Gerry Roach's guidebook, so Mark wanted more details. We talked about the initial scrambling up the steep and at times loose gray granite that was required to attain the ridge. I also shared with him that we had previously stuck fairly close to the ridge crest toward the summit since the rock was more solid there, albeit also more exposed. I wished Mark well, with my final words to him, "Be safe."

We know that Mark reached the summit of Snowmass Mountain that day because his camera survived the fall. Mark's one summit photo was a spectacular shot that his family had enlarged and prominently displayed at his memorial service. Mark's parents would later write to me, commenting about that photo, "It is easy to see the beauty and peace that Mark found at the top of a mountain." We don't know much else about Mark's fall. His hiking companion that day stopped part of the way up the ridge and agreed to meet Mark back at the car after Mark had completed the climb. When Mark didn't return to the trailhead that evening, his climbing partner reported him missing. The next morning, thirty-one volunteer search and rescue team members set out to try to locate and rescue him. At about 4:00 p.m. Sunday, he was spotted on a precarious ledge at about 11,000 feet, but was unresponsive to the rescuer's attempts to make contact. Due to the difficult terrain, they were only able to get to within a few hundred feet of him that day.

Me looking upward at Snowmass Mountain years later.

Arvada climber falls to his death on Snowmass Mountain

By Jerry Roys
ROCKY MOUNTAIN NEWS

SNOWMASS — An Arvada man plunged more than a third of a mile to his death Saturday near Snowmass Ski Area, according to Gunnison County sheriff's officials.

His body was recovered Monday afternoon.

Mark Golden, 32, fell between 1,800 and 2,000 feet while descending Snowmass Mountain near Aspen. He had reached the summit of the 14,092-foot peak and may have been looking for a shortcut on the way down when he fell, Gunnison County Undersheriff Rick Besecker said.

A hiking companion who accompanied Golden part of the way up the peak, turned back and waited to meet him at the trailhead. He reported Golden missing Saturday night after Golden failed to arrive at their designated meeting place, Besecker said.

At dawn Sunday, West Elk Search and Rescue Group began a search of the area where Golden was climbing. His body was located in a snowfield on the west side of the mountain about 4 p.m., Besecker said.

Besecker said there is no trail leading to the summit and the climb is a difficult one. Snowmass Mountain is part of the Elk Mountains in the Maroon Bells-Snowmass Wilderness.

Thirty-one people from eight rescue agencies and an outfitting company in Gunnison and Pitkin counties were involved in the recovery of the body Monday.

Golden's father, Peter, said his son was "the outdoors type" and that he had spent five years in the U.S. Coast Guard and was an Eagle Scout.

Golden was employed as a computer consultant.

Golden, 32, fell more than a third of a mile.

On Monday, the mission had been reclassified from a rescue to a recovery, and the search and rescue volunteers used special equipment to reach his body. The rescuers found "obvious catastrophic trauma consistent with a fall" upon reaching his body, words that still haunt me to this day. The volunteers carried Mark's broken body down through scree and snowfields until they reached a place where it could be loaded onto a horse. Rescue personnel believed that Mark may have been looking for a shortcut on the descent when he fell an estimated 1,800 to 2,000 feet. Years later, Melissa and I had the opportunity to speak with one of the volunteers who recovered Mark's body (it was Aron Ralston, the guy who cut his own arm off to free himself from a slot canyon in Utah, who my company had brought in to tell his inspiring story) and was told that they believed Mark had been trying to descend a steep snow couloir from the crest of the ridge, possibly even trying to glissade down, but not having an ice axe with him. He must have realized that he was sliding out of control and attempted to stop, ripping his fingers down to the bones.

I have told this story many times over the years to those I have met on Colorado's highest peaks that were thinking about glissading down the snow without an ice axe. It is far too easy to gain speed sliding down a steep snowy hill and extreme care must be used to ensure that: a) you know where the snow leads and b) you have the ability to manage your speed and safely stop yourself with your ice axe. Mark's tragic and premature end has helped me to steer many others over the years away from his path, but I unfortunately can't go back in time and share that advice with Mark via phone on that Thursday before he died when I gave him my input on the route.

Mark was a great friend and colleague of mine and I know he was a loving and caring son to his parents. He had spent five years in the U.S. Coast Guard and was also an Eagle Scout. I think of Mark often. Every time I record a new peak climbed in my Excel spreadsheet, I see my note from 2004 indicating the date he passed away. He was my climbing partner on ten of my first forty-one peaks (second only to my dad) and I still miss his company.

Mark Golden on the summit of Crestone Peak in 2002 before our traverse to Crestone Needle.

CHAPTER 10

Life Goes On (Again)

Melissa and my father attended Mark's funeral with me in early July. Mark's death shook me up and I didn't climb again for a month. Mark was the first person my age that I had known who had died. I asked myself whether I should keep climbing or whether I should give it up. Each time I thought about stopping, all I could think of was the beauty, peace, and serenity that I feel when I am in the wilderness, and especially high up on a summit ridge. Melissa and I discussed it as well and she told me that climbing was too important to me and my mental well being for me to not do it. "Just be careful" is all she asked. It was even more important now since we had just learned that Melissa was pregnant with our first child. To celebrate the news, we raced out and bought Melissa a shiny new Subaru Outback station wagon.

My next time out was not until July 31 when Dad and I decided to drive up the Mt. Evans road to a shoulder at about 13,000 feet and park. We descended down into the valley to the west toward Mt. Bierstadt's east ridge. As we climbed the steep, exposed ridge, high off the valley floor, I began to freak out and think about Mark and his fall. I was having trouble moving across the exposed ridge, at times stopping, looking down and imagining falling from such a high place. Dad was instrumental in calming me down and focusing me on the task at hand. It reminded me of some of my first Class 3 climbs where my dad really did the heavy lifting of getting me safely down. After reaching Mt. Bierstadt's summit yet again, we traversed across the famous Sawtooth Ridge, then ascended the west ridge to Mt. Evans' summit, this time via the proper route rather than the erroneous route that we had followed back in May of 2001. What a difference being on the trail makes.

We were just two weeks out now from the trip to Aspen to attempt some of Colorado's most dangerous peaks, in the same range as Snowmass Mountain, from which Mark fell. Melissa knew I really wanted to climb all of Colorado's 14ers, but she also understandably didn't want to be a widow raising a child. I offered to check and see whether there were guides in Aspen that could accompany us up the two most difficult peaks we were going to attempt—Capitol and Pyramid. She agreed that this was an appropriate compromise, so I quickly lined up a guide from Aspen Expeditions, a reputable guide service in the area. Melissa recalls:

> Mark's death and talking with Aron Ralston at Brad's work function took on a new tone for me in the light of my pregnancy. Of course there were the expected concerns about Brad dying and leaving me a single mother, but those were actually trumped by my sudden and deep connection with their mothers. Before I became a mother I had not fully appreciated what my mom, Brad's mom, Mark's mom, and Aron's mom had experienced. To this day I balance my hope that our children grow up loving the outdoors like we do with my anxiety that I do not want to be in these wonderful mothers' shoes, not knowing where our child is and if they are hurt. The love that we feel for our children and our desire to keep them safe is primal. At times I find it hard to temper it with cheering our kids on as they fly farther from the nest.

We decided to start with Capitol Peak, widely viewed as one of Colorado's hardest 14ers, primarily due to the infamous "knife ridge," a sharp stretch of ridge about 100 feet long with a 1,000-foot drop off on either side. Our guide was a wonderfully mellow guy named Bob Sloezen, nicknamed "Slow Man." Slow Man was the exact opposite of our guide on Orizaba—there was nothing drill sergeant about him. He was in his late forties or early fifties (not much younger than my dad at the time). He had a long, shaggy beard and a down to earth, easy to get along with personality. When we arrived at our camp near Capitol Lake the night of August 14, he actually pulled three cold beers out of his backpack for us to enjoy.

On the morning of August 15, we got an alpine start and climbed the initial easy slope to Capitol's northeast ridge in the dark. Slow Man then roped us up as we descended some steep terrain down into the basin below our next destination—the 13,664-foot point on the ridge known as "K2." After climbing down the steep west face of K2, it was time to cross the famous knife ridge. This is a place where you don't want to linger too long. Pausing here and looking at this dramatic ridge can quickly cause you to reconsider whether this is really a mountain you want to climb. We were very glad Slow Man was with us and had us tied into the rope! We started across the ridge and found that the rock was extremely solid with footholds seeming to

Dad crossing Capitol's famous knife ridge.

magically appear right where they were needed on one side of the ridge crest or the other. It was clearly not somewhere you wanted to fall from, but we felt oddly secure moving slowly and steadily across the solid rock toward easier ground on the other side. Once Dad and I were across, we looked back to see Slow Man walking upright across the knife ridge that we had just gone across with our hands never leaving the rock. Wow.

The rest of Capitol receives almost no mention in the guidebooks or climbing posts—everything is about the knife ridge. We actually found the next stretch up the eastern face of the peak to be more unnerving due to the loose rock. Shortly after we came off the knife ridge and got onto the face, a climber above us accidentally sent a bowling ball-sized rock down toward us. Slow Man was out in front and moved to the side as the rock whizzed past. That was too close for comfort. Slow Man yelled up to the climber above us, "That one didn't kill us—send down another if you want to try again!!!" Thankfully, no other rocks were released and soon we were on Capitol's tiny summit (my forty-eighth), looking down over the northwest face toward Capitol Lake and our tent far below.

When we got back to the guide shop in Aspen that afternoon, we asked whether Slow Man was available to be our guide later that week for our attempt on Pyramid—we were thrilled to learn that he was, so we bid him farewell for a few days and made plans to meet for Pyramid at the end of our week in Aspen. That night, we enjoyed a big celebratory dinner and a game of cards back at our condo with my mom and Melissa. The bond between Melissa and my dad was growing stronger and stronger as time passed. They had a riot being pinochle partners against Mom and me; frequently Dad would be on the verge of tears from laughing so hard as he took the pair "set" on a fairly regular basis. It was wonderful to see my dad's increased comfort level being around Melissa. It seemed like he was beginning to forgive himself for what happened to her.

U.S. Forest Service plaque for the Maroon Bells. Photo courtesy of Bernie Towne.

In between our guided climbs of Capitol and Pyramid, Dad and I planned to attempt the Maroon Bells on two separate days. On August 17, we started our climb up South Maroon Peak, the taller of the two at 14,156 feet. The Maroon Lake trailhead is a scenic place known to people around the world from all of the photographs. Many people come here to have a first-hand look at the Maroon Bells—their beauty is simply stunning. Many of these same people have been tempted over the years to go just a little bit closer and a little bit closer and maybe even attempt to climb these picturesque peaks. Many of them have died trying and today, a bronze U.S. Forest Service plaque just past the main loop around the lake morbidly greets would-be climbers with the message entitled, "The Deadly Bells."

Every time I see that sign, it has its intended effect on me—fear. Here I was back for a second attempt at South Maroon Peak, wondering if I was truly qualified. I had done all but six of Colorado's highest peaks already, but boy does that plaque get you thinking. Up the trail we went, past Crater Lake, then onto South Maroon's eastern slopes. The trail ascends steeply up the grassy slopes toward the south ridge. This is where it gets tricky.

South Maroon is rated a Class 3, meaning some scrambling and hand and foot climbing are required—an easier ranking than Capitol, Pyramid, or North Maroon, all of which require some Class 4 climbing to reach their summits. The key, however, to keeping South Maroon a Class 3 climb is staying on the proper route. We found this no easy task—we found it nearly impossible. The plaque is correct that the rock is downsloping. Each ledge on which you travel is covered with loose rock and is eager to escort anyone not careful right off the ledge. Massive rocks hang above you everywhere on the slope, somehow staying put for the moment, but seeming ready to fall at any time. We coined these the "widow maker" rocks and we used extreme caution as we ascended. We did our best to follow the trail, constantly searching for the next cairn. Unfortunately, many a lost hiker on South Maroon Peak has made himself a cairn to mark his way back down and we soon found ourselves cliffed out below a "death trap" gully on the west face of the mountain.

As we were backtracking to find the correct trail, we saw a climber about 50 feet above us who told us that he was confident he was on the right trail. Glad to know where we were supposed to be, we backtracked until we found our missed upward turn and regained the main trail. It was 3:00 p.m. by

Dad among the loose rock in one of South Maroon's countless deadly gullies.

the time we reached the summit, my forty-ninth. The weather had held so far that day, but didn't look great to the west. The climber who we had seen above us was on the summit with us and was contemplating doing the difficult but famous traverse over to North Maroon Peak. He turned to us, and in a German accent said, "Are you going to do zee traverse?" "Hell no!" we replied and quickly headed back down the south ridge. We were again astonished at how easy a trail is to follow from above. It was 6:00 p.m. by the time we reached the trailhead again—a whopping thirteen hours after we had started. We drove back to Aspen and had a wonderful celebratory dinner that night with Melissa and my mom.

Two days later we drove Melissa's brand new Outback to Maroon Lake again, this time to attempt North Maroon Peak. We planned another alpine start, so it was still pitch black as we drove up the road. About a mile from the trailhead, we saw someone running down the hill toward us. He flagged us down and told us that his friend had fallen the day before and had wounded his leg. They had been descending through the night trying to get him down and had finally reached the trailhead. However, they had parked their car down at the shuttle bus parking area many miles down the road. He asked if we could please go up the road, get his wounded friend, then drive them down to their car so they could get him to the hospital.

We of course agreed, so he jumped in and we raced up the road, with the smell of our new guest (who I later learned was one of Aron Ralston's roommates) nothing compared to the "new car smell" that Melissa's car was still sporting. We got to the trailhead and found the wounded hiker. His leg and knee were badly cut by his fall on the sharp rocks and they had put on a tourniquet to stop the bleeding. He was placed in Melissa's car and we barreled down the road back to the shuttle bus parking area and their car. We offered to take them straight to the hospital, but they declined and said they'd handle it from there. We bid them well and turned around and drove back to the trailhead once more, not yet realizing we would need to clean blood off the tan leather seats of Melissa's brand new car after our climb.

As we passed the "Deadly Bells" plaque for a second time that week, I was really hoping that this would be the last time I would ever need to attempt one of the Bells. But it was not to be. As we ascended the steep slopes of North Maroon above Crater Lake, then traversed across a stream and over a rocky moraine to the start of the more difficult areas of the upper mountain, it began to rain. We knew that this was no place to be when the rocks were wet and slippery, so we immediately retreated. It began to rain harder and harder and soon were drenched. It was then that my father chose to teach me one of the most enjoyable lessons he has ever taught me—how to cross a stream.

I was in front leading us down in our retreat along the narrow trail with thick shrubs on both sides of us. When I arrived at the stream, which we had crossed earlier that morning, I found that it was running much wider and deeper than before. The rocks on these peaks get extremely slippery when they are wet, so I wasn't sure about trying to jump from rock to rock in order to cross over. My dad had now caught up to me and was standing close behind me, but couldn't tell why I had stopped. As I continued to study the rocks and test my footing, looking for the best course of action, I could actually *feel* him fidgeting behind me, getting anxious. He finally said, "What the hell are you waiting for?!?" I replied, "The rocks are really slippery and I'm not sure how to get across." He saw his opportunity for a valuable fatherly lesson.

With his right arm, he brushed past me so that he was now in the front. Then he said his now famous words, "Well, how about this?" as he leapt from the trail to the first rock visible above the stream. When his foot hit that slippery rock, he reminded me of a cartoon character on a kid show. Dad froze before my eyes, nearly horizontal, but suspended in mid-air as his feet rapidly backpedaled, looking for anything to grip. There was nothing of course and he fell into the stream with a splash. Madder than a wet hen now, he jumped up and finished the stream crossing demonstration, not really caring anymore how wet he got. Once I had stopped laughing and thanking him for showing me the way, I went back to my careful study of the best way across, eventually finding a rock I was comfortable with and crossing without issue. Of course, my father finds this story funny now and I have told it to many friends over the years as one of my favorite father/son memories.

Another two days later, with one of the two Bells to our credit, Slow Man picked us up at the condo for our final attempt that week—Pyramid Peak. We told him about having climbed South Maroon earlier in the week and being rained off of North Maroon. His response was, "You climbed South Maroon without a guide? That's the one out of all of these mountains that *I would have hired me* for." We quickly agreed with him that it would have been great to have him with us that day!

But today was about climbing Pyramid. The trail to Pyramid starts the same way as the approach to the Bells, so we passed the Deadly Bells plaque for a third time. Pyramid shares the same rotten rock and downsloping ledges of the Bells and has a reputation of having very difficult route finding on the upper mountain with no room for error, as falls in the last 1,000 feet are usually fatal. The weather forecast showed the customary 30 percent chance of rain, which seems standard near Aspen. The 30 percent chance is high enough so that the weather forecasters can always say, "We told you it might rain," but low enough that you convince yourself that it means there's a 70 percent chance of sunshine.

On this morning we were climbing well, having acclimatized nicely over the past week. There were low clouds almost like fog drifting through the valleys and around the peaks as we climbed to Pyramid's north shoulder, then around to the east face where the real climbing would begin. Slow Man roped us up for a couple of steep pitches and across a three-foot gap in one of the ledges that we had to jump across. We reached the summit of this rotten rock pile before 9:00 a.m. and looked across the valley to the west. "What's that mountain over there?" I asked Slow Man, pointing to the large rocky face across from us. "That's the Maroon Bells" he replied. I was astounded. From this angle, the picturesque Maroon Bells that looked like two separate bell-shaped mountains from Maroon Lake now just looked like a long ridge of rotten rock with a large bump on the southern side (South Maroon Peak) and a small bump on the northern side (North Maroon Peak). The Bell Cord couloir that runs up the center was mostly melted out for the year, but was still a visible diagonal line up and across the face. I guarantee that no one would come from around the world to photograph these mountains if this was the view of them that they saw.

With fifty of the fifty-four peaks now climbed, it was time to head home to Denver and prepare for the winter and the birth of our first child. Melissa was glad the Aspen trip was over and that I had three fewer dangerous peaks left on my list to climb. I had also just changed jobs, joining the largest Denver-based public accounting firm, EKS&H, as a senior manager while embarking on the final year of my MBA program at the University of Denver. North Maroon would have to wait, as would Culebra, Mt. Wilson, and El Diente.

CHAPTER 11

Finishing the Quest

Our son, Connor, was born in January of 2005 and he was exactly what Melissa needed to continue moving beyond our accident. In 2002, about a year after the accident, Melissa put pen to paper and wrote out her own story of what happened. She concluded her story with the following:

> Just a little while ago, I went on a three-mile hike with Brad and Malcolm. I am still dealing with a lot of emotional healing. I have not yet fully learned to accept that a part of my body is gone forever. I have found a wonderful counselor [Todd] who is helping me with that part.
>
> I'm looking forward to putting this all behind me. For nine months now, it has consumed me. I'm working toward a time when the accident isn't my world. Each day I'm getting closer to that time. I now go for hours at a time without thinking about it. Sometimes I go an entire day without my feet bothering me.
>
> While this has been a life-altering event for me emotionally, it's not going to be physically. I will be able to do all of the things I did before the accident. I'm looking forward to much more hiking this summer with Brad and Malcolm. Right now, I'm still not hiking much because I get cold so quickly that it's not comfortable. My friend from Everest [Ed Webster] told me that after about two years, he stopped feeling cold all the time. I'm looking forward to that. I know that this, like everything else, will get better with time.
>
> The best thing the accident did for me was to make me realize what a wonderful family I have. We were all tested by the accident in our own ways and we used it to grow closer together. This has especially been true for Brad and me. We have used the accident

to make our young marriage stronger. I know this will help us with any other crisis we may face in the future.

It really took her pregnancy with our son before Melissa stopped thinking about her feet each and every day. She had something new and exciting to focus on, and soon her fetal girth actually obscured her feet from her view. This was wonderful for her and she has never looked back from that point.

After Connor arrived in January, Melissa and I had our hands full juggling everything. I was again working public accounting busy season hours all the while going to school two nights a week to finish my MBA program. I recall one night when Melissa told me that it was much harder than she thought it would be—having a baby and having me gone as much as I was. I felt bad and tried to get up even earlier in the morning to do my homework for school and my work at EKS&H while still having time to spend with her and Connor when I was home (and they were awake). Eight months, I thought. We can do anything for eight months until I'm done with the MBA. For me, Connor's arrival was a wonderful gift, but also a great responsibility. I remember when the nurse first handed him to me and I looked down at him, thinking, "Wow! This little person is mine to take care of—I won't let him down."

Melissa and I worked together, and with great support from both sets of grandparents, we made it through until the summer when Melissa's school year was done and my busy season at work was over. I got out and hiked when I could find time that summer. Most of the hikes were duplicate 14ers for me, but ones that my dad had not done with me the first time around. We planned another attempt on North Maroon in August of 2005, so we wanted to be physically fit and ready to go. We had also paid our fee and made a reservation with the private ranch on which Culebra Peak lies to attempt to climb it in mid-September 2005. I was starting to think about finishing up my last several 14ers and had decided that I didn't want Culebra, an easy Class 2 hike, to be my last one simply because it was remote, near the New Mexico border, and inaccessible without permission.

When August rolled around, Dad and another climbing friend of mine, Rob Norris, headed up North Maroon for what I hoped would be my last time. We crossed that same stream again where my father had taught me the lesson the previous year; I chided him in good fun and asked him if he would please demonstrate once again just so I could be sure I had the technique down. He declined and told me I should have paid attention the first time. Unlike our attempt the previous year, the weather held beautifully and we carefully picked our way up the steep northeast ridge with Rob generally leading the way. Toward the summit there is a large block that must be climbed with a few Class 4 moves, which we negotiated fairly easily. Soon we were on the summit, looking to the south at the bigger of the two Bells and taking in the spectacular view back down toward Maroon Lake. Fifty-one down, three to go!

I finished my MBA program with a perfect 4.0 GPA that month as well and looked forward to September when the partners at my firm would be voting on whether or not to admit me to the partnership as their youngest partner. The common theory during this stage of possible admission to the partnership was "hide under a rock and don't do anything to screw up." I figured the mountains were a great place for me to be to avoid any missteps at the office.

In September, on the way down to Culebra Peak, Dad got our one and only speeding ticket in all of the driving we did to get to 14er trailheads. Rob again accompanied us and we camped out for a night before our summit attempt. Culebra is a Class 2 walk-up, but requires a 13-mile roundtrip day, gaining 4,800 feet of elevation, so it is certainly no picnic. On September 17, 2005, the wind was absolutely howling all day as we ascended Culebra's slopes. From the summit we looked across to the southeast at 13,908-foot Red Mountain less than a mile away and one of the Centennial 13ers; we really thought about doing the easy traverse as long as we were there. The wind was at our backs for the ascent, which was nice, but we knew we would be hiking into the wind the whole way down. Given that we were already 6.5 miles from the trailhead, we opted to take a pass on Red Mountain and call it a day. Fifty-two down, two to go!

Days after our Culebra climb, the partner vote was taken and I was admitted to the partnership of EKS&H. Things were looking up for sure. I was done with my night school program, Connor was sleeping through the night (which meant Melissa was also sleeping through the night) and I had achieved a huge goal of making partner in my firm. Now I just needed to figure out how to finish up my 14er goal ...

The last two Colorado 14ers for me were 14,246-foot Mt. Wilson and 14,159-foot El Diente Peak (Spanish for "the tooth"). These peaks are in a group southwest of Telluride along with Wilson Peak, which I had already climbed back in 2002 while vacationing in Telluride with my brother, Todd. Mt. Wilson and El Diente are connected by a ridge, and the Class 4 traverse between these two peaks is considered one of the four classic 14er traverses in Colorado (along with the Maroon Bells traverse, the Crestone Peak/Needle traverse, and the Blanca/Little Bear traverse). I had done the Crestone traverse and thought that doing the Wilson/El Diente traverse would be a fitting way to achieve my goal of climbing to the summit of all of Colorado's 14,000-foot peaks.

We planned a trip to Telluride for August of 2006, renting a condo large enough for Melissa, me, our son, my parents, my brother and his wife, and their young daughter. Again, my 14er training started early in the season that year so I would be in prime condition when August rolled around, logging in nine duplicate summits between May and August, many of them new for my dad, who was making good progress on his list toward all fifty-four as well.

On July 15 of that year on one of those training hikes, we set out for Mt. Bierstadt and Melissa joined a group of us for the climb. She had never climbed Mt. Bierstadt, which bothered her since it was on its lower slopes that she had frozen her feet in the willows five years before. She did amazing on the ascent, periodically pausing to look back down to the west, over the vast expanse of willows in which we had spent the night. This was the first time she had really gotten a good look at the area since the accident and she found herself doing what Dad and I had been doing for years, each time we climbed Mt. Bierstadt—trying to visually retrace our path descending from Mt. Evans, into the willows, and finally to the clump of trees on the small hill where we had spent the night. Like us, she was never able to pinpoint where exactly we had gone wrong or where exactly we had ended up. After successfully climbing Mt. Bierstadt that day in July, she felt as if another phase of healing after the accident was behind her. Standing on the summit and looking down over the willows, she knew she could do anything she wanted to do with the rest of her life.

August rolled around and we all headed out for our vacation in Telluride, hopeful that I would get my last two peaks and finish my eight-year 14er quest. Todd and Dad wanted to do the last two with me, as did my climbing partner Rob. I was thrilled that Todd was willing to travel up from Phoenix to join us for this finale to the 14er goal. The four of us packed into Kilpacker Basin on August 16 and set up camp just below treeline. We woke up early and set off in the dark for Mt. Wilson, wanting to have plenty of daylight on the difficult upper slopes; we also wanted to allow plenty of time to get across the Class 4 ridge to El Diente before any afternoon storms rolled in. We were all climbing well and actually had to take a break at about 13,500 feet to wait for daylight since the terrain was getting steeper and the route less clear. As the sun came up, gradually lighting our way, we continued upward toward the ridge crest and the crux of the route. We roped up for the final scramble across the ridge to the summit, hopping from refrigerator-sized block to refrigerator-sized block until we could climb no farther. It was about 8:00 a.m.

when we reached Mt. Wilson's summit and we were optimistic about the traverse to El Diente.

In his classic *Colorado's Fourteeners* guidebook, Gerry Roach describes the traverse as "long and time-consuming," adding "escape from the ridge is difficult, and this is a bad ridge to be stuck on during an electrical storm. Consider the weather carefully before launching." Safety was our top concern, but the weather looked good and was forecasted to stay that way, so we launched toward El Diente. Descending down Mt. Wilson's eastern slopes required scrambling down steep Class 3 terrain in order to bypass a 60-foot cliff. We slowly and steadily worked our way across the ridge, losing elevation at times and having to regain it not long after. We finally reached the 13,900-foot saddle, which was the start of our planned descent route down El Diente's north slopes. After a few hundred feet more of Class 3 climbing from the saddle, we were on the top of the last of my fifty-four Colorado 14ers. It was a wonderful feeling to have accomplished a goal so long in the making—it had taken me eight years, one month, and two days to complete all fifty-four, a far cry from the current speed record for climbing all of them in just under eleven days.

Dad and my brother, Todd, on the traverse between Mt. Wilson and El Diente Peak.

A common climbing saying coined by Ed Viesturs goes, "Getting to the top is optional, but getting down is mandatory." These simple words ran through my head as we began the second half of the climb—the descent from El Diente, which is one of my least pleasant memories out of all of the 14ers— not nearly as bad as our May 2001 accident, but sufficiently unpleasant none- theless. From the saddle, we descended down the north slopes of El Diente. Basically we were in a wide gully filled with scree and loose rocks. We stayed together and tried to stay on the edges of the gully where the loose rock in the middle met the more solid steep walls forming the gully. We couldn't see anyone below us, but we were still being extremely careful not to send loose rocks down, just in case. It was mid-August, so the snow was all melted by then, and I found myself longing for the gully to be filled with compacted spring snow and to be walking on top of that snow with a pair of crampons firmly attached to my boots. But no such luck. The gully was dry and loose.

At one point, Rob and I got a few hundred feet ahead of my father and brother, who were hugging the edge of the couloir. We had all talked about the importance of alerting climbers below us if we accidentally sent a rock down by yelling, "ROCK!!!!"

My brother recalls hearing something far above him that sounded like the crack of a gun. He looked up the gully and saw a rock hurling down the center toward me. He screamed, "ROCK!!!" at the top of his lungs to alert me to the danger. When I heard this, I turned and saw a football-sized rock go whizzing past my shoulder. Wow! That was close. We were all wearing hel- mets, but with the momentum that rock had when it went past me, it would not have mattered. That rock would have killed me instantly, literally taking my head off. I wanted to get the heck out of that gully. Rob and I quickly talked about whether we were better off waiting until Todd and Dad caught up to us, or just hightailing it the rest of the way down. We opted for the lat- ter and got down and around the corner and out of the gully as quickly as we could without risking twisting an ankle or knee. Todd and Dad joined us not long after and we all breathed a sigh of relief to be out of there, all in one piece. Now I felt as if the 14er quest was officially done. We descended down to timberline, packed up our camp, and drove back to Telluride for a feast with the girls and the kids.

CHAPTER 12

What Now?

I was finished with my goal of climbing all the Colorado 14ers. Friends and family kept asking me, "Now what?" Because I am a big believer of finishing what you start (remember Inspiration Point?), I am also quite cautious about committing to new goals. I thought about maybe doing all of the Centennial 13ers in Colorado (the next highest set of mountains ranging from 13,800 feet to 13,999 feet), but several of those required Class 5 moves to reach the summit (which I had never done before) and many of those peaks are in the San Juan Mountains in the southwest corner of Colorado, far away from Denver. I pretty much took 2007 off from climbing mountains, only doing two mountains that entire year (by far my lowest on record since I started in 1998). Melissa was pregnant with our second child that summer, so we were busy getting ready for that. Once our daughter, Megan, arrived in mid-July 2007, I quickly learned that anywhere I went, I was generally going to be accompanied by my two-and-a-half year old toddler son, and I didn't think he was *quite* ready to start climbing with me. I wasn't quite sure what to make of Megan, not having had a sister growing up, but I was excited to see what the future brought with one son and one daughter. Perhaps Megan would be the one who wanted to climb mountains with me when she was older ...

Melissa and I still enjoyed spending time in the mountains, so we found ways to get up to the hills. We spent some time that summer enjoying the scenery at my grandfather's fishing cabin on Kenosha Pass, about an hour west of Denver. We also spent a week in the mountains with Melissa's parents near Aspen, in a town called Snowmass, just a few weeks after Megan was born. You might think that a new mother would want to rest, but Melissa is not a typical person. She wanted to get out and move around while we were in Snowmass. One day, we drove to the shuttle parking lot for the Maroon Lake trailhead (the same lot where my dad and I had deposited the injured hiker a few years before) and took the bus up to Maroon Lake. Melissa strapped Megan to her chest with a Moby Wrap and Connor walked with me up the trail to the "Deadly Bells" plaque, which I had told Melissa about, but which she had never seen. She was happy that I was done with these nasty mountains as we stood there admiring them, re-reading the plaque about all of the things that can go wrong.

In addition to the short Maroon Lake hike, Melissa had a bigger adventure in mind for us on that trip. She had always wanted to try paragliding, having seen people floating down from the sky above Aspen over the years. We knew that the Aspen Expeditions guide shop I had used for Pyramid and Capitol also did tandem paragliding flights in Aspen, so we agreed to give it a try. You may find it surprising and counterintuitive for a guy who loves climbing mountains, but I'm actually terrified of heights. I have never had an interest in sky diving as I just don't think I could convince myself to jump out of a perfectly good airplane. I wasn't sure how this tandem paragliding thing was going to go, but I was willing to try it for Melissa. The way it works is that you have a pilot with you (that's the "tandem" part) who works the controls on the parachute. Instead of jumping out of an airplane, you start high up on the side of a mountain and fly from there back down to the valley floor. The flights are usually scheduled for first thing in the morning or dinner time because that is when the thermals, warm currents of air moving up the mountain from the valley floor, are best and most predictable.

We arrived at the guide shop that morning—Melissa excited and me terrified. Melissa's parents graciously agreed to watch the baby and the toddler while we went, asking only that we be sure to return from our little flying adventure. We filled out the usual waivers of liability, reading the various warnings of serious injury or death, signed them, and waited for our tandem pilots. Minutes later, a young, good looking Argentine man walked out from the back of the shop, and in his Spanish accent, said "Are you Melissa?" She could not believe her good fortune—he looked as if he *must* have done some male modeling!

Melissa and Jaime on their tandem flight.

He introduced himself as Jaime and told her that he would be her pilot. I naturally got my hopes up that perhaps my pilot would be a young, attractive woman who took a break from underwear modeling to pilot clients like me on paragliding flights in Aspen. Boy was I disappointed.

Instead, a short, stocky man named Alex came over and introduced himself to me as my pilot. Alex was about five-foot-seven and two hundred pounds, a much different build from my six-foot-four, hundred eighty-five pound frame. He told me that he was their "big man specialist" and explained to me that it is much more difficult to land the parachute with a tall guy like me as the passenger. Oh dear. I was not feeling good about this and thought about backing out. I felt a tiny bit better when he told me that he was very good at this and had just taken a seven-foot tall NBA player up the week before. Melissa gently reminded me of the importance of finishing what I started and asked me whether I really wanted to leave her all alone with her former male model pilot Jaime. Seeing her point, I reluctantly got in the back seat of the quad-cab truck that would drive us to the top of Aspen Mountain. Just before we departed, a few other guys threw their parachutes in the back of the truck and hopped in, hitching a ride to the top. Alex and Jaime informed us that the other guys were locals who were experienced fliers and the guide service allowed them to dead head up the mountain in the truck if there was room.

We headed up Aspen Mountain on the steep, bumpy dirt road, slowly but steadily climbing toward the top of the ski mountain. When the truck stopped along a steep hillside, I glanced over and saw a ski run marker sign indicating that the run below was rated as a black diamond expert run. That meant it was going to be steep! The dead headers quickly jumped out and began readying their rigs for the flight. They clearly planned on taking off before we did, which was just fine with me. I was excited to watch someone else do this before it was my turn, thinking it would help ease my mind. It ended up doing quite the opposite.

Alex and Jaime were busy spreading out our tandem parachutes on the steep hillside when the first dead header went to take off. He started running down the grassy, treeless ski slope and I could see the parachute behind him starting to catch in the wind. But something went wrong—one side of his parachute wasn't opening up as it was supposed to and the guy had to abort the takeoff by pulling on the control cords to collapse the side that was open (and getting ready to provide him with lift-off). The whole thing happened very quickly and soon the dead header was tumbling down the slope head over heels before coming to a stop another 20 feet down the slope. Alex turned to me, and seeing the look of utter horror on my face, said, "Don't worry—that almost never happens." I didn't feel a lot better about this little adventure, but I decided to trust my guide/pilot, subtly reminding him that I was the father of two young children.

After watching the rest of the dead headers take off, this time without any issue at all, it was Melissa's and my turn to go. Alex and Jaime asked which one of us wanted to go first. I didn't figure sitting there and thinking about it more was going to make me less scared, so I volunteered to go first. I would later regret that. Alex got me all strapped into my harness and explained to me that he would be handling all of the flying and showing me that my harness would actually fold out into a seat once we were airborne. His instructions were quite simple, "When I tell you it's time, just start running downhill and don't stop until I tell you it's okay to stop. It will get harder and harder to run as the wind catches the chute, but don't stop until I tell you it's okay to stop. Got it?" I assured him I had it.

Giving Melissa one last look of "Help! Don't make me do this!" over my shoulder, I awaited Alex's command to run. He was strapped into our tandem harness behind me, so when he said, "Run!" I was in the lead and sprinted downhill as fast as I could. Sure enough, the parachute behind us began to catch the thermal air coming up off the valley floor and I felt as if I was being pulled backward up the hill by the force. But I kept running as I had been instructed until only my toes were hitting the ground with each step. Soon after, I couldn't touch the ground any longer. Alex hadn't told me I could stop yet, so I just kept running in place in the air until he finally chuckled that I could stop now. He folded down my seat and told me to sit back and enjoy the twenty-minute flight down to the valley floor.

My paraglider high above Aspen.

The feeling of flying was unbelievable! Alex used his anemometer, a strange beeping device used for measuring the air current and air temperature while paragliding, to "read" the currents and gain altitude for us at the start of the flight (I was quite surprised to be gaining altitude rather than losing it). I saw that the dead headers were several hundred feet above us, ascending in spiral circles using the warm thermal air to gain enough elevation for their planned trip up and over West Maroon Pass and down into the mountain town of Crested Butte—a journey that would have taken them five to six hours by car. I also checked behind us to make sure that Melissa and Jaime had successfully taken off—luckily they had fared better on takeoff than the first dead header and were airborne behind us. Melissa had a HUGE grin on her face as she waved to me. Apparently sitting practically in the lap of her former male model pilot while floating above the gorgeous green valley below was agreeing with her!

After Alex had gained all of the altitude he wanted, he decided it was time to offer to do some "tricks" for me. His first offer was something he called a "wing over." I wasn't sure what it was, so I said, "Sure, go ahead." He proceeded to tug on the cords for one side of the parachute, basically collapsing that side. As you would expect, we began falling in that direction until he released the cord and allowed the air to come back into that side of the chute. Then he pulled the cord on the other side, causing us to fall in the opposite direction. Nausea hit me like a brick wall—oh this was not going to end well. I asked Alex to please not do that again. He offered another trick and this

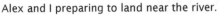

Alex and I preparing to land near the river.

time I declined and asked if we could just float gently down to our landing spot on the grassy area next to the river below us. He seemed a bit disappointed, but agreed that we could just do a normal ride the rest of the way.

When it was time to land, Alex informed me that my job was to stay out of the way and let him do the work. Apparently clients have injured their legs by trying to "help" on the landing. I was glad to let him drive, but my stomach muscles got quite fatigued at the effort of holding my legs up and out of the way as we approached the ground. Alex was true to his reputation of being a "big man specialist" and expertly landed us. It was then that I had my most terrified moment of the entire ordeal. I looked up and saw Melissa still hundreds of feet above me. I knew I had a three-week old baby and a two and a half year old waiting for me back at the condo—and I knew that I had no chance in the world without their mother! I should have had her take off (and land) first. I helplessly looked upward and willed Melissa and Jaime to land. Luckily, they were on the ground next to us a few minutes later and I breathed a big sigh of relief. Melissa had thoroughly enjoyed the ride and talked on the way back to the condo about how maybe someday we should learn to paraglide on our own so we could do this again. "Maybe someday" I told her. But my mind was already shifting back to climbing mountains and wondering what I should do next.

CHAPTER 13

Mt. Rainier—Take One

In September 2007, Melissa and I were driving home from a visit to REI in downtown Denver when I turned to her and told her that I was seriously thinking about attempting Mt. Rainier in 2008. We talked about it for a little while and she was very supportive of me attempting this 14,410-foot volcano outside of Seattle, Washington. My father was talking a lot about his retirement from climbing mountains, having been turned back by deep spring snow on Mt. Columbia in June of 2007, one of his nine remaining Colorado 14ers, so I seriously doubted that he would consider going to Mt. Rainier with me.

I was sad that Dad was talking about retiring from doing 14ers. He and I had been on sixty-seven 14er attempts together from 1998 through 2007, not to mention the hours in the car driving to and from the trailhead. My dad was definitely my favorite hiking partner during that time. We talked, laughed, and joked around on every trip we took. I understood that his deteriorating fused ankle was bothering him more and more, and that the ibuprofen (affectionately known as "Vitamin I") before and after the climbs was simply not cutting it anymore, but I still felt that I was losing my favorite hiking partner and time with my best friend.

I asked Melissa if she could think of anyone else that we knew who might want to go with me. Much to my surprise, she paused and said, "I think I'd like to go." "Seriously?" I asked. She replied affirmatively and we launched into the next phase of our lives together. I could hardly control my excitement!

I wondered what caused this shift in her views. Melissa recalls a time visiting with an old family friend, Dr. Will MacPhee, shortly after the accident on Mt. Evans. Dr. MacPhee is a huge race car buff and Melissa has watched him enjoy this hobby since she was a child, going over to the MacPhee home to play with her best friend Alex. On this day, Dr. MacPhee was trying to help Melissa deal with her feelings after the accident on whether or not she could and should continue to hike and climb mountains. Melissa was initially afraid that if she couldn't or didn't hike and climb, it would hurt our relationship since the mountains are my primary hobby. Dr. MacPhee, in his usual calm, soft-spoken words, said to Melissa, "You know, Lois and I have been married for a long time and she doesn't even like racing cars."

This was a pivotal moment for Melissa because those simple words showed her a clear path to a long-lasting, great marriage where one spouse's hobby is not shared by the other. This was a huge relief for her—she now realized that it was a simple choice that was hers to make—did she *want* to hike and climb or not. Who did she want to be? She knew that either way, we could be married and enjoy our time together. She had only climbed two 14ers since the accident—Humboldt Peak in August of 2002 and Mt. Bierstadt in July of 2006—both of which she climbed just to prove to herself that she could still do it. She had been thinking a lot lately about whether she actually enjoyed hiking and climbing and had decided that she did. She wanted to climb Mt. Rainier with me. It had been six years since the accident and we were talking about it less and less frequently. When we did talk about Melissa's feet, the focus began to shift to joking about Melissa being the best two-toed person at this or that. We both thought it would be very cool if Melissa could climb a mountain like Mt. Rainier with only two toes.

We signed up for a June 2008 summit climb of Mt. Rainier with a local guide service, Rainier Mountaineering, Inc. (RMI) and began our preparations. We had a great time purchasing all of the gear that we needed from the provided pack list, ordering thousands of dollars of new clothes and equipment to keep us warm and safe. With two young children at home, we did much of our physical training separately. I am generally averse to indoor workouts in gyms, so I started climbing two 13,000-foot peaks near Denver almost weekly to get ready (taking advantage of the wonderful flexibility my job offers outside of tax season). Melissa worked with a personal trainer at a local gym and did smaller hikes in the mountains as often as she could get away for a few hours. We supported each other's training efforts and excitedly looked forward to being able to be together in the mountains.

At the end of May 2008, we arranged two weekends in a row where the grandparents could watch the kids so Melissa and I could climb 14,000-foot peaks together to better our acclimatization in advance of our early June departure. First, we chose Quandary Peak and made a critical discovery for hiking together that has led to far more happiness in the years since. We learned that Melissa should *always* hike in the front of the two of us. It doesn't sound like much, but oh the difference it has made. Previously, I would always go in front and set the pace. My natural pace tends to be a bit faster than hers due to my six-foot-four frame versus her five-foot-six build. I would frequently look back over my shoulder to see where she was and to make sure I wasn't going too fast. She took these head turns to signify impatience with her slower pace, which agitated her and made her go even more slowly. It was a downward spiral from there.

When she suggested on Quandary that maybe she should go in front, I said "Sure," just happy to have the opportunity to hike with my lovely wife. Whatever pace she set was just fine with me—I could easily keep up and had the added benefit of getting to look at my wife's cute backside while enjoying the natural beauty around me. She found that she enjoyed hiking in front tremendously—she could go however fast or slow she wanted and enjoy the view around her. We easily reached the summit together that day, both of us pleased with our separate training programs, and we genuinely enjoyed the ability to climb together. We did the same thing on a much longer hike of Pikes Peak the following weekend and declared ourselves ready for Mt. Rainier.

We chose RMI's five-day summit climb, which included a day of mountaineering skills training such as rope travel, self-arrest, and crampon skills, and which also included two nights on the mountain to help acclimatize to maximize the chances of a successful summit bid. With our duffels packed, we flew to Seattle, then drove to RMI's Ashford, Washington, headquarters. We had arranged to stay at the quaint Whittaker's Bunkhouse for the nights that we weren't on the mountain. We nervously gathered up our gear the following morning to go meet the other seven clients in our group as well as our guides. I had assured Melissa that other women climbed Mt. Rainier and I was certain she wouldn't be the only one in our group of nine clients. Oops. There were no other women in our group, nor were any of our three guides women either. It is a good thing Melissa is mentally tough and likes a challenge (I already knew this of course—anyone who could manage our house, two little kids, my busy work schedule, teach a classroom full of kids, and still have time to train for a climb such as this was *far tougher* than me).

She started to feel much better when we drove through the falling snow to the base of the mountain for our mountaineering skills workshop where she realized that she could do everything they were asking just as well (if not better) than the guys in the group. We nicknamed one of the guys in the group "The Human Snowball" during self-arrest practice. Self-arrest is the technique whereby you stop yourself from sliding down a snowfield using a mountaineering tool called an ice axe. Self-arrest practice on Mt. Rainier consisted of the guides lining the clients up at the top of a 30-foot moderately steep snow slope above a large flat area, and then sending us down what had quickly become a bobsled run down the slope. We practiced falling from various positions—feet first, head first, face up, face down, etc.

Our fellow climber, The Human Snowball, failed to stop himself even once with his ice axe in all of those tries. Over and over again, he took the guide's instruction, nodded his understanding, and then threw himself down the slope, rapidly accelerating all the way to the bottom where each time he landed in a large puff of fresh powdery snow. He would stand up, snow covering his entire body, even his face, shake it off, acknowledge that he had failed to stop yet again, and return to his place in line at the top of the hill. Yes, indeed, Melissa was going to do just fine on this trip—it turned out she was excellent at stopping herself with her ice axe—there was only one Human Snowball in our group.

Our clothes were soaked from the heavy, wet snow by the end of the day, so we took them to the small local laundromat back down in Ashford so they would be dry the following day for our summit climb departure. While we waited, we found a restaurant close by that had homemade fruit pies, which became one of the highlights of the trip for me. Melissa recalls:

> That night at dinner I told Brad that any fears I'd had about be-
> ing the only woman, and the weak link, on our trip were quickly
> dashed. The team could not have been more welcoming to me. It
> was also apparent that with my training and home altitude advan-
> tage I was going to be able to keep up with the guys. "Expedition
> pace" works as a wonderful equalizer for leg length; I was not
> going to have to worry about the rest of the team taking off up the
> mountain and leaving me in the dust. After dinner I insisted upon a
> trip to Ashford's market to purchase Fritos. One of our guides had
> pulled out Fritos after the skills workshop for a snack. It turned out
> that they were everything that had been missing from my hiking
> snacks! When we are hiking, my taste buds crave salt. Unfortunately
> most snacks that transport well tend toward the sweet (e.g. granola
> bars). Chips don't work well because they smash in a backpack
> and you end up with a pile of crumbs. But Fritos ... they are oily
> and salty and their shape makes them fairly durable—in short, they
> are perfect. Now that I knew about the beauty of Fritos as a hik-
> ing snack, I was not going to head up the mountain without them.
> Thankfully, the market was open and stocked; the trip could begin!

The next morning we set out again through more snowfall toward the Paradise Ranger Station at 5,400 feet. We had seen on the TV news that morning that the newscasters were referring to the month as "Juneuary" because of how much snow had fallen so far in the month of June. We hadn't even been able to see the mountain because it was so socked in. In hindsight, that might have been a good thing. Starting to climb a 14,000-foot mountain from only 5,400 feet was not something we were used to—most trails in the Colorado Rockies start between 10,000 and 11,000 feet, leaving 3,000 to 4,000 feet of climbing typically required to reach the summit. Here we had almost 10,000 feet of climbing above us—the equivalent of climbing one of Colorado's 14ers from the Mile High City of Denver!

The nine clients got out of the shuttle bus at Paradise and began our final preparations for our ascent. Our group was getting along well and consisted of an ER doctor from Seattle, another gentleman from Seattle who was on his third Rainier attempt, having suffered from severe altitude sickness on the first two, a fifty-something-year-old father and his two adult sons along with an adult nephew from the East Coast, Melissa, me, and The Human Snowball. Right before we were to begin our hike up to Camp Muir at 10,060 feet, the guides handed us each a pair of snowshoes and said we would unfortunately need to start in them due to the recent snowfall. Little did we know it at the time, but that pair of snowshoes being handed to him was pretty much the last straw for The Human Snowball. After hiking for the first hour, we stopped for a short break and realized we were down to eight clients. The Human Snowball had turned around in the first mile, accompanied back to Paradise by the most junior guide (who then hustled to catch back up to the group after making arrangements to get The Human Snowball back to Ashford).

We lost our second client on the headwall just below the famous Muir Snowfield. The fifty-something-year-old father was having knee pain flaring up from an old skiing injury and chose to turn around rather than risk preventing his sons and nephew from reaching the summit by continuing up. We were already down two clients, with seven continuing on. The remaining clients got into a nice rhythm once on the Muir Snowfield and marched in unison up toward Camp Muir. Midway up the snowfield, we got another treat. We were starting to climb through the top of the cloud. Every now and then I would catch the faint outline of something big up above me, and the guides told us we were about to get a look at the upper part of the mountain. When we finally punched through and I got my first clear look at Mt. Rainier, I nearly buckled from the joy and beauty! This was a *far* bigger mountain than anything I had climbed before in Colorado or even the much taller Orizaba in Mexico. Mt. Rainier's slopes are covered with glacier after glacier of bright white snow and ice, occasionally pierced by a jagged rock fin vertically splitting the massive rivers of ice.

Melissa and I punching through the clouds on Mt. Rainier.

We could see the little hut at Camp Muir now, too, and our strong group got there with relative ease. We arrived as another RMI group was packing up for their descent, having reached the summit early that morning and Melissa saw that there was a woman in that group. She felt even better upon learning that the other woman had reached the summit—Melissa was climbing well and feeling strong. Our high-altitude training in Colorado had definitely given the two of us a distinct advantage over the other five in our remaining group who had all come from sea level.

RMI has two sleeping huts at Camp Muir—a larger one for the clients and a smaller one for the guides. They are little more than shacks with plywood bunks on the inside, but they felt luxurious to us as we took off our packs and settled in. The others in our group told Melissa and me that we could have our pick of the sleeping spots since we were the only couple in the group.

We found a cozy area big enough for both of us directly above the entrance to the hut and quickly named it the "honeymoon suite." We explored Camp Muir a bit after unpacking and enjoyed a wonderful dinner prepared by our guides, then turned in for the night. The next day was to be our "rest

Melissa in the "honeymoon suite" at Camp Muir.

day" with only a short hike to review the glacier travel skills that we would need for summit day. But there is no such thing as a restful night's sleep in a community mountain hut. Around midnight another RMI group sharing the hut with us got up and began preparations for their summit attempt.

We lost another member of our team first thing the next morning. The poor guy who was on his third try, whose body just doesn't acclimatize to the altitude well, had had a miserable night and his head was killing him. He had come to the mountain almost a week before this trip and had camped as high as he could for several nights in advance, hoping he would be able to reach the summit this time. Unfortunately, his physiology just didn't allow it. Again, the most junior guide was sent down with him with orders to race back up as quickly as he could so as not to leave us a guide short. Luckily guides, especially young, junior guides, are in phenomenal shape and he was back in no time!

After breakfast, the talk turned to the weather. The guides were getting updates from Ashford and there was apparently a storm that was due to move in that night. The sky was cloudless currently and I heard the guides discussing our plans for the day. I overheard our lead guy say something about "maybe sneaking one in" as he wrapped up his communication with base camp in Ashford and I suspected I knew what he had in mind.

Our lead guide gathered the remaining six of us up for a team meeting to discuss the day's agenda. He said we were just going to go for a walk and see how far we got. "Maybe sneaking one in" kept going through my head and I had a hunch that he planned to go for the summit today if we could. My suspicion was confirmed when one of the others asked what we should bring and his response was, "Oh, just bring whatever you would bring if we were going for the summit." He said it in such a calm, matter of fact manner that it took awhile for it to register to everyone that we might just be setting out on our summit climb. I was getting excited, feeling that we had a strong group now with less than a two to one client/guide ratio!

We set out from camp, crossed the Cowlitz Glacier and began climbing toward Ingraham Flats. Melissa and I had previously discussed and agreed that we wanted to be on separate ropes as we climbed higher up the mountain. This served two purposes: 1) it was good risk management for parents of young kids, and 2) if one of us needed instruction or to have our technique corrected, it was better for our marriage if this came from a guide rather than a spouse. We were moving very well and feeling strong as we climbed toward the base of the Disappointment Cleaver, the crux and namesake of the standard and easiest route on Rainier. The guides again conferred on the weather, our progress, and the safety of the snow slopes above us. The two junior guides dug a snow pit to evaluate the avalanche danger and then gave us a mini-seminar in evaluating the snowpack. Since it had snowed so much in the days right before our climb, the question was whether or not that new snow had had a chance to consolidate, or bond, with the stable base layers.

We were all disappointed when the guides shared their decision with us that we should turn around. They were confident that the weather would hold and the snow would be safe to ascend to the summit, but they were concerned about the slopes avalanching under our weight on the descent during the heat of the afternoon. Although disappointed, Melissa and I thanked them for putting our safety first (we had young kids at home after all) and we descended back to Camp Muir, grateful for having had the chance to come and see this beautiful massive mountain first-hand and get a small taste of what climbing it was like. Melissa recalls:

> As we hiked across the glacier that day, I felt good. I was roped in behind our lead guide, Gary, in the front rope team. I was not having trouble keeping up and the views were breathtaking. I have seen many movies and read many books about mountaineering, but until you have seen a glacier up close, it is hard to understand the size and beauty. As we were coming to the end of the Flats and getting near the bottom of Disappointment Cleaver, we had to cross a narrow ledge. As we crossed, there was a steep drop off to my right and an overhanging cliff on my left that I felt was pushing me toward a long fall from this narrow snow-covered ledge. There was a fixed rope at this part, but for some reason we didn't clip in. I was scared out of my mind the whole way across, but didn't say anything. "Just get across," I thought. The terror was so encompassing in that moment that all I could do was try to get out of that spot. I would not allow myself to be paralyzed by it. My anxiety was compounded when Gary turned back to the next rope team and told them that they "Better clip in," for that section. In my mind, this justified my paranoia that we had a near miss crossing the ledge. Soon everyone was across and the guides did their snow assessment and determined that we should turn around.
>
> I was not excited to go back across the ledge as my nerves and adrenaline had not had a chance to calm back down. A sense of immense relief washed over me when Gary told our rope team that we would clip in on the way back. "At least if we fall the rope will catch us," I kept thinking. The return across the glacier was uneventful, but I still couldn't shake my fear from the ledge. I kept thinking

about my babies back home and how the most important thing was making it back to them. It is common for people who survive an accident to be scared of things that they were not scared of before. Once you are forced to acknowledge that you are not invincible and will someday die, there is a certain fear that can overtake you if you allow it. I have had to work over the years to temper that fear. At times it can be very unhealthy; like when I read about a car accident while I was in recovery and became afraid of riding in a car for a short period. Other times the fear is healthy and helps you make safe choices. I believe that on Rainier the fear helped me make a safe choice. Megan was not quite a year old yet and Connor was just three. I did not need to push myself for the summit; I needed to make it home to raise them.

Once Brad and I were back in the "honeymoon suite" for a rest, I told him that I would not be going for the summit with the team the next day. I was too scared and couldn't do it. Brad was disappointed, but understood. It was a little harder to convince the guides and other members of our team that I wasn't going. They each argued that we hadn't really been in danger and that we would clip in the next day. They also assured me that I was one of the stronger members of the team. I was flattered that the guys wanted me to be with them on the summit attempt, but I would not be swayed. I was going to stay at Camp Muir while they tried for the summit. In the end, it didn't matter since no one was able to try for the summit the next day due to the storm.

When the new RMI team joined us in the hut that night, I counted my blessings that I was on such a great team. The other team was all men, and they spent a large part of the night trying to prove who had more testosterone. They were loud and told offensive stories and jokes late into the night. I quietly listened, thankful that I had not needed to spend five days with these "men."

Back at Camp Muir, the guides updated us on the progress of the incoming storm. Our original summit day was supposed to be the following day, launching around midnight that night, but it didn't look promising due to the weather. Another group arrived at Camp Muir that afternoon, this time a group of guys who were also shooting to leave for the summit that night. We went to bed early just in case we got lucky with the weather and agreed that we would get up at midnight to see if we might be able to make a second attempt.

We could hear the wind howling outside during the night, so it wasn't a big surprise when the guides came in at midnight and told us there was no way we were trying to go up the mountain. They told us to sleep in and that we would head down sometime during the next day. The next morning, we took our time packing up our things and had a nice leisurely breakfast. The wind was still blowing and the snow was falling fast. It was time to get out of there. The other group of guys was disappointed to not even have gotten above Camp Muir. The guides decided to join our two groups for the descent back down to Paradise.

By the time we started down, the storm was going full force, creating near whiteout conditions. This brought back bad memories for Melissa and me, but we trusted in our guides and warm clothing and headed down with the group. The guides were using GPS units to navigate back down the Muir Snowfield, which can be quite disorienting in such conditions. One guide took the front and one took the rear, acting like a safety on a football team—no one, absolutely no one gets behind you if you are the safety! The other four guides flanked the clients, two on each side, herding us downward and keeping us all together in a pack. We paused briefly when we saw a group of three people climbing up the snowfield in the storm so that the guides could attempt to convince them to turn around. The group of three continued upward. Melissa shook her head and said to one of our guides, "The only thing crazier than descending in this weather is going up in this weather!" The guide replied to her, "I am very happy that you understand that."

Melissa (center with goggles visible) preparing to descend in the storm.

Ice crystals on one side of my face from the storm.

Melissa had proven herself as one of the strongest members in our group and we thoroughly enjoyed traveling and climbing together.

Sadly, a newspaper headline caught my eye at the airport in Seattle two days later as we were traveling home to Denver. The article was about someone perishing on Mt. Rainier after getting disoriented and lost on the Muir Snowfield during a whiteout. The person who lost his life was in a group of three and perished sacrificing himself to keep his wife and friend warm, offering his body to shield and warm the other two, who survived the incident. Those were the three people who had passed us on their way up. Their tragedy hit close to home as it was a husband, wife, and friend who were hiking together. The husband perished, leaving his wife alone to raise their two kids, ages five and three.

CHAPTER 14

Kilimanjaro

Upon returning from Mt. Rainier in 2008, I was named the head of EKS&H's audit practice, a huge honor considering I was still the youngest partner in the firm. With the recession already in progress, I threw myself into my work to help navigate the downturn, putting in yet another nearly three thousand–hour year at the office.

I was ready for a short break by the summer of 2009 when I was due for my first sabbatical from my firm, a wonderful benefit offered to the partners so that they can enjoy four consecutive weeks off once every three years. Melissa had been thinking about what we should do on my sabbatical and I genuinely thought she was joking when she said that she thought we should go to the summit of Africa and climb 19,340-foot Mt. Kilimanjaro in Tanzania. "I'm serious," she said, "I really think we should go." As I thought more about it, I realized she was right and we began making plans for a trip to Africa in August 2009. Melissa had accepted a job at a new school as a fifth grade teacher and was scheduled to start work two weeks before we would be back from Africa. Somehow, her new principal agreed that she could miss the first two weeks of school.

She and I climbed two more 14ers together late in the summer of 2008, then divided again for our separate Kilimanjaro training programs. We synched up our training hikes again in July 2009 and climbed three 14ers together, culminating in Melissa's first climb of the long, tough Longs Peak in early August shortly before we departed for Africa. We had both trained hard again and felt ready for our next adventure.

Kilimanjaro is not known as a particularly difficult or technical mountain, but its height certainly requires good physical conditioning. We signed up with RMI for an eight-day climb of the mountain with a safari afterward, which would require us to be gone for just over two weeks in total. We know we are incredibly fortunate to have supportive parents who enjoy spending

Melissa on Kelso Ridge on Torreys Peak in late summer 2008.

time with their grandkids to allow us to be able to travel like this, and we also recognize how fortunate we are that we can afford to take guided international trips now and then.

After arriving in Arusha, Tanzania, we met our American guide and the rest of our climbing group. This time Melissa was in luck—she was not the only woman! There were three others on the trip—a female couple and a retired school principal. The others in our group were a retired police chief (the husband of the retired school principal, both of whom were in their sixties), a sixty-something-year-old gentleman from Hawaii who was immediately nicknamed "Baboo" (meaning Grandpa) by our African guides, a pair of brothers, and another solo climber from Virginia. Including the two of us, we had a group of ten clients heading into our climb up the Machame Route (also known as the "whiskey route") of Kilimanjaro. We would spend six and a half days slowly ascending the mountain from its base at 5,000 feet above sea level, taking our time on the ascent to ensure proper acclimatization. We would descend the much shorter "Coca-Cola Route" in just a day and a half when we were finished with the climb.

The most amazing part of the Kilimanjaro climb was watching the porters, who would carry all of the supplies we would need for well-supplied camps all the way up and down the mountain. We had forty to fifty porters carrying supplies for the ten of us, enabling each of us to carry only a small fifteen to twenty pound daypack—just enough for our snack food, water, and an extra layer of clothing. As the ten of us loaded into the back of a shuttle bus with our American guide, we watched as *at least* ten porters climbed into the far smaller cab area of the vehicle.

Once on the mountain, it was amazing to watch them pack up their loads for the day and place them firmly on top of their heads for carrying. Some carried our larger duffels with food and clothing that we wouldn't need until high on the mountain, while others carried tubs, chairs, cartons and even the portable chemical toilet that we would use while on the mountain. Melissa and I joked with our lead guide that it must be the low man on the porter totem pole who had to carry the toilet. Much to our surprise, we were told that this was actually one of the best, most highly sought after jobs. Apparently with some guide services (not RMI), the guy who gets the toilet is one of the few porters who is guaranteed work throughout the entire trip—far different than someone who is carrying the food for the first dinner that will be consumed the first night, leaving him out of a job the next day (many outfitters send them down when no longer needed rather than redistributing the loads).

Porters carrying their loads between camps.

The first day's journey was uneventful until right after lunch when Melissa began to feel ill. By the time she was lying in bed that night, she had diagnosed herself with a urinary tract infection and began to panic that she was going to have to turn around and go down. The next morning, she told our lead guide that she wasn't feeling well. Our guide said he would go through his medical kit to find some antibiotics, and word of Melissa's illness began to spread to others in our group. One of our fellow climbers was a medical doctor from Atlanta, so he and the guide conferred on the best treatment. Ultimately, the doc decided to give Melissa a strong antibiotic that he travels with to make sure the infection was killed quickly.

Our lead guide, Dave, had one of the African guides take her pack from her to lighten her load, but she struggled that whole day waiting for the medicine to kick in, actually lying down on the ground at each break. Melissa recalls Dave and me standing over her talking about whether she was okay each time she laid down. She insisted that she was, but it was less than convincing given she was lying on her back. Luckily, by the next morning, Melissa was feeling a world better and knew she would be able to continue. As spirits lightened, the female couple joked with Melissa that the infection was the result of having relations with boys. Melissa recalls:

I was so relieved that the antibiotics had worked and I was going to be able to proceed on the climb. Lying in my sleeping bag that first night in camp, I did not get much sleep because of my discomfort, so my mind kept mulling over my situation. I could not believe that after all of the training and planning to make the trip happen, I was not going to be able to do the hike because of a UTI. I knew that I would convince Brad to continue with the climb without me. I would not allow him to miss this experience just to sit back at the hotel with me while I waited for the antibiotics to work. My thoughts wandered to what I would tell my students back home. How would I explain to them why I had been unable to do the climb? How would I feel about missing the first two weeks of school to sit in a hotel?

I was also intimidated at the thought of having to be alone back in Arusha. I knew that the hotel would take care of me in terms of getting me to a doctor and putting me up, but I did not want to spend seven days sitting alone in the hotel. I was incredulous that I was going to be unsuccessful in another hike: the accident, our Bierstadt attempt after the accident, Malcolm getting hurt on Humboldt, and the failure on Rainier. How did this keep happening? So many odd things have happened to us on hikes that I frequently turn to Brad in difficult situations and say "But I already have enough character!" It is a joking way of reminding myself that I will choose to use setbacks to make myself a better person instead of being a victim of them. I became resigned that this was going to be another character building experience. When the doctor on our team produced the antibiotics the next day and told me that they would enable me to continue, I was overjoyed! Hiking that day, while I still felt sick, was no easy task. The simple hike the second day became the crux of the trip for me. But, with each day, I felt better and better.

Our progress up the mountain was quite modest each day, so Melissa had no trouble keeping up the third day while the infection was being killed. Our modest progress up the mountain was good for another reason—the female couples' luggage had not arrived at the airport until after we had departed for the mountain. Porters were reportedly going to be racing up the mountain with their luggage any day, but until it came, the rest of the group was outfitting them. Thankfully, the duffels arrived before we needed any of our cold weather gear. By day four, Melissa was her normal self and was asking if she could please wear her daypack again rather than having her African guide, Hadison, carry it for her. Each time she asked, Dave talked her out of it, saying, "There's no reason to push it just yet—save your strength for summit day."

Our climb up Mt. Kilimanjaro was far from "roughing it" we quickly learned. Each morning, the porters woke early and began preparing breakfast in the cook tent. When we awakened, we all congregated in the community tent where a long table with chairs was set up, table cloth and all.

Melissa with her personal porter, Hadison.

Breakfast was a feast of eggs, bacon, pastries, coffee, and juice. After breakfast, we returned to our tents to gather our snacks and extra clothing for the day to include in our daypacks. We then zipped up our large duffels containing the things we wouldn't need for that day and gave them to our porters. The climbers departed camp while the porters were finishing the breakfast dishes and re-packing their loads for the day. Once we were out of camp, the porters broke down the community tent and all of our sleeping tents, quickly packed up the entire camp, hoisted their assigned loads on the top of their heads and started up the trail. Within an hour, the porters generally passed us each morning, rushing up ahead so that they could get the lunch tent set up before we arrived at our designated stopping point. As a group, we were not at all hard to pass. We walked incredibly slowly, our guides constantly reminding us, "Pole, Pole" (pronounced Po-LE, Po-LE), which means, "slowly, slowly" in Swahili.

We generally hiked for another couple hours after lunch, again quickly being passed by the porters after they had broken down the lunch tent. By the time we arrived at our camp for the night, all of our tents were set up for us and our personal duffels were carefully placed outside of our assigned tents. We had some free time in the afternoons before dinner that we spent playing the card game Hearts in the community tent, setting up our solar chargers for our iPods, and calling loved ones when we could get cell service. One of our party even had the regular afternoon routine of calling her grandmother, who she talked to daily until her grandmother died a few years later. Dinners were fit for a king and consisted of a soup each night, then fish, potatoes, vegetables, and bread. We also learned that we had three birthdays out of the ten clients on the trip and were treated with birthday cake on each of these nights. After retiring to our tents for the evening, we got one more treat which Melissa came to enjoy perhaps the most—hot water bottles to put inside our sleeping bags to keep our feet warm. This was definitely not roughing it.

Melissa and I were having a wonderful time together on the trip, laughing and talking without our kids interrupting us. Life was simple—it was all about eating, drinking, sleeping, and hiking. The hiking made us very excited for the eating, even to the point where one day we realized we had a tin of sardines in our food bag, which we devoured using a broken piece of plastic we found. We were also thoroughly enjoying the company of the rest of the climbing group. We were both feeling strong as we climbed higher each day, with Melissa eventually bypassing her 14,421-foot personal altitude record as we ascended toward our 15,000-foot camp near the Barafu Hut the day before our summit attempt. We were all a bit nervous about summit day,

Melissa enjoying a warm foot bath at camp.

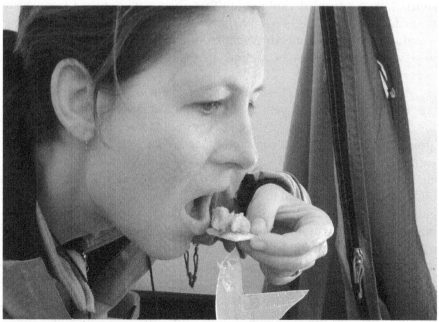

Melissa eating sardines with a piece of broken plastic.

Melissa and I with Mt. Meru in the background, and an ocean of clouds below.

knowing that it was a twelve to fourteen hour day versus our previous days of hiking roughly six hours between camps. We had an early dinner at Barafu Camp during which our guide told us the plan for summit day in terms of departure time (just after midnight so that we could reach the summit about sunrise), recommended clothing (all that warm stuff that had been safely stashed in our duffel bags each day, never seeing any action), and answering questions that the group had. We retired to our tents early that night to try to get a few hours of sleep before waking up for the summit attempt. No one slept much.

At midnight, my watch alarm went off in our tent and we powered on our headlamps and began getting dressed. It was quite cold at this altitude in the middle of the night, so we dressed as quickly as we could. Soon the whole group was convened in the community tent for a quick breakfast of instant oatmeal and coffee, then we were off for the summit, some 4,300 vertical feet above us. We all stayed together, flanked by our guides who constantly reminded us, "Pole, Pole" and to use the pressure breathing technique they had taught us. This breathing technique is used at higher elevations and consists of pursing your lips and quickly exhaling through your mouth, followed by a slow, deep inhale through your nose. The technique stimulates the oxygen exchange through the lungs while ridding the lungs of stale air at the bottom that normally does not get fully exhaled in our everyday lives.

At around 17,500 feet, two of the clients in our party began to have some trouble—one with her breathing and the other with cold hands that would not warm up. We learned that the woman who was having trouble with her breathing was a lung cancer survivor who had actually lost part of one lung through the illness. That she had made it this far was a huge tribute to her strength and toughness. She told us that she had already made it farther than she thought she would on the trip and that she was going to turn around and head back down to high camp along with one of the guides. The man with the cold hands was instructed to swing his arms vigorously back and forth to stimulate blood flow. I was hiking behind him at the time and took on the role of encouraging him while simultaneously dodging the flailing arms swinging toward me. This technique eventually worked and his hands warmed up nicely.

One of my favorite times on the entire climb was looking over my shoulder to the east as the first hint of light touched the horizon, illuminating the layer of clouds far below us. There is just nothing in the world like enjoying the sunrise from high up on a mountain ridge! The stunning view provided me a much needed second wind as we ascended toward the crater rim at Stella Point. I was definitely feeling the altitude at this point and was concerned at how Melissa must be feeling if I was struggling. To my surprise and delight, Melissa was doing phenomenally well and was among the strongest in our entire group on summit day. She was definitely kicking my butt as we made our way to our last break before the true summit. She took on the role of encouraging me that I could make it, very much the opposite of our normal roles when we hiked together, but I welcomed the kind motivational words nonetheless. After a quick snack and some water, we were moving again, with one last hour to go as we traversed the crater rim to the true summit, Uhuru Peak, at 19,340 feet (5,895 meters). Melissa recalls:

> At the summit I felt joyously strong physically and emotionally. I had hiked for over six days through illness and altitude to reach the top. Sitting at the summit, Hadison handed me a piece of obsidian that he had picked up along the trail. He told me that I had done a good job and I thanked him for helping me get there. For the entire climb, he had been a quiet force helping me. He was always right there, waiting in the background in case I needed him or my pack. I don't know if I would have made the summit without my quiet cheerleader.
>
> After the numerous photos and summit snacks, I decided that I needed a restroom break before heading back down. I walked a couple hundred feet down from the summit for a little privacy and to not pollute the summit. That moment alone looking at the

glacier was so peaceful. It truly feels as if you are on top of the world when you summit a peak like Kilimanjaro. I was looking down on the clouds and all of Africa. As I finished and turned to head back up to the summit, I had a renewed appreciation for the lack of oxygen at 19,000 feet. The stretch I had just easily descended was actually difficult to get back up. I even had to stop for breath at one point. Huffing and puffing back on the summit, I jokingly told the others that they should wait and pee in camp instead.

We felt a huge sense of accomplishment and relief upon reaching the summit around 7:00 a.m. that morning. We ate, drank, and took tons of photographs. Nine of the ten of us had reached the summit and we shared hugs and high-fives. As the sun rose in the sky, the temperature climbed to the point where it was quite pleasant hanging out on the summit for about an

Melissa and I on the roof of Africa.

hour. Once all the photos were done, it was time to descend back to Barafu Camp where we would have lunch and gather up our belongings for the 5,000-foot descent to Mweka Camp at 10,000 feet where we would stay the night, before descending the final 4,000 feet to the Mweka Gate at 6,000 feet where our shuttle would be waiting to take us back to our hotel in Arusha.

I actually find descending mountains far tougher on my body than ascending them. I rely heavily on my trekking poles for the descent, turning myself into an awkward-looking four-legged creature as I lean forward and plant my trekking poles down in front of me before each step. As expected, descending nearly three vertical miles in a day and a half had my knees aching in no time. But I was not the worst off in our group—one of our climbing partners had to resort to walking down the hill backward to provide his sore toes some relief from the blistering that his boots were causing on the way down. Melissa of course poked fun at him, joking, "What I wouldn't give to have toes that could be getting blisters right now!" Another climbing partner's knees were really bothering him and he had to be escorted down by two of our African guides.

After one last celebratory dinner at Mweka Camp, we had the tipping ceremony where we rewarded our wonderful guides and porters for their hard work. The next morning, we descended to the gate, and it was on to the safari portion of our trip in which we visited three game parks in Tanzania: Lake Manyara National Park, Ngorogoro Crater Conservation Area, and Tarangire National Park. While riding around in pop-top Land Rovers in our casual clothes, our drivers pointed out the various animals to us. The first day we were incredibly excited every time we saw a pack of zebra or wildebeest. By the third day, we realized that zebra and wildebeest are plentiful in number and had narrowed our focus to finding the elusive jaguar or watching an active hunt by lions. One zebra that we did find interesting toward the end of the safari we nicknamed "Zeek." Zeek, we decided, owned the title of the "slowest living zebra," as evidenced by his narrow escape from death by some predator. Zeek was marked by a massive gash in the flesh of his hindquarters, revealing bright red tissue in contrast to the rest of his black and white hide. I suspect that Zeek was still the slowest zebra

"Zeek," the slowest living zebra.

the next time a lion came looking for lunch, and that he probably lost the "living" part of his title.

Our accommodations on the safari portion of the trip were amazing, consisting of fine lodges in beautiful country near the national parks. The night before visiting Tarangire National Park, we slept in a platform tent with doors, windows, and running water situated on the border of the national park. After dinner at the community hut, we were informed that we needed to be escorted back to our platform tent by an armed lodge worker because we were close enough to the park that lions were often seen in the area. Wow! This was scarier than climbing Kilimanjaro! I turned to the young man next to me, carrying his bow and arrows, and asked him if he was a good shot. "I am *very* good" he assured me. But I have to admit, I felt much better after entering the tent and securing the door. It had been an amazing adventure and Melissa and I were ready to return home to see our kids.

We were also beginning to think about what we wanted to do next. As usual, Melissa already had a few ideas beginning to float around in her mind, and if it involves mountains, I'm generally game.

Melissa and I enjoying the thicker air on safari.

CHAPTER 15

Winter Solo and the Grand Teton

After two years in a row of traveling outside of Colorado during the summer to climb mountains, we decided to take a break in 2010 and stay close to home. Melissa didn't do any peaks with me that summer, so I found myself solo a few times and climbing with other people that I met along the way. A good friend of mine, Tony, was getting close to finishing all of Colorado's 14ers, having just a few of the hardest ones left to go. He asked me if I'd consider accompanying him on some of these and I jumped at the chance to climb them again.

In July of 2010, we were scheduled to make an attempt on the rotten, loose, and dangerous Pyramid Peak with a friend of his and a friend of mine. Unfortunately, at the last minute Tony had to cancel due to a significant acquisition that his company was doing. His friend (who I'd never met) still wanted to go, so we ended up being a party of three climbing Pyramid for my second summit of that mountain. Like Tony, most people save Pyramid for one of their last ten peaks due to its difficulty. We were astonished to meet up with a young dating couple at the summit, learning that the young man had opted to bring his new girlfriend up this scary mountain as her first ever 14er. Bold move! She was still speaking to him on the summit, so hopefully it stayed that way after she did the descent, which is the tougher direction for sure.

A few weeks later in August, Tony and I got another climb on the calendar, this time for him to attempt two of his remaining tough peaks—Crestone Peak and Crestone Needle. Thankfully, this time neither of our jobs interfered and we headed down toward Great Sand Dunes National Park for the climb. Tony's college-aged son and another friend would also be joining us. The four of us went up and over Broken Hand Pass, on the shoulder of Crestone Needle, then dropped down on the south side to reach the trail for the "red couloir" route up Crestone Peak, which we planned to climb first. The Crestones are amazingly steep, rugged mountains, but their reddish, knobby conglomerate rock provides ample (and generally fairly stable) hand- and footholds. We celebrated briefly on the summit of Crestone Peak with a snack and some photos, then, as I've done so often, we looked west to gauge the weather. The sky was clear and blue, so we set off across the rugged traverse toward Crestone Needle, carefully scanning the areas ahead for the proper route (which is quite difficult to find). I had done the Class 4 traverse once before with Mark Golden, but that had been way back in 2002, so my guiding left something to be desired.

We traversed across and eventually climbed back up to the ridge crest and readied ourselves for the 150-foot Class 4 crux pitch. About 30 feet above me as I started up, one of the guys weighted a knobby handhold to test it and it came right off in his hand. The rock that had dislodged was about the size of a football and would have done some serious damage had he not managed to keep it from falling. Yikes! This was a good reminder to always test your planned holds and take extreme care to not send rocks down on people who may be climbing below you. The rest of the crux pitch was uneventful and we stood on the summit of Crestone Needle, getting the two tough mountains logged off for Tony while giving me my second time across the famous traverse.

In October of 2010, Melissa stepped awkwardly off of our back porch stairs and broke a bone in her foot. She spent the next six months wearing a boot around, having trouble getting the bone to heal. We didn't know it then, but this would prove significant the following summer. By New Years, Melissa was itching to be able to exercise and get out into the mountains again even though her foot was not yet healed. We decided (okay, really *she decided*) that we would take a trip the following July to Jackson, Wyoming, and try the 13,770-foot Grand Teton. The reason that the Grand Teton appealed so much to Melissa was that the upper part of the mountain is all technical rock climbing, with the two most popular routes being the Owen-Spalding route (OS for short) that is rated at 5.4 and the Upper Exum Ridge, rated at 5.6 in difficulty. She and I had both rock climbed just a few times before, me just once in 2009 and again in 2010. We had climbed up to 5.6 before and I have to say that I viewed this as about my limit. As someone who is actually quite afraid of heights, I usually find rock climbing to be "Type 2 Fun"—fun when it's over. But I was super excited to get to do another climb with Melissa, so I swallowed my fear and we scheduled the trip.

I got out a couple of times that winter for some high altitude training, climbing Mt. Bierstadt again in December 2010 and accidentally doing my first winter 14er solo a few weeks later in January 2011. How does one "ac-

Cold "selfie" on Mt. Bierstadt in December 2010.

cidentally" do a solo winter climb of a 14,000-foot peak? I had actually set out that morning of Thursday, January 6, to climb a 13,000-foot peak called Grizzly Peak from the summit of Loveland Pass near the Eisenhower Tunnel; however, as I got closer to the Loveland Pass turnoff, it started snowing hard and I saw a sign flashing next to the highway that said "Loveland Pass Closed." Bummer! I had driven about an hour from my house already and it seemed a shame to turn around and go home. It was still so early that it was pitch black. I thought, "Well, I'll just turn around and drive back down the highway a few miles to the 9,800-foot Baker-ville exit and the road that leads up to the Grays Peak trailhead." Knowing my car would not make it up the snowy, unplowed road, I parked my car in a small lot right off the exit and figured I'd just take a short hike up the road so that the day wasn't a total waste.

I kept my snowshoes strapped to my backpack as I began walking in the dark up the packed snow in the center of the road. I didn't see another soul as I walked up the road for 3 miles to the summer trailhead at 11,200 feet. When I got there, I checked my watch and saw that it was only 8:30 a.m., so I decided to go a little farther. The snow was getting deeper as I climbed higher, so I strapped on my snowshoes to keep me on the surface. I had never been in this area in the winter, so I was scanning my surroundings carefully to make sure I didn't climb into avalanche danger. About thirty minutes above the summer trailhead, I saw that prior snowshoe tracks forked from the summer trail and led off to the left across a snowy meadow. I knew the summer trail climbed steadily up to the base of neighboring Kelso Mountain before traversing to the southwest along the base of Kelso and up into the basin beneath Grays and Torreys Peaks. I decided to follow the snowshoe tracks and was relieved by two things: first, there had been enough foot traf-fic across the area to keep my snowshoes firmly atop the snow—a HUGE benefit over the post-holing that could easily have been my fate in this area, even with snowshoes on, and second, the trail that I had found was clearly designed to meet back up with the summer trail after passing well below the chutes that occasionally send avalanches down from Kelso's upper slopes.

Because of the favorable snow conditions, I was making pretty good time and soon reached the sign for Grays and Torreys that stands at about 12,000 feet, warning of the dangers of summer afternoon thunderstorms. I had a snack at the sign and checked my watch again. Only 9:30 a.m. I thought about turning back at that point and calling it a day, but another thought was beginning to creep into my mind—how cool it would be if I could pull off a winter solo ascent of a 14,000-foot mountain! I had a good view of the upper reaches of Grays Peak from my resting spot and could see a thin line of snow switchbacking up the windblown face. There sure didn't look to be any other avalanche chutes above the trail the rest of the way up, so I decided I'd walk a bit farther.

My appetite for reaching the summit this January day was definitely growing as I continued to walk along the firm, snow-packed trail higher into the basin. As soon as I could, I took off my snowshoes (I truly hate the things and only wear them when I absolutely have to), tucking them under a couple of rocks alongside the trail and kept gradually gaining elevation. Soon I was on the shoulder of the mountain at about 13,000 feet, high enough that my cell phone had service. I sent Melissa a quick text indicating my position and letting her know that I was planning to try for the summit. On summer hikes, I often find that I get my second wind at about 13,000 feet and feel fairly strong for the final 1,000 vertical feet. Today, however, I had already climbed 3,200 vertical feet in the 6 miles I had traveled from my car, all of which was across snow. There was no second wind for me that day.

As I climbed higher, the westerly wind picked up and I was no longer sheltered from it as I had been down in the basin below. I was determined to get to the summit though, so I kept advancing one step at a time. I checked my watch and saw that it was about 11:15 a.m. I had forty-five more minutes to get to the top to comply with the normal rule of thumb of being on the summit by noon. I continued to struggle up, against the wind and cold, but it felt like my pace was in a slow motion time warp as the time on my watch seemed to accelerate in the opposite direction. At noon, I checked my altimeter and saw that I was at 13,900 feet. Although it was windy and extremely cold, the sky to the west was clear and blue, so I kept pushing toward the top. A gust of wind knocked me off balance about 50 feet below the summit, so I dropped to my hands and knees and crawled the rest of the way to the 14,270-foot summit. It was 12:20 p.m. and I had done it—my first winter solo 14er summit! I was elated but exhausted and began to feel isolated as I looked down at my ascent route running all the way down to the highway nearly a vertical mile below me, where I knew that my car was waiting. It had taken me six hours to reach the summit and I knew I had another three hours of descent time staring me in the face. I never saw another person the whole way down to my car—I was truly isolated up there.

I was relieved to get home that night and have this feat under my belt, but it was time for me to focus on my accounting work for the next few months leading up to the annual tax deadline. Melissa and I trained separately through the winter and spring for the Grand Teton climb, with me generally sneaking workouts early in the morning and during the week and her working with her trainer and catching an occasional hike on the weekends while I hung out with the kids. January through March ended up being exceptionally snowy months in the Rockies that year, which is wonderful for the Colorado ski resorts, but made us wonder whether it was all going to melt in time for us to climb the Grand Teton the first week of July. In June, I started calling our guide service weekly to check on conditions. I was informed that things were changing daily on the Grand Teton, but indeed, there was still a ton of snow up there. The guides weren't all that concerned though—the climb could still be done as a steep snow climb if need be—it just changed what we would need to pack. They told me to start planning on bringing our crampons just in case.

We had chosen to do the standard two-day climb of the Grand Teton (some incredibly strong climbers can do this monster car-to-car in a single day) and since we had not climbed with Exum Guides before, they asked that we also do an additional two days of rock climbing instruction before the climb. I was all for the extra instruction since I had only done technical rock climbing on two prior occasions. We would be in a small group for the first rock climbing instruction day with a guide named Rick Wyatt, then we would have a guide all to ourselves for the second instruction day and actual climb of the Grand Teton.

We began the first training day with the basics of rock climbing including footwork, knots, belay techniques, and the standard verbal commands to ensure that there are no miscommunications between the climber and belayer. This was all review for us and we were anxious to get onto the rock after lunch and do some actual climbing to practice our skills. We had been instructed not to bring our true rock climbing shoes for the Grand Teton climb or the training day, but rather our "approach" shoes. Both types of shoes have sticky rubber soles that help them to better grip the rock since the real climbing is done with the legs and feet rather than with the arms and hands. Rock shoes are much smaller and fit much tighter on your feet than approach shoes, which are more like slightly smaller cross training shoes with the sticky rubber sole. Every other time I had climbed, I had been wearing my rock climbing shoes, and while I was enjoying the increased comfort of the approach shoes, I was a little worried about not having the same level of proficiency with them as I had with my rock shoes. Keep in mind that my level of proficiency on rock is pretty weak anyway.

Since the accident, shoes tend to be a tricky thing for Melissa. She often has to buy two pairs of the same shoes in different sizes so that she can pair the smaller size right foot shoe with the larger left foot shoe. Even with a smaller right shoe, she generally has to stuff the toe of the shoe with foam or tissue. Melissa actually misplaced her keys once at a swimming pool and couldn't find them for a few minutes. She had tucked them in the toe of the shoe and didn't notice them when she put her shoe on to leave.

The final thing we had to do that first afternoon was a 50-foot rappel, since the descent from the Grand Teton requires what is known as "the big rappel." Gravity was obviously on my side for this one, but I still had to get over the mental fear of stepping backward off a cliff, trusting a rope and a small device on my harness to keep me from plunging to certain injury or death at the bottom. I "put my big boy pants on" (a favorite saying of a former boss of mine and which has become a favorite saying of Melissa's as well) and got the rappel done. For some strange reason, Melissa finds rappelling fun, so after everyone in our group had done their rappel, she asked if she could please go back up and do it a few more times. Strange woman. She was having Type 1 fun—fun while she was doing it.

The second day, we did a couple of easy warm-up pitches with our new guide, Mike Abbey, that went well for both of us and soon it was time for the "assessment" pitch that would determine whether or not they let us do the climb of the Grand Teton. I was always a good test taker in school, but this had a different feel to it. If I couldn't climb up this rock pitch, they weren't going to let me do the climb I had traveled here to do. Mike asked which of us wanted to go first and I quickly volunteered, figuring it was better to get it over with rather than sitting there on the ground thinking about it while I watched Melissa. I tied my figure-eight follow-through knot, yelled, "On belay," then after hearing the return call indicating I was on belay, yelled "Climbing!" "Climb On!" he yelled back and it was go time. I had tried to sound confident yelling the commands, but inside I was a mess. My palms were sweating and my mouth was dry as I executed the first few moves without much trouble. Next I had to traverse about eight feet across a narrow rock ledge as I continued my assessment climb. Then I got stuck.

The next move required a long reach up and to the right to the next handhold. No problem—I've got long arms on my six-foot-four frame. The problem was that I needed a foothold and there were none to be found. I knew there had to be one there somewhere, so I tried a thin protuberance from the rock and had my foot immediately slip when I tried to weight it. I knew in my head that I was on a top rope and couldn't fall more than a few inches, but I couldn't get my body to ignore the natural instinct to avoid falling at all costs. I tried the move a couple more times without a better outcome. Now my legs were beginning to shake visibly as I yelled up to Mike above me that I was having trouble finding a foothold. He couldn't see me from his belay ledge and just yelled down to me to keep trying. He pulled me a bit tighter on the rope, which was somewhat reassuring, but the panic had set in too much already. I was seriously thinking that I wasn't going to get to climb the Grand Teton because I couldn't do the stupid practice climb, and I was getting frustrated and angry. Melissa was yelling encouragement from below, clearly seeing from my bouncing legs that I was in need of it!

I finally decided to get this over with and threw good form out the window. Rather than find the proper foothold (which I was convinced didn't exist), I threw my foot up on top of the fixed bolt in the rock that is used to protect the leader from a fall and lunged up and over the section I was finding so difficult. I was extremely relieved to find that the route was much easier above that point, and quite soon I was sitting next to Mike on the belay ledge, safely affixed to the anchor he had built. He tossed the rope back down to the ground so that Melissa could tie in. This wonderful two-toed woman then climbed up the pitch much more quickly than I had and joined us on the belay ledge. After anchoring herself, my lovely wife turned to me and said, "Boy, you made that look hard. No one should have to climb after you!" Apparently seeing me struggle on this pitch had made her expect it to be quite difficult—she of course did not find it difficult at all. But we had passed the assessment, so we were going up the Grand Teton in the morning. We really liked Mike and hoped that maybe he would be our guide the next day for the actual climb. Melissa recalls:

> Back at the hotel that night, Brad and I relaxed in a small common area to read. I wasn't really into the book I had brought, so I leafed through some of the magazines that were on the coffee table. One of them had a story about a horrible accident that had happened on the Grand Teton the previous summer. Three climbing teams were near the summit when a fast-moving storm unleashed rain, hail, and lightning on top of them. An explosive blast killed one of the climbers, injured several others, and trapped all seventeen on the upper reaches of the mountain. Working collaboratively, park rangers, helicopter pilots, and three Exum guides staged the largest rescue in the park's history. Reading about another mountaineering disaster quickly ate away at the good feelings I had from our two training days. Here was another thing that I needed to worry about. I discussed my concerns the next day with Mike. He pointed

out to me that none of the parties had been with a guide service. Continuing, he stated that he had been in Jackson at the time of the accident and guides had not taken clients up that morning given the weather reports. Additionally, he informed me that a guided climber had not died in the range since 1986. Knowing these additional facts made me feel better, but the concerns were now there in the back of my mind.

After a nice dinner in town that night and a good night's sleep, we headed back to Exum's headquarters early the next morning. We were excited to see that Mike was going to be our guide. He took us inside to do a final equipment check. There was still enough snow on the upper part of the mountain that we would be doing a snow climb of the OS route, which meant that we needed to carry crampons and wear our hiking boots instead of our approach shoes. I was almost relieved by this since I was more comfortable on snow than I was on rock. Melissa was just the opposite though. She had signed up for a technical rock climb, not a steep snow climb on crampons, which she had only worn a few times before.

We started from the Lupine Meadows trailhead up through green meadows with gorgeous purple, yellow, blue, and red wildflowers surrounding us; Melissa perked right up, forgetting for a moment that the approach hike is 7 miles and climbs 5,000 vertical feet to reach the lower saddle where we would spend the night. She has always been the type of hiker who wants to take the time to stop and smell the flowers, whereas I tend to be driven and anxious to get to my destination. We steadily gained elevation off the valley floor and soon rounded a corner above a steep ravine that was still carrying snow. This was definitely where the casual hikers turned back—we witnessed several arrive at the first snow, take one look down the steep snow slope with jagged rocks at the bottom, and spin around. Mike roped us up here and we continued across the mushy early July snow. We climbed up into an alpine basin at the foot of the Middle Teton and from here we donned our crampons, veered right, and began to climb the first of two headwalls.

On the first headwall, Melissa began to complain of fatigue, thinking that maybe she had overexerted during our rock climbing practice days. She was a trooper and kept putting one foot in front of the other, but she was clearly getting tired. After finally topping out on the first headwall, our route turned left and we traversed across a relatively flat snowfield to the base of the second headwall, on top of which was the upper saddle and Exum's hut where we would be spending the night. Off to our right, we would occasionally catch a glimpse of snow avalanching off the upper slopes and down into the gully

Melissa ascending the second headwall on the Grand Teton.

Melissa near the lower saddle and Exum hut.

across from us. Those were the only live avalanches I had seen in all my time in the mountains at that point and it would stay that way for several more years. As we climbed the second headwall toward the saddle, Melissa would occasionally ask Mike how much longer we had. Each time he answered, she briefly shut her eyes in discouragement, then took a deep breath and plodded along up the snow.

When she got her first glimpse of the Exum hut on the saddle, she asked anxiously, hoping against hope, "Is that it?" Tears came to her eyes when Mike answered, "Yep, that's it. We'll be there in ten or fifteen minutes." When we arrived, we were the only ones there, so we had our pick of sleeping pads and spots on the floor. Mike encouraged us to rest for a while before dinner to prepare for our early start the following morning up the more difficult part of the climb. Melissa and I ate a snack, then listened to some music and relaxed for a while. We eventually grew curious where Mike had gone and came out of the hut to take a look. We saw him across the saddle practicing some bouldering moves on a rock the size of a semi-trailer—clearly he had more energy left over after today than we did.

After dinner, Mike asked how we were feeling and whether Melissa's strength was returning. She indicated that she was still extremely fatigued and wasn't sure whether she was going to be able to do the summit climb the next day, another 2,100 vertical feet above the saddle. We all agreed not to make any decisions that night, opting instead to wait until morning to see if a night's rest might be just what the doctor ordered. I could tell that Melissa didn't think she was going to bounce back in time and she was very upset about it. She was also concerned that if she started toward the summit in the morning, but couldn't make it, all three of us would have to descend.

When the alarm went off around 4:00 a.m., Mike heated water for coffee and oatmeal and asked Melissa how she was feeling. She indicated that she felt a little better and wanted to give it a try this morning. But she was quick to ask what the latest point was that she could turn around and still have Mike and me continue on up to the summit. Mike had pointed out the previous night a rocky outcropping called the Black Dike that was across the lower saddle and a few hundred feet up. In response to her question, he told Melissa that he would need to know by that point whether she could get to the summit or not. The trail was easy to follow from there back to the hut, so she would be able to descend that on her own if she didn't feel up to the summit climb. Melissa was glad to have clarity now and know that if she was still too fatigued, I could continue on to the summit with our guide while she waited for us in the hut.

After breakfast we headed out across the lower saddle and reached the Black Dike within about thirty minutes. Mike asked Melissa how she was feeling and she indicated that she didn't want to risk going higher up and having to spin the entire group. Knowing she was making the right decision and eager for a few more hours of rest, she turned around and we watched her headlamp as she descended down the easy trail back to the hut. Mike and I climbed a bit higher until we reached the snow in the approach gully. We put on our crampons and began ascending the snow couloir, eventually reaching the upper saddle. Now the fun really began.

Mike led me around the corner to the first of several famous moves on the OS route—the "belly roll," which is a large flake of rock that must be bypassed on the airy west side by grabbing onto the top of the rock and hugging it while scooting your mid-section around the bulge that threatens to push you over the cliff. Have I mentioned that I am afraid of heights? Next up was the "crawl" section where you literally take off your pack, lie on your stomach on an 18-inch wide ledge with an overhanging rock roof and crawl across like a worm. It is again open to your left side and the exposure is incredible—we're talking thousands of feet! After crossing these two obstacles

Me on the summit of the Grand Teton.

with massive exposure, I was actually pretty happy to get to the crux "double chimney" pitch, which consisted of more traditional rock climbing moves on good solid rock. We continued up steep slabs, finding a mixture of rock and snow as we scrambled up the final several hundred feet to the tiny snow-covered summit of the Grand Teton.

I was astonished at how fast the mountain fell away into nothingness in every direction from the summit. This was one steep mountain! After a snack and summit photos, the reality sunk in that I was only halfway done and still had to descend those steep slopes back to the lower saddle (including the big rappel) where Melissa was waiting for us. As we started down, Mike was behind me holding the rope I was still tied to so that he could stop me if I began to fall. In hindsight, I should have asked Mike if I could please put my crampons back on for this part of the descent down the steep snow slopes leading away from the summit. I felt uncomfortable walking down the steep snow with just my boots, so I was going very slowly, often lowering my center of gravity to the point where I was nearly crab walking down the snow.

Mike began to get frustrated with me and said, "Come on! The stairs in your house are steeper than this slope! Stand up and walk downhill!" I have learned that one of the attributes to be a successful mountain guide is to have a generally laid back, easy to get along with personality, while also having a switch that can be turned on when needed to be incredibly assertive when a client needs a little "tough love." I was a little annoyed at first when Mike yelled at me, but I also knew that he was right. The weather can change in a flash up there and I certainly didn't want to be high on the Grand Teton in a lightning storm. I redoubled my efforts and we started making better time down the mountain toward the spot where we would do the big rappel—a 120-foot rappel that bypasses the double chimney, crawl, and belly roll sections and deposits you back at the upper saddle.

When we got to the big rappel, I understood why Exum mandates that their clients do both the climbing assessment as well as complete a practice rappel before attempting the summit climb. I cannot imagine never having rappelled before and arriving at that spot, then having your guide rig you up to the rope with your belay device and abandoning you on the ledge in order to provide a fireman's belay from below (with a downward tug on the ropes from below you, a guide can put enough friction on your belay device to stop you). Yes, it was a good thing I'd done this a couple of times before. I'm not sure that I will ever be able to step backward off a cliff into open air without my heart rate rising and my mouth going dry, but I am getting to the point where I can do it when I have to. That first step backward is always the worst—once I had started down and got my rhythm controlling the speed of the rope through my belay device, I almost enjoyed the rappel down to the upper saddle. Almost. It was fun when it was over (Type 2 Fun). From the upper saddle, Mike instructed me to put on my crampons for the final descent back down the snowy couloir to the lower saddle. I impressed him with my downhill pace during that stretch. What a difference it made having sharp metal spikes on my feet for traction!

Melissa waved like a madwoman when she saw us descending toward her and she hiked back up to the Black Dike to greet us. She was feeling a bit better after resting some more, but knew that she had absolutely made the right decision not to try for the summit. After a quick bite to eat, we packed up and descended the first headwall. At the top of the second, Mike suggested that we could safely glissade down, sliding on our butts using our ice axes as a brake. It was amazing how much faster (and more fun) it was to descend that headwall compared to the time it took us to ascend!

We reached Lupine Meadow in mid-afternoon and thanked Mike and bid him goodbye. Another spectacular climb was done for me—this one unfinished for Melissa. But I don't expect it to stay that way.

In the months after we returned from the Grand Teton, Melissa's energy level continued to gradually decline. She said, "I can't feel like this anymore. Something is wrong with me and we have to figure out what it is." She finally went to the doctor in November and the doc went to work, running blood work and other tests to try to determine the cause of Melissa's fatigue. Melissa was quickly diagnosed with anemia and put on iron pills, which provided a boost in energy and some hope. We didn't know what was causing the anemia however. If it were socially acceptable, Melissa would eat bacon with darn near every meal and she gets plenty of protein in her diet, so the iron deficiency was puzzling.

Finally, in February of 2012, she went in for a colonoscopy that her primary care physician had ordered. Just before the procedure, the gastroenterologist came in and said, "I've been studying your chart and I don't think I'm going to find anything on the colonoscopy. I would bet that you have Celiac Disease, but to know for sure, I would need to biopsy your small intestine." He told her he was so sure this was what she had that if the insurance company would not pay for the additional procedure, he would pay for it himself. Melissa agreed, and sure enough, she was diagnosed with Celiac Disease, which is a disorder whereby the body attacks the absorptive surface in the small intestine in response to the protein "gluten."

We don't know how long she had had the disease already, but we now knew that her body had slowly been starved of vital nutrients. The doctors were sure that she had been suffering from this disease when she struggled up to the lower saddle of the Grand Teton and they also told her that her bones had been weakened by it as well, which explained the broken bone in her foot that took so long to heal the previous fall. It took Melissa over a year to start feeling better again after cutting gluten out of her diet. I knew she was finally recovering when one night she made a quick-witted sassy comment to me after dinner for the first time in a long time. I was so happy to have her back, even if it meant that her quick-witted humor would disarm me from time to time.

It is not on the calendar just yet, but I fully expect that Melissa and I will return to the Grand Teton so that she can join me in having reached the summit. She recalls:

I came home from the Teton trip feeling empty inside. Was I really not strong enough to climb big mountains? This was not the image I had of myself, but increasingly it was looking like my reality. Brad, ever my support system, tried to rationalize my failure. He pointed out that we had been scheduled to have a rest day after the two days of climbing school before the main climb. Because of Exum's annual guide meeting, we had agreed to move our climb up a day so Mike would be back for the meeting. Surely I would have been able to make it if I had the rest day, he argued. Additionally, he reminded me that I had done most of my training with a broken foot, which had prevented me from training like I had for Rainier and Kilimanjaro. I quietly agreed, but on the inside I was in mourning for my climbing career that I was imagining was gone.

By Thanksgiving, when I went to my doctor, I had a lengthy list of my ailments. After talking, my doctor told me that she thought I was suffering from depression. I told her that I certainly was, but that I wanted to rule out any medical causes. I agreed that if she ran tests and couldn't find anything physically wrong with me, I would pursue a doctor who could help me psychologically. When the anemia and eventual Celiac diagnosis came and were easy to fix, I mentally and physically started to feel better almost immediately. I was happy to know that it wasn't all just in my head.

Since the accident, my general approach to change is to jump in with both feet. When I left the doctor's office with my diagnosis, I vowed that gluten would never again cross my lips. Unfortunately it has on occasion, but true to my word, it has never been on purpose. In hindsight, jumping right in might have been a bit extreme. I drove straight to Whole Foods that day to restock our house with gluten-free food items. Unfortunately, because I had not taken the time to educate myself first, I ended up standing in the aisle completely overwhelmed and ended up leaving without anything, since I wasn't sure what to buy.

While I was relieved to have an answer as to why I had felt so bad, there was a part of me that was frustrated at my new diagnosis. Externally everyone saw "strong" Melissa who was taking another thing in stride and powering through it. Internally I was frustrated and angry. At my worst I would quietly rage about how it wasn't fair that these things kept happening to me. At my best I would wonder if this was now enough "character." Several times I thought of the movie *Unbreakable*. In it, Bruce Willis' character is virtually invincible, even surviving a train crash that kills everyone else on board. He is the counter to Samuel L. Jackson's character "Mr. Glass," who is quite literally fragile and is hurt by the slightest thing. In the pity party in my head, Brad's body was strong and mine was weak. Fortunately, as my body healed, my mindset improved. I now know that one of my side effects when I eat gluten is that I get irrationally emotional. I do not have the typical stomach problems associated with Celiac Disease. Instead, I get headaches and become upset. This is probably part of the reason why I was sick for so long before my diagnosis. I never once complained to the doctor about my stomach.

CHAPTER 16

Mt. Rainier—Take Two

Melissa's hiking and climbing was on hold while she recovered from Celiac Disease. My 2012 climbing season began in February in preparation for my second attempt on Mt. Rainier, which I had scheduled for July. My friend, Mark Dunning, and I had decided to go back to Mt. Rainier that summer for both of our second tries. Another friend, Ryan Chase, was training to do a Denali preparation class in Alaska in May of 2012, so the three of us were seriously motivated to get our training started during the winter. On February 24, we loaded up heavy packs with our warmest sleeping bags, stoves, and a couple of tents and began walking up the road from I-70 toward Grays Peak. Our plan was to take the packs to about 12,000 feet, set up camp for the night, then make a summit attempt on Grays the next morning.

Mark and I were sharing my two-man three-season tent (I didn't yet own a four-season). Unfortunately, we were in the "fourth season"—winter—at the moment and this tent would not make for a great night because the screen mesh sections on the tent body allowed fine snow crystals to come through. Ryan had just purchased a new two-man tent that he planned to use for himself. As he was setting up his tent, a gust of wind came down the cirque and caught the tent, lifting it into the air like a kite and blowing it a hundred yards or so to the east of us. Ryan took off to retrieve it while Mark and I worked together to get our tent set up and tied down to rocks so that it didn't suffer the same fate as Ryan's. Luckily, Ryan's tent was unharmed and he got it set up and tied down before the next big gust of wind came up. We used our stoves to melt snow so that we could eat our dehydrated meals and have a cup of tea for dinner, and then we settled into our sleeping bags for the night.

Around 9:00 p.m., the wind really started to pick up and it began to snow. Mark and I knew for sure that it was snowing because the wind was blowing it underneath the rain fly of our tent and through the three-season mesh, lightly coating our sleeping bags in a fine white powder. We were still toasty warm in our zero-degree sleeping bags, so the snow and the wind were more of an annoyance than anything. That changed at about 11:00 p.m. when a malevolent gust ripped down from the west and pulled a corner of the rain fly off of the rock to which I had tied it. The fly was now flapping wildly in the wind and this new parachute-like quality of the fly was making me wonder if the next gust was going to rip the whole thing off the tent, or even worse, lift the tent up with us still in it.

Grudgingly, I unzipped my nice warm sleeping bag and put on my head-lamp, pants, boots, and jacket to go outside and secure the fly. I worked as quickly as I possibly could since it was incredibly cold outside at 12,000 feet in February in a windstorm. I was able to get the fly securely fastened and tied the guy line to an even bigger rock and got back into the tent and into my sleeping bag. There wasn't much sleep that night as the wind continued to howl and thicken the coat of white powder on our bags inside the tent, but the fly held and I didn't have to leave the tent again.

Our plan was to wake at 4:00 a.m. to prepare for our summit attempt. However, when the alarm went off, the wind was still howling just as it had been all night long. I told Mark and Ryan that I was pretty tired of lying there listening to the wind howl and that I was thinking about heading up a ways toward the summit to see how far I could get. I asked what they thought and got different answers from each. Ryan agreed with me that he couldn't lie there anymore listening to the wind, whereas Mark was the logical one, pointing out that if it was this windy at 12,000 feet, it was bound to be worse higher up. That made good sense and I honestly wasn't expecting that Ryan and I would get very far, but he and I still decided to get dressed and go have a look up the trail a ways. Mark bid us well and said he'd hold down the fort while we were gone.

Ryan and I climbed out of our tents in the dark, with headlamps illumi-nating the alpine world of snow and rock around us. We made final prepa-rations quickly, threw on our packs, and started hiking up the trail into the wind, shielding our faces from the biting gusts as best we could. Yes, this was going to be a *very* short hike indeed!

We began to climb into the basin below Grays and Torreys and an odd thing happened—the higher up we went into the basin, the more the wind seemed to die down. As we traversed around the bend to the south toward the shoulder of Grays, we were high-fiving each other on our decision to get out of the tents and give it a try—there was no wind at all anymore. It was as pleasant as 5:30 a.m. on a 14er in February gets (many of my friends tell me that "pleasure" is not a word they think of when I describe some of my winter outings to them). Ryan and I gradually gained ground, reaching about

Ryan Chase on the summit of Grays Peak in February.

13,300 feet before the sun colorfully lit up the sky to the east. On we went to the 14,270-foot summit of Grays Peak, occasionally looking down to see if we could spot our tents a couple thousand feet below us and wondering if Mark was cursing himself for not coming with us. We figured Mark was probably pretty bored sitting there by himself in the comforts of the tent, so we snapped a couple of photos on the summit and had a quick snack before heading back down as quickly as we could.

It was nearly 9:00 a.m. by the time we approached our tents again on the descent. We rounded a corner and suddenly the wind was fiercely raging once again. Yikes! What were the chances of that—the wind died down long enough for our summit climb, but then kicked back up when we returned to the tents. We greeted Mark when we got back and I climbed back into our tent to get out of the wind. He asked how far we made it and we told him that we had reached the summit with the weather quite nice. "Really????" he asked, incredulously. "It has been blowing just like this down here since you guys left!" Now he was clearly disappointed that he hadn't joined us for the summit climb. Apparently we had camped in a small wind tunnel—I won't be camping there again. We packed up camp and descended, with Ryan and I trying to hold back our smiles from sneaking in the summit climb that morning and Mark still pretty bitter that he had spent an extra five hours lying in a sleeping bag in the wind while we did so.

On March 30, I continued my Rainier training with a solo climb of Kelso Ridge from I-70, marking my first and as yet only Kelso Ridge climb in the month of March. On my May 6 wedding anniversary, Ryan and I climbed Kelso Ridge again and three days later I soloed Dead Dog Couloir, a steep snow route directly up the face of Torreys Peak, then spent hours helping rescue an injured climber that I encountered on the way down (more about that later). I climbed Kelso Ridge two more times in the month of May that year, and I also set a new personal speed record up Mt. Bierstadt that month, round tripping the 7-mile climb in two hours and fifty-four minutes without stopping once on the way up or down. Trail runners do it much faster I'm sure, but I'm a mere hiker.

On June 9, Mark and I went for a big training climb together, seeking to do Torreys Peak from the top of Loveland Pass. The thing that makes this tough is the vertical feet—it requires 5,500 vertical feet of climbing over a 10-mile round trip hike (almost twice the normal vertical feet of a summer 14er climb), requiring you to climb 13,427-foot Grizzly Peak twice—once on the way to Torreys and once on the way back to Loveland Pass. We did the roundtrip climb in seven and a half hours and were feeling cautiously optimistic about our conditioning in preparation for Mt. Rainier. Three weeks later though, I climbed Longs Peak with a couple of friends and noted in my climbing log, "Not feeling ready for Rainier in three weeks!" My fatigued legs felt heavy with each step and I was having trouble getting into a good breathing rhythm. I guess just like anything in life, you have days when you feel great and others when you don't.

On June 14, I had a new climbing partner with me—my then seven-year-old son, Connor. He and I hiked a ways up the Grays Peak trail, with me not pressuring him into going any higher than he wanted to go. At around 12,000 feet, he asked me, "Daddy, where does this trail lead?" I pointed to the summit of Grays Peak, nearly 2,300 feet above us and told him that if we kept walking, we would end up on the summit. He said, "That looks far. I don't think we should go there." I said, "Of course we're not going that far." I asked if he wanted to keep walking and he said he did.

A bit higher up, he pointed at another mountain, nearby Kelso Mountain, the 13,164-foot neighbor of Torreys Peak and whose connecting ridge I have climbed so often. Connor said, "How tall is that mountain?" When I told him it was just over 13,000 feet, he said, "I want to climb that one." "Really?" I asked. He repeated that he wanted to climb Kelso Mountain, so we ascended to the saddle between Torreys Peak and Kelso Mountain and turned right instead of my normal left turn for Kelso Ridge up Torreys. We scrambled up over some steep rock bands just above the saddle, but were soon having a leisurely walk toward the grassy summit. Connor was very proud of himself (as was I) for climbing his first 13,000-foot mountain. My time climbing with my dad over the years has been extremely special to me, so I was quite emotional about this first summit with my own son. Perhaps someday he will be my regular climbing partner just as I was for my dad. I would certainly enjoy his company if he chooses to climb with me more in the future.

Connor and I on Kelso Mountain with Torreys Peak in the background.

On July 5, I was back on Kelso Ridge and tied my personal speed record of two hours and eight minutes to the top. I was feeling good and wanted a big training day, so I headed over and also climbed Grays. Still feeling good and wanting more, I decided to continue east on the ridge to see if I could also climb the Centennial 13er, Mt. Edwards (13,850 feet), before going down. En route to Edwards, I encountered a mama and a new baby mountain goat and watched with awe as they both ran down the rocky cliffs on the north face. I felt a strange connection to these two goats, having just climbed with my son for the first time. It was just incredible to watch a baby mountain goat negotiate these cliffs so easily! They were long gone by the time I topped out on Mt. Edwards and returned to Grays for my descent, but I think I saw the same two goats over on Torreys Peak a few days later.

I was back on the same mountain the next morning, July 6, this time with a new hiking partner, Chelsea May, who is a trail runner. Her husband and my wife had been joking that it would be interesting to see who was faster up the mountain since I was beginning to hit my Mt. Rainier stride and she was a very fit trail runner, routinely running fifteen to twenty mile stretches at high altitude. As she and I pulled into the crowded Grays Peak parking lot on this summer morning, I noticed a group preparing to head out on a hike and put down my window. It was one of my partners from work with a small group of friends and family. "Hi Kreg," I said. He got excited and turned to his group and said, "You know the guy I was just telling you about who I said I wouldn't be surprised if we saw up here today? This is him!" My partner then came over to my car, bent down and looked in the window, preparing to greet my wife (who he had met on a number of occasions). It was quite an awkward moment being "caught" with another woman so early in the morning. I introduced him to Chelsea and quickly tried to explain about the bet our spouses had made as to which one of us would be faster that day.

Chelsea and I parked, got geared up and started up the trail. We passed Kreg and his group fairly quickly (larger groups are always slower), then Chelsea announced that she was going to run for a stretch. Grr! I hate running. But I was determined to try to keep up so I ran, too. Soon it was clear that she had no intention of slowing back down to hiking. I guess this must be how Melissa used to feel when I would hike in front of her at a much faster pace. I didn't know how I was going to get Chelsea to stop—she was too far away for me to throw a rock at her, so I yelled to her that I conceded that I could not keep up. I suggested that she go ahead and run up Grays, descend to the saddle, then climb Torreys. I would take my favorite Kelso Ridge route and meet her on top of Torreys. She told me that it wasn't actually a race to the top and that she would stop running so we could hike together. Relieved that we would no longer be running, I agreed.

She continued to stay in front, though, and set the pace just slightly faster than I would have comfortably been going without her. We arrived at the top of Grays in an hour and a half and I was drenched in sweat (which I really don't do much while hiking). We posed for a couple of awkward "We're both married to other people and by the way, you're sweaty" summit pictures, and then headed over to Torreys Peak and on down. I told Melissa about the

uncomfortable meeting with Kreg and the sweaty hike with Chelsea when I got home and she thought it was funny. A couple of weeks later Melissa and I were having dinner with Kreg and his wife and I made sure to bring up the awkward moment at the trailhead in front of Melissa, just so Kreg knew that it was not a secret that I had gone hiking with another woman. He breathed a big sigh of relief and we laughed about it more at dinner.

Chelsea and me "awkwardly" on the summit of Grays Peak.

On July 9, I was back again for one last climb before leaving for Mt. Rainier. This time I soloed Kelso Ridge in one hour and fifty-six minutes, shattering my previous personal speed record by twelve minutes. Thanks Chelsea! Now I was ready for Rainier. One problem emerged however ... my climbing partner, Mark, was no longer joining me.

I got his text while Melissa was driving us down the highway to a dinner party about two weeks prior to our departure date. He had been on

Mt. Bierstadt that day doing a training climb with several gallons of water in his backpack for extra training weight. Rather than pour the water out on the summit to lighten his load, he decided to carry the extra weight down the mountain with him (legs need to be strengthened for downhill with weight also—it's just harder on your knees). He stepped down onto the rock below him and in a freak accident, his kneecap dislocated and moved to the side of his knee joint. Luckily, people are aplenty on Mt. Bierstadt in July and one of the next people coming down the trail after him was an EMT who offered to help pop the kneecap back into place by extending Mark's leg. Sure enough, when the EMT started to straighten Mark's leg, the kneecap popped back into its rightful place, but the damage had been done. Mark dumped all of the water at that point and was able to limp back down to his car in a valiant self-rescue. But once he stopped moving, his knee swelled rapidly and he knew that Mt. Rainier was not in the cards that year. The doctor confirmed his suspicion the next day, so Mark was out.

I got an e-mail a couple of days later from one of the other guys on our Rainier climb asking if anyone had a hotel room he could share—it seemed they were all booked up in Seattle that weekend. Mark and I had reserved a room with two queen beds, and since one of them was now to be vacant, I offered the extra bed to the guy who had e-mailed. He and I texted a couple of times to share flight information and it turned out that he was on a flight from New Orleans with a layover in Denver, then he would continue on to Seattle on the same flight as me. He offered to save me a seat on the plane when the folks departing in Denver got off, so we had the opportunity to sit together on the flight. My new roomy was a bigger guy who shared with me that he has always struggled to keep weight off, which is why he likes training for mountains—it keeps him motivated and keeps the pounds off. He told me that he had lost fifty to sixty pounds preparing for the Mt. Rainier climb (and even after that he still probably had fifty pounds on me).

After deplaning in Seattle, we picked up our luggage—two large expedition duffels each—and loaded into a cab to go check in at our hotel. Gear check at the Alpine Ascents guide service office a few blocks away was at 2:00 p.m., so we had time to grab some lunch, then headed over carrying pretty much everything we owned. Since Mark had been unable to come, our team was only seven clients instead of eight. As we were discussing group gear, the subject of tents came up and the guides asked if any of the thinner guys were willing to go three to a tent instead of two so that we didn't have to carry the weight of an extra tent. There were two other pretty thin guys who offered to share their tent with me, which left my hotel roommate sharing a tent with another single guy from California while we were on the mountain. That turned out to be a great move for me.

We returned to the hotel to drop off our stuff in the room and began sorting our gear out between mountain stuff (the vast majority of it) and city stuff like clean clothes, tennis shoes, etc., that we wouldn't need again until we got down. We then met up with the guides and the other clients at a nearby restaurant for an early dinner. We needed to be at the Alpine Ascents office at 6:00 a.m. the next day to load into the shuttle bus to begin our adventure. I go to bed pretty darn early anyway (8:15, 8:30, or maybe on a late night 9:00 p.m.), so it doesn't take much of a pep talk from the guides about what a big day tomorrow is to get me into bed early.

My roommate was apparently a night owl, however, and he began to fidget as I did my nighttime chores preparing for bed. After ten minutes of pacing the room, he abruptly announced, "I've got to get out of here for a bit" and he left the room. I flipped on his bedside light, turned off all the others, then got into bed around 8:30 p.m. I turned on the TV for some background noise in hopes that I wouldn't wake up when my roommate came back. It doesn't take me long to fall asleep—it is generally when my head hits the pillow. This night was no exception. I didn't turn on the sleep timer on the TV, figuring my roommate would be back before long and turn it off when he went to bed. Oddly though, he didn't come back anytime soon. I woke up at about 11:30 p.m. and noticed that the TV was still on, as was the light by his still unoccupied bed.

I got a little grumpy with my roommate at that point. It was only five and a half hours until we were to wake up and we had a big climb ahead of us. I wanted and needed my sleep that night. I checked my phone for texts, thinking maybe he was in trouble or something—none. I decided that he was a big boy (both physically as well as having fifteen to twenty years on me in age), so I turned off the TV and the other light and went back to sleep. Finally at around 2:00 a.m., my roommate returned to the hotel room, took a shower, got ready for bed, and fell soundly asleep. I thought, "This guy must be a machine to be able to stay out this late, then get up early the next day and climb!"

Then the snoring started. Oh, how he snored! It was noisy for sure, but it was also disturbing, sounding like a gasp for air on each breath. Luckily the pack list for the climb included earplugs and I had mine handy. Problem solved. But I did feel bad for the guy he would be sharing a tent with on the mountain.

When the alarm went off at 5:00 a.m., we both jumped right out of bed, got dressed, and gathered our things. I never got up the courage to ask him where the heck he'd gone that night and what took him so long getting back. I'm still quite curious actually. After a quick run to the nearby 24-hour market for some breakfast and final snacks for the climb, we headed to the guide service and prepared to get on the shuttle for the drive to the White River Campground at 4,300 feet, where we would begin our ascent. Only 10,100 feet to go!

Our first day's task was to reach a camp at 8,500 feet on the Inter Glacier. We started off climbing gradually through the forest on a good solid dirt trail with an occasional switchback. I think everyone is checking everyone else out at the start of these climbs (I know I am). The clients are hoping they trained hard enough; the guides are hoping the clients trained hard enough. The clients are wondering whether everyone will make it to the top. The guides know better. Not everyone will make it to the top. They are probably wondering which ones won't (and beginning to form educated opinions as they watch the clients make their way up the trail). My goal when I'm training for a climb like Mt. Rainier is to be in strong enough physical condition that, weather and mountain willing, I can reach the summit and safely return. As we took breaks on the way up to the glacier, I was feeling good and could have skipped a break or two and been just fine. My hotel roommate did not seem to be feeling the same way. Early on, he was falling slightly behind the main group, with a guide playing "safety" (no one gets behind you) accompanying him behind the main pack. Our hourly breaks were long enough initially that they always caught up before we departed. Guided trips are definitely more of a team sport than an individual thing. The ratio of clients to guides is carefully monitored and there is always the possibility that the whole team will have to turn around if enough clients are struggling. Because of this, I find myself paying attention to how other clients are doing.

When we got to the edge of the glacier and crossed from the dirt and rock onto the snow and ice, we took one final break before making the last push to camp. Each of us put on our crampons, which is another time the guides are watching closely to see who is struggling and who looks as if they've actually done this before. I've watched many a fellow climber put their crampons on the wrong feet. Another goal of mine is to never be the last one ready to go. Whether it is layering up or down at a break, putting on or taking off crampons, or just getting water and a snack, I like to be ready to leave again before my guide suggests that it's time. The six clients and two guides in the main pack set off up the Inter Glacier just as my roommate, huffing and puffing and drenched in sweat, along with the third guide, arrived at the break spot; it was pretty clear that we weren't going to see them again until later at camp.

When we reached our camping spot at 8,500 feet, we had to level out four platforms in the snow for our tents. It was hard work chipping away at the glacial snow with our ice axes and shoveling it out of the platforms with the shovels we had carried up—it took a good hour with everyone tagging in and out when they needed a breather. Our lead guide, Dave, used another shovel to dig himself out a little cooking area, where he could stand in a thigh-deep hole in the snow and use a small snow bench that he created at waist level for the stove. About the time our dinner of chicken burritos was ready a couple of hours after we got to camp, my hotel roommate and the last guide rolled in. Maybe his late night outing the previous night had caught up with him. Dinner was amazing, as most meals are after a big day of exertion, and we went to bed with full bellies, ready to move up to Camp Schurman at 9,500 feet the next day.

In the morning, I woke at sunrise and enjoyed the views around me, which were not obscured by clouds as they had been the previous afternoon and evening. I looked down below our camp at the rocky outcropping just below and saw that two of the guides had spent the night out in the open under the stars, with just their sleeping bags. I was a touch jealous. After breakfast we practiced our crampon technique on the steeper slope above camp and did a quick refresher on self-arrest. I was pleased to see that no one in our group impersonated our first Rainier trip's "Human Snowball." We packed up our camp, roped up, and moved on up the glacier to go up and over the ridge, then onto the Emmons Glacier and around the corner to Camp Schurman.

Climbers avoiding a massive crevasse en route to Camp Schurman.

Traversing along the edge of the Emmons Glacier, I was amazed and humbled by the sight of the monstrous crevasses all around us. We never got close to any of the edges of these massive fractures in the frozen river of ice that was slowly moving down the mountain, but I could see enough to know that I never wanted to be in one of them.

Camp Schurman consists of a rock hut perched on a rocky ridge that separates the Emmons Glacier from the Winthrop Glacier and is occupied by the climbing rangers in Mt. Rainier National Park. Thankfully, there were several vacant tent platforms that had already been leveled and used by previous climbers just below Camp Schurman on the edge of the Winthrop Glacier. My tent mates, Josh and Jeff, and I selected a spot and got our tent set up. Our guides went into the small hut to visit with the climbing rangers to get the latest on the conditions for the Emmons Glacier route to the summit that we planned to follow, beginning at about 1:00 a.m. that night.

We had heard that the conditions on the upper Emmons route had been fairly tricky so far this season, which had cost a climbing ranger his life just four weeks prior. The route was still icy and slick toward the top, where it is also steepest, and a group of four climbers had gotten themselves into trouble on the descent. The four climbers had been roped together when they slid out of control down the mountain. Two of them went into a crevasse, actually preventing the whole party from a likely fatal fall down the icy slope. Climbing rangers were dispatched to the scene and they eventually called for a helicopter evacuation of the injured party. Sadly, a thirty-four-year-old climbing ranger named Nick Hall slipped and fell to his death in the process of attempting to load an injured climber onto a litter to be hoisted into the helicopter. For more information and analysis on this accident, read the American Alpine Club's *Accidents in North American Mountaineering,* 2013 edition. We were hoping that the slopes were less icy up top for us than they were the previous month, but all reports indicated that the route was still tricky and harder than normal.

Three hours later, in mid-afternoon, my hotel roommate and our final guide arrived at Camp Schurman and our team was all together again. At dinner, the guides briefed us on the plans for our alpine start for our summit attempt later that night and provided advice on clothing and gear to pack. After the group discussion, the three guides fanned out individually to check on how each of the seven clients was feeling about the summit climb. I had a feeling this was when they were going to tell my hotel roommate that he wasn't going on the summit climb (and frankly I was hoping they would).

The way it works on guided climbs like this is that if someone starts on the summit climb, but ends up not being able to make it, one of the guides has to go down with him or her. That means less guides are left with the remaining clients. If someone else has to go down also, it can get to a point where everyone has to turn around because there are client to guide ratio limits set by the National Park Service (rightly so for safety reasons), preventing too many clients from roping up with a single guide. Seeing that my hotel roommate was three hours behind the rest of us on a fairly easy day up to Camp Schurman didn't leave me all that optimistic that he was going to be able to reach the summit and safely descend.

Sure enough, the lead guide took him aside and explained to him that his pace was not quick enough to safely climb to the summit and back, so he would need to wait for us in camp (but on the bright side, he did get to sleep in). We also had a strong climber who had come on the trip with his adult son who decided not to attempt the summit climb. He had previously reached Rainier's summit (along with the summits of many other high mountains in Ecuador and other places) and didn't want to risk pushing his knees for the summit climb without a rest day in between (which wasn't in the itinerary). It was more important to him that his son, Rob, have a good chance at reaching the summit since this was Rob's first big mountain climb. We were all disappointed to hear that John was opting out of the summit climb because he had been such a strong performer each of the first two days, but we certainly respected his decision. That meant that we had five clients and three guides going for the summit.

Everyone is curious before a summit climb as to who they will be on a rope with (myself included) and the guides tend to maintain the suspense until the last minute. Once everyone was ready to leave camp after a quick breakfast of oatmeal under the midnight stars, they told us where they wanted us to tie in on the three ropes. Our lead guide Dave told me to tie in at the end of his rope and Rob tied into the middle. My tent mates, Josh and Jeff, tied onto our Kiwi guide, Dennis's rope. The other solo climber from California, who was sharing a tent with my snoring hotel roommate, tied onto our Swiss guide, David's (pronounced DA-veed) rope. I was excited to be on a rope with Rob and Dave, and was honored to have the caboose spot (usually the guide leads the rope and the second most experienced person takes the other end).

We started up the Emmons Glacier in the dark, headlamps illuminating the rope and packed glacial snow path in front of us. Our first real challenge was an icefall that we had to traverse in order to continue on up to the upper part of the mountain. The icefall consisted of narrow ledges in and around massive blocks of ice that were leaning downward toward the crevasses that awaited them when they fell (in this place, it was clearly *when* they fell, not *if*).

We moved as quickly through this dangerous place as we could, only feeling slightly more comfortable knowing that everything should still be frozen solid because of the cold clear night sky above us. On the rope right behind me as we weaved through the ice fall, I could hear David coaching his client and rope mate on proper crampon technique without seeming to have much success in doing so. I felt a little awkward that I could hear the coaching, but I was also comforted that the guides were addressing safety issues promptly. Once out of the ice fall, we climbed a bit higher on the open expanse of glacier above us, with the sun beginning to illuminate the sky to the east.

We took a break to eat some food and get some water, with the three rope teams parallel, running vertically down the mountain. That put me right next to Jeff for the break as we sat on our packs, snacking and looking down at Camp Schurman far below us. This was also Jeff's first glaciated climb and he was becoming uncomfortable as we moved higher on the steep snow. He told me that he wasn't sure he wanted to go any higher and I tried to tell him what a great job he was doing and to just take it one step at a time. I remember telling him that it was a good sign that he was a little scared when he looked down the steep glacier below us—that just meant he was human and his instincts were still functioning properly! He told Dennis that he wasn't sure he could do the summit climb, but Dennis convinced him to stick with it a little longer. Jeff really was doing great—he was physically strong and his climbing technique was good. Jeff agreed to keep going until the next break—but he reserved the right to ask to go down at that time if he wasn't feeling better.

As we started up again, I could tell that things weren't going much better on the rope behind mine in terms of the California guy's crampon technique. David kept telling him to stand up straight and use the rest step as the guides had demonstrated the previous day, but the client insisted on bending over forward, almost at a right angle, putting as much weight on his trekking pole and ice axe as he was his crampons, the very devices that, if used properly, would keep him firmly affixed to the glacier. I thought, "Here comes a spinning," meaning the guides telling a client that it was time to turn around and head back down the mountain. The client managed to continue his awkward hunched-over stride until it was time for our next break.

Slightly above me, I heard David conferring with the lead guide, Dave, and David expressing his safety concerns for his client. Dave agreed with David's spinning recommendation and David came back down and told his client that his crampon technique was a safety issue for himself and his rope mate and thus, they would be turning him around at this point and heading back down to Camp Schurman when the break was over. Dennis also checked in with Jeff to see if he was feeling any better about continuing on up to try for the summit. Jeff apologized and said that he would really prefer to go down. Jeff had performed extremely well on the climb and I know he would have reached the summit had he continued, but he decided it was time to go down. This was absolutely the right time for Jeff to make the call given that David and his client were preparing to head down anyway, so Jeff tied onto their rope and the three of them set off down the slope toward our camp, a few thousand feet directly below us.

That left us with two rope teams continuing on for the summit—Dave leading me and Rob, and Dennis leading Josh. Out of the seven clients who started the climb, we were down to three, but all three of us were feeling strong and climbing well. The weather was lovely that day without a cloud in the sky, so we continued up the ever-steepening slope toward the crater rim. As the incline steepened, Dave shortened the rope between each of us so that if someone slipped, he would be able to prevent a fall more easily than having a long rope length where a client could gain speed and momentum and potentially pull others from their feet; we were now about six feet apart from each other.

After another forty-five minutes or so of ascent, Rob hollered up to Dave that he unfortunately thought he was going to need to use one of Mt. Rainier National Park's famous "blue bags." Blue bags are basically a double plastic bag for human excrement with the inner bag containing some odor-controlling powder and the thick outer bag equipped with a ziplock to prevent the blue bag's contents from leaking. Dave initially asked Rob if there was any chance it could wait until we were on the crater rim where the slope was not nearly as steep, but Rob declined, saying it was time now. Dave anchored the rope and looked down expectantly at Rob as if to say, "Okay then, get on with it." Rob looked back and asked whether there was a corner or something he could go around for some privacy. Slightly agitated, Dave pointed out that we were on the steep slopes of a glacier and there really wasn't anywhere to go. And by the way, if you need to go, go because we need to keep moving.

Dave instructed Rob to turn so he was facing down the mountain, squatting on his crampons. He also thoughtfully offered a basketball analogy to Rob on the use of the blue bag: "Remember, we're going for a slam dunk here. No trying to shoot three pointers! Get that bag right up in there to make sure it gets in the bag!" Out of respect to Rob and not having any desire to watch, I also turned to face down the mountain. That's when Rob informed me that he thought he would need to pee also. "Just don't pee on me, my friend. Point that thing straight down into the snow!" I replied. Thankfully, the process was fairly quick and my rope mate had his pants back up and his blue bag safely packed away in no time. On the mountain, there is just nature and its callings. The mountain has little use for modesty or privacy.

A few minutes later we reached the steepest, iciest part of the route, near where the party of four had fallen in June along with the climbing ranger who was trying to rescue them. Dave told us that the route was still not in great shape, but that he would keep going up with us if we made him a deal. "You guys can't fall," he said. "I need you concentrating on what you are doing one hundred percent with each crampon placement." Rob and I agreed. No falling. Dave had the two of us anchor ourselves firmly with our ice axes into the snow, then he let out the coils of rope between himself and Rob. He told us to wait there while he climbed ahead up the steepest part. At the top, he grabbed a snow picket (a two- or three-foot aluminum shaft) from his pack and hammered it into the snow with his ice axe to serve as an anchor. He then clipped the rope through the carabiner at the top and told us to climb up to him. No falling. I drove my ice axe as deep as I could get the shaft with each step and made sure that all of my crampon points were engaged. In just a few minutes we had rejoined Dave. He had us do the same drill one more time while he climbed the last steep pitch and pounded in another snow picket. Rob and I were careful with our steps, climbing on when Dave gave us the okay.

We could see that we were close to the crater rim now, the incline lessening with each step until finally we reached the rim. The summit was still a few hundred feet higher and we would need to traverse to the left along the crater rim for a while, then veer right to climb the last few hundred feet to the summit. I was elated because I knew at this point that we were going to reach the top. I tried to put out of my mind any thoughts of the descent back down the glacier, especially down the steep, icy pitches we had just ascended. When we veered to the right for the final summit push, we could see across the broad, snow-filled crater of Mt. Rainier all the way over to a point on the opposite side of the mountain where we saw people standing. We asked Dave what route they were on and he told us that we were looking at the top of the Disappointment Cleaver (DC for short) route that Melissa and I had attempted back in 2008. I was pretty happy to be on the Emmons route that day because we had a much shorter walk to the true summit at Columbia Crest than the DC route folks, who still needed to cross the massive crater before having the opportunity to stand atop the state of Washington and the Cascade Range.

Dave, Rob, Dennis, Josh, and I reached the summit together and congratulated each other. We took off our packs, put on our puffy down jackets for warmth, ate our snacks, and took lots of pictures. When it was almost time to head back down, my body told me it was time for me to spend a bit of my own time with my "blue bag." I was quite relieved to be able to do so unroped and tucked behind a rocky outcropping just below the summit, with about as much privacy as one can get on a popular mountain. I was thrilled not to have to mess with my blue bag need on the steep glacier on our descent!

As we descended the crater rim back toward the top of the Emmons Glacier route, Dave reminded us to pick up our feet with each step on the way down, make sure that we kept our feet about shoulder width apart, and to use all of our crampon points. The guides were at the back of the ropes for the descent, and with Rob taking the middle again, I was in front with a bird's eye view the whole way down. My oh my was Camp Schurman a *long* way below us. I concentrated hard on every step, not wanting to catch a crampon point and trip. Practicing self-arrest with an ice axe can actually be kind of fun, but I had no desire whatsoever to try it out now with my life and the lives of my rope mates on the line! We went down as fast as we safely could since the ice fall we had crossed before sunrise that morning was now getting baked in the late-morning sunlight and becoming less stable with every minute. It was a huge relief getting through that stretch without any of the seracs dislodging, and soon we were on much easier ground with Camp Schurman just one long, mild snow slope below us.

It is always a bit awkward coming back to camp having reached the summit on a climb, knowing that some others in the party didn't. Everyone congratulated us for making the summit and we fielded many questions as to what it was like in the areas past where each climber had been. I was thrilled at having summited Mt. Rainier on my second try, but tried to temper my excitement while talking to the others who hadn't been so lucky. I had to do this again once I got home and shared the experience with Mark, since I felt bad that he had not been able to join me after injuring his knee. I snuck in a short nap in the tent that afternoon, not having slept much at all the night before our summit attempt. That afternoon and evening at Camp Schurman we feasted, recognizing that any food we didn't eat that day would need to be carried out with us the following morning. After a quick breakfast the following morning, we packed up our camp and roped up one last time to descend the short stretch of the lower Emmons Glacier before we climbed back up and over the ridge and onto the crevasse-free Inter Glacier. At that point, the guides gave us a treat and said that the Inter Glacier would be safe for glissading, so we did a quick skills review, then sat down on our butts, ice axes at the ready, and slid down roughly two thousand feet of soft glacial snow. What a way to end the climb!

After leaving the glacier and continuing onto the remaining stretch of dirt trail through the forest, we hustled down toward the parking lot, dreaming of a big lunch on the drive back to Seattle. Our guides had their favorite local establishment with giant hamburgers and hundreds of beers on tap. We all ordered hamburgers with far more decadent toppings than we would normally allow ourselves and enjoyed a cold frosty beer. After that, most of us were asleep in the shuttle for a good stretch of the remaining drive to Seattle, where we bid each other farewell. Rob and I had become friends on the trip, so it was more of a "see you later" with him. I was of course already pondering what was next …

Rob and I back on terra firma after summiting Mt. Rainier together.

CHAPTER 17

Ecuador

Within a week after I returned home from Mt. Rainier in July 2012, I asked Melissa her thoughts on me signing up for a trip to Ecuador in early January 2013. I explained that I really enjoy having something on the calendar to look forward to and that this helps my motivation to stay in shape. Ever the supportive partner, she agreed, but with one condition. "I've never been to South America either," she said, "so if you are going, I want to go, too—but not to climb mountains." She jumped online and found that the Galapagos Islands are only 800 miles off the coast of Ecuador. She asked whether we could swing it to go to the Galapagos together for a week before I needed to meet up with the climbing group. She would return home the same day I was to meet up with the guide and other clients in Quito (the capital of Ecuador). We both liked our win-win solution—I was going climbing again soon and Melissa was going to get to go to the magnificent islands made famous by Charles Darwin and his studies of evolution.

I signed up for Alpine Ascent's sixteen-day climb of the Ecuadorian volcanoes called Antisana (18,874 feet), Cotopaxi (19,347 feet) and Chimborazo (20,701 feet) and continued my training in Colorado right where I left off before Mt. Rainier, climbing North Maroon Peak with my friend Tony in early August and helping him reach his fifty-third Colorado 14er summit. The next week, I climbed my old favorite Kelso Ridge on Torreys and for the first time ever (after climbing the route thirty-one times), descended the ridge instead of going down the easy standard trail. Once the snow came in October, Grays Peak became my training ground for the rest of the year, registering five more summits there between October 26 and December 12. Mark blowing out his knee two weeks before leaving for Mt. Rainier earlier in the summer was still fresh on my mind in mid-December and I decided to call my Ecuador training complete after the December 12 climb.

Melissa and I packed our bags right after Christmas, dropped the kids off with their wonderful grandparents, and headed to the airport on December 28 for our South American adventure. I packed two large duffels with primarily climbing gear while Melissa packed everything she thought she would need for the Galapagos Islands. We were to fly from Denver to Miami then Miami to Quito, where we would spend the night. The next morning we would catch a flight from Quito to the coastal city of Guayaquil and finally on to the Galapagos Islands. Ah, the best laid plans …

In Denver we requested that our bags be checked through only to Quito so that we would have them with us in the hotel that night before re-checking them the next morning on the flight to the Galapagos Islands. No problem the airline agent said. The flight to Miami was uneventful. We wandered around the Miami airport for a while since we had a three-hour layover, frequently checking the departure board to see if our flight to Quito was on it yet so that we would know where our next gate was. Our tickets showed that we were on an American Airlines flight to Quito departing at 7:30 p.m. Not seeing it on the departure board yet, we got chair massages at an airport shop offering to help relax stressed-out travelers. We checked again after our short massages and still didn't see the flight on the board. We decided we'd walk over to the American Airlines counter (which, it turned out, was at the opposite end of the terminal) to figure out why our flight wasn't listed.

When we finally got to the American Airlines desk fifteen minutes later, we saw that it was dark and deserted. We decided to try to go through security where the other American Airlines flights were, but were told when we got to the checkpoint that our flight was not an American Airlines flight at all, but a Lan flight instead. It was about 6:30 p.m. at this point and we were beginning to get concerned that we were supposed to board an international flight for departure in an hour and we couldn't figure out where the gate was. We headed to the Lan Airlines counter (at the opposite end of the terminal from American) to see if they could tell us where we were supposed to be.

When we reached the front of the line, the attendant looked concerned and told us that we must be on an American flight since their only flight to Quito for the day had just departed at 6:25 p.m. Now we were freaking out. I had all sorts of time in Ecuador, but for Melissa, if we didn't get out that day, she was losing a full day of her week in the Galapagos (not to mention that we hadn't yet gotten one of these two airlines to acknowledge that they were responsible for taking us there). The Lan agent got on the phone and began speaking quickly in her native Spanish to see what she could figure out for us. Melissa is fluent in Spanish, so she was giving me the play-by-play in English throughout the conversation. The Lan agent was absolutely wonderful in her customer service spirit; through much hard work, she ended up salvaging the trip for us. It turned out that our boarding pass printed in Denver by United was wrong on the departure time and flight number and we actually were supposed to have been on the Lan flight that had just left. There was some mix-up between the travel agent we had booked through and the three airlines that were involved in getting us to our destination.

This gracious woman went to work on figuring out how to get us to Guayaquil by the next morning to catch our flight to the Galapagos. After typing on her computer for a while, she said she could get us on the red eye flight that night to Lima, Peru, with a tight connection for a flight from Lima to Guayaquil that would get us there just in time to board our original Lan flight from there to the Galapagos. We said, "Great!" when she also mentioned that she was putting us in first class for our trouble, so she booked it all the way through and gave us all of our boarding passes and showed us which way to go to the gate. First though, she informed us that we should go try to get our bags back from American since the bags would have been taken off the earlier flight once they realized Melissa and I were not on the plane. She instructed us to run down there, get our bags, then run the bags back to her so that she could make sure they got onto our new flights.

We raced back over to the other end of the terminal and went downstairs to American's baggage claim area. Yes, they confirmed, they had our bags, but they were still en route back to the baggage claim area. It could be up to an hour they told us, so we waited, spying through the large silver window every time the guy opened it to reveal bags on the other side. But our bags never came and we were determined not to miss the flight to Lima, so we finally gave up on the bags and headed to the Lan concourse to board our flight. We figured our bags would eventually find their way to us, and it wasn't a big deal if it took an extra day for them to show up.

As we boarded the flight to Lima that night, our moods were definitely much improved. We were even joking that since things hadn't worked out to go to Ecuador as planned, we'd just say, "Screw it! Let's go to Peru instead!" The first class seats afforded us the ability to catch a few hours of sleep during the night. When the pilot started our descent into Lima, Melissa and I started stretching out for our sprint through the airport (this one would be easier than the one in September 2001 with Melissa running on her bandaged feet). Melissa's Spanish skills were instrumental in getting us quickly through customs in Lima and we raced to our next gate, arriving just in time to board our flight to Guayaquil. We plopped back into the first class seats and prepared for the much shorter flight, all the while becoming more optimistic that we might actually be on our originally scheduled flight to the Galapagos. Sure enough, all went smoothly in Guayaquil and we were back on our original itinerary and heading west over the Pacific toward the Galapagos by mid-morning.

With a huge sigh of relief, then a deep breath of fresh ocean air, we stepped off the plane in the Galapagos and followed the crowd to baggage claim. It wasn't terribly surprising to us, given the altered flight plans, that there was no sign of our bags, so we filled out the lost baggage claim forms with our hotel information before boarding the shuttle to the ferry that would take us to the island of Santa Cruz. There we would catch a taxi to Puerto Ayora and our accommodations at the Hotel Red Booby. We learned that Lan had an office just around the corner from our hotel, so we decided to swing by and introduce ourselves after checking in at the hotel. We showed them the lost baggage claim forms and a young man assured Melissa that our bags would come in on the flight the next day. No problem—we had our toiletries with us in our carry-on bags, so we could manage a day or two in the same clothes.

We explored Puerto Ayora a bit that afternoon, realizing that most U.S. tourists see the Galapagos Islands from a ship-based tour, whereas South Americans vacationed in the Galapagos as we were—staying in the city and venturing out for day trips. Yes, indeed, Melissa's Spanish skills were going to be incredibly valuable while we were here.

The next day we walked to the Charles Darwin Research Station and checked out the amazing tortoises ("galapagos" in Spanish) and birds and learned lots about the famous last-of-his-species galapago, Lonesome George. In the afternoon, we swung back by the Lan office to see if our bags had arrived. It turned out that the same young man Melissa had talked with the previous day had absolutely no information for us, including an utter lack of knowledge about where our bags currently were and whether they had even been put on the flight that day. We left frustrated, not realizing at the time that this would become our daily ritual during our week in the Galapagos—venturing off to do something fun every morning (including Melissa's request to go cliff diving and to see more massive turtles), then returning to the Lan office each afternoon so that Melissa could terrorize the poor young man who probably felt as helpless as we did. I know very few Spanish words, but listening to these daily interactions definitely put suitcase, "maleta," into my Spanish vocabulary for good.

That afternoon we washed our clothes (the only ones we had and the same ones we'd been wearing since we left Denver) in the sink at the hotel. On day three, Melissa announced that we were purchasing bathing suits and a change of clothes. Knowing this was not the battle to fight, I acquiesced and bought two shirts and a new bathing suit for myself while Melissa did the same. I generally don't mind wearing the same clothes over and over

Melissa cliff diving with teenage boys in the Galapagos.

Melissa getting ready for "lunch" in her galapago shell.

again, so I was finding it mildly amusing that we had no luggage yet. A good friend and former neighbor used to joke with me that I only had three outfits—business suit, pajamas, and t-shirt/jeans that I wore on the weekends. This trip for me was about climbing three volcanoes in Ecuador—the Galapagos leg of the trip was just kicking back for a few days before the climbs. I did finally start to get nervous about where all of my thousands of dollars of climbing clothing and gear were when the bags still hadn't arrived by day five.

One of our biggest issues was that our phone chargers were in our checked bags rather than in our carry-on bags (never again). We had been powering our phones off to conserve what little battery they had left. I finally decided to use some precious battery to get an e-mail off to Alpine Ascents in Seattle on day five. They sprang into action, getting me connected via e-mail to the local program coordinator in Ecuador, who turned out to be the wife of our lead guide, Jose-Luis. After a couple of e-mails describing our predicament, they asked that I take a picture of the baggage claim forms and our passports and e-mail them so Jose-Luis could go to the airport in Quito to see what he could figure out. My biggest fear was that we were going to leave the Galapagos to head back to Quito in a couple of days and that the day after we were gone, our bags would be delivered to the islands.

Jose-Luis has good connections in Ecuador and the next day figured out that our bags had been sitting in Quito at the American Airlines baggage claim desk for several days. Since we had originally checked our bags to Quito for our initially planned overnight stay there en route to the Galapagos, the airline thought they had gotten the bags to where they were supposed to be. Since we had not claimed them for several days, American was actually getting ready to send them back to Miami when Jose-Luis arrived. He showed them our passports and the lost baggage claim forms and miraculously, they let him take our bags to the Hotel Quito so that they would be waiting for us when we arrived there the next day. I let out a huge sigh of relief when I got the e-mail that our bags (and all of my climbing gear) were safely at the Hotel Quito! Now I knew that the climbing part of the trip would go on. Melissa of course was a little bummed that she would have to finish out her trip to the Galapagos without any of the stuff she brought for the trip.

Sure enough, when we arrived in 9,350-foot Quito (the highest capital city in the world), Melissa set her sights on her long lost bag and I quickly checked to make sure that all of my most important climbing gear was still secure in my duffels. Melissa and I went out for a nice dinner in Quito that night to celebrate having clothes to wear again and went to bed nice and early since she was being picked up at the hotel at 5:30 a.m. the next day for her flight home to the states.

When I went to the hotel restaurant for breakfast later that morning, the stark reality hit me that my translator had returned home to our kids and her teaching job. I was now in a foreign country with Spanish skills at the preschool level. Certainly I was doing better trying to speak and understand some Spanish than I would have been doing without spending a full week with everyone speaking Spanish around me in the Galapagos, but it was still a challenge any time I needed to do anything more complicated than ask for more coffee or another beer.

After breakfast I went to the hotel lobby to meet Jose-Luis and the other clients. One of the guys in the lobby had on an Alpine Ascents t-shirt, so that made him an easy first one to find. We soon located another client and the three of us sat together talking excitedly about the upcoming climbs. Jose-Luis approached us and we now had our guide. We were still missing one other client though, so Jose-Luis went off to have the front desk call his room. No answer. Jose-Luis had a cell number for our final team member and called it. A phone rang nearby and a gentleman sitting about six feet from us answered it and we had our fourth. This quickly became a joke among us and we adopted the team name "The Lost Boys" for our webcast updates for folks at home to follow our daily progress.

That day we did a gear check and then Jose-Luis took us for a wonderful tour of the colonial district of Quito. We were all getting along very well and Jose-Luis was a wonderful tour guide and ambassador for his home country of Ecuador. We got back to the hotel in the early afternoon and I decided to head down to the spa to see if my Spanish was good enough to figure out how to get a massage. There was a lot of pointing and gesturing, but I eventually got my appointment scheduled for later that afternoon and had a semi-successful conversation with my masseuse about our spouses and kids during the massage. There was more pointing and gesturing when it was time to settle up, but it all worked out. I was glad that the currency in Ecuador is the U.S. dollar, which eliminated any need for me to worry about currency exchange rates.

The next day we would ride a gondola up to about 13,000 feet on the shoulder of an old dormant volcano called Ruca Pichincha and climb to its summit at 15,413 feet as an acclimatization hike. I had been fighting a headache ever since I had been in Quito and I was hoping it was just the city air and not the effects of spending a week at sea level then going straight to almost 10,000 feet. I knew this was quite possible though, since skiers coming to Colorado from sea level occasionally get acute mountain sickness. I was drinking lots of water and was really hoping that getting outside and getting some exercise on the acclimatization hike would help. I'm not sure whether it was getting out of the city air or getting the exercise (or a combination of both), but once we were hiking on Ruca Pichincha, I started feeling much, much better. Thank goodness! It would have been a real shame to not even get to try one of the big volcanoes I had come here to climb.

Everyone did well on the acclimatization hike, and afterward we boarded our shuttle to travel into the Ecuadorian highlands toward our destination for the night—the hot springs of Papallacta. The rustic cottages of the resort surrounded a series of natural hot springs pools of varying temperatures, which we enjoyed after a delicious dinner. The next morning we ate breakfast then drove to a nearby trailhead where we did another acclimatization hike up to just over 13,000 feet. We returned to Papallacta well in advance of dinner and I got another massage at their spa. "I have to bring Melissa back to Ecuador to the highlands for the hot springs lodge," I thought. Dinner was outstanding as were the hot springs pools afterward. This was living!

The next morning we met our other guide, Freddy, and headed to Antisana base camp at 13,500 feet. On the way we stopped in a small town for a quick lunch and some supplies. One of the other clients, Nader, had a very tough stomach, which we saw in action for the first time. Nader saw a street vendor across the street with some peeled hard-boiled quail (or some other bird) eggs floating in a pool of suspect-looking liquid and said, "Those look pretty good." He told us he wanted to try one and headed off across the street. Jose-Luis got Nader's attention and shook his head "No." Nader insisted that he wanted to try one and proceeded to purchase a couple and eat them. He told us they were pretty good, but the rest of us were just waiting for something bad to happen. Thankfully, Nader made it the rest of the way to Antisana Base Camp without issue.

While Jose-Luis and our cook were setting up camp, Freddy took us on another acclimatization hike to the 14,870-foot Advance Base Camp. We returned to camp that afternoon and had a wonderful dinner and talked about our itinerary for the next couple of days on Antisana. The clients were getting along very well. The others were Bruce, who was in his sixties and also from Colorado; Andy, an air force captain of about forty-five; and Nader, an offshore drilling rig worker from Houston who was not yet thirty.

The next morning after breakfast, we drove up to Advance Base Camp, and then hiked for forty-five minutes to reach the edge of the glacier. We could tell from the landscape, and Jose-Luis confirmed for us, that the glacier is receding. There is a very distinct area in between where the glacier ends and where vegetation begins. Since it was covered by snow and ice not that long ago, vegetation had not yet grown. We put on our crampons and divided into two teams for skills review. Andy and I were the more experienced of the clients, so we were paired together with Jose-Luis, while Nader and Bruce went with Freddy. Jose-Luis refreshed us on the "French crampon technique" of moving almost sideways up the mountain using the rest step as well as the "duck walk"—pointing your toes outward when things get steeper—and finally the "American technique" of plunging the pick of your ice axe into the snow in front of you and front-pointing up the snow when it gets really steep.

We also practiced self-arrest with our ice axes and finally moved up the glacier to join Freddy and the others for crevasse self-rescue training. This consisted of trying to climb as far up an ice cliff as possible on top rope, knowing that you would eventually fall off, be suspended in the air by the top rope, and practicing tying on your prussic knots to climb the rope and self-rescue. Boy was that exhausting! I sure hope I don't fall in a crevasse and have to do this for real. That afternoon back down at our lower base camp we practiced our running belays before dinner by pounding some pickets into the ground and practicing clipping and unclipping from them while walking roped together in a circle. After that, it was time to get packed for the real thing.

Me practicing crevasse self-rescue on Antisana.

In the morning we broke camp and headed for Advance Base Camp, where we had driven the previous day. We set up the tents and prepared for a few short hours of sleep before our summit climb of Antisana. It was to be an alpine start again, which meant lying in my tent for a few hours after dark doing my best to relax before it was time to get up around midnight to leave for the climb. After Mt. Rainier, I made one meaningful improvement in my preparations, however. I set up a special playlist on my iPod called

"Mountain Rest," which had all of my favorite softer songs on it. This plan worked beautifully in Ecuador; each night, I would put in my earbuds and close my eyes. I'm pretty sure that I at least drifted off to sleep for a little while every night before a climb using my new playlist.

We set off in the dark from camp, donning our headlamps for the same forty-five minute hike to the glacier that we had done the previous day. We were all excited to reach the glacier and put our crampons on and rope up. Jose-Luis put Andy and me on one rope with Freddy, while he led the other rope with Bruce and Nader. We set off at a slow but steady pace up the frozen glacial snow. Freddy was first on my rope with Andy in the middle and me bringing up the rear once again. Our rope team led the way. My only gauge of where we were and what we were climbing was looking up to see where the two headlamps above me were. On a few occasions, I couldn't find them at first because I wasn't looking up high enough—yikes this was steep! Through the first two breaks, the other rope team was keeping up with us, albeit at a slightly slower pace.

At each break we would self-anchor with our ice axes, put on our puffy down jackets, then get some food and water out of our packs. I would sit on my pack and look down into the darkness, watching the headlamps from our other rope team approach and eventually pass me. Just like on Rainier, the ropes ended up parallel at the breaks, so the guides could converse at the front. I ended up next to Bruce at the end of the rope on the first couple of breaks. I asked him how things were going and he said he was feeling good and as long as the pace was slow, he knew he could get to the top.

The third break was very long and cold for me—even with my puffy down jacket on (the one I refer to as the "Big Kahuna" at home). The other rope team was still a long way below us. When Jose-Luis passed me while leading the second rope team up, he asked how I was doing and I told him I felt great while I was moving, but I was getting pretty cold on a long break such as this. He apologized and told me that they were struggling a bit with equipment and pace. As soon as he reached Freddy, Jose-Luis sent Freddy on with Andy and me while his team took their break. This would be the last time we saw the other rope team until the climb was over. Andy and I were climbing well with Freddy in the lead and Jose-Luis had clearly given the guidance to Freddy to not wait for the second rope team any longer. Jose-Luis would turn Nader and Bruce around not long after this break and the three of them descended back to Advance Base Camp.

Freddy, Andy, and I moved onto more difficult terrain as the sun started to illuminate the horizon. For the first time I could actually get a look at some of the crevasses we were crossing on narrow and seemingly delicate

Me and the penitentes on Antisana's summit.

snow bridges. I stayed focused on climbing well on the way up and figured I'd worry about the way down later.

As we reached the saddle between the main summit and the south peak of Antisana, Andy's stomach started bothering him, so we had to stop so he could relieve himself. I flashed back to Mt. Rainier, thankful that at least we were a lot more than six feet apart this time. Andy felt better afterward and he, Freddy, and I advanced to Antisana's penitente-covered summit (tall thin blades of snow or ice oriented toward the general direction of the sun). One Ecuadorian volcano down, two to go!

Of course, I still needed to descend this one, so I stayed focused. I was on the front of the rope on the way down, with Andy behind me, and Freddy bringing up the rear. I felt much more comfortable descending Antisana than I had on Rainier. The only part I truly didn't enjoy was getting to one narrow snow bridge across a three-foot crevasse. I was about to step on the snow bridge when I looked down and saw how thin it was. I'm sure I stepped there on the way up and it obviously held me, but it was dark then and I couldn't see it. A trekking pole had punched through it just inches to the right of where I was going to step and I could see that it was only an inch or so thick. There's no way I'm stepping on that! Freddy asked me what the holdup was

Antisana's lower south summit with Cotopaxi in the background.

and I told him I was trying to figure out how to get across. "Jump," he said. That was fine—it was only three feet across after all. The problem was that the slope dropped off into 45-degree snow immediately on the other side and I wasn't sure I would be able to "stick the landing." I finally told myself to just keep moving, so I reached across with my trekking poles to stabilize myself and keep as much weight off of the snow bridge as I could, and then stepped gently on and across it. It held and I finally breathed again.

The rest of the descent was uneventful and we were met by Nader, Bruce, and Jose-Luis at Advance Base Camp with a hero's welcome. We boarded our bus at Advance Base Camp and drove to the Los Mortinos lodge, close to our next volcano objective, 19,347-foot and picture-perfect coned, Cotopaxi. This lodge was absolutely amazing, with climbing memorabilia on every wall and astonishing views of Cotopaxi from the windows. We had a relaxing dinner and caught up on our reading and e-mails. The next morning we would move up to the 12,356-foot Tambopaxi Lodge, from which we could see climbers high on Cotopaxi's slopes through the powerful telescope in the dining room. We relaxed here and prepared to move up to the Jose Ribas hut at 15,750 feet on Cotopaxi's slopes the following day.

We arrived at the hut via our shuttle the next afternoon around 4:00 p.m. and found it to be quite a crowded place. We staked out bunks upstairs and dropped our packs, then came back down the steep wooden stairs to the dining hall. We enjoyed trying to fix Nader up with a few of the young ladies, who were also there to climb Cotopaxi, before, during, and after dinner, until it was finally time to settle in for a few hours of rest before another alpine start up this massive conical volcano. Having had Antisana all to ourselves, it was quite a shock to have climbers all around us in the Cotopaxi hut, moving throughout the night. I tuned out to my Mountain Rest playlist once again and got as much rest as I could have hoped for—which wasn't much.

Bruce offered to pay for a third guide for this climb to provide the group and himself more flexibility in case people were going at different speeds or someone wanted/needed to turn back. Both he and Nader were determined to get to the summit of Cotopaxi to share some of the views that Andy and I had gotten from the summit of Antisana a few days before. Andy and I roped up together again, this time with Jose-Luis guiding us. Freddy was leading Bruce and our new guide was leading Nader. Unfortunately, the Antisana and Cotopaxi climbs proved too close together for Bruce and he and Freddy decided to turn back, not satisfied with their progress up toward the most challenging part of the climb, the "Khumbupaxi" ice fall (named for the famous Khumbu ice fall on Everest). This was another stretch where time was of the essence—the more quickly you moved through it, the safer it was.

Not surprisingly, given Cotopaxi's nearly perfect cone shape, the slope was absolutely unrelenting. There were no ledges, lips, or even traverses to take some of the load off of our leg muscles. Instead, it was just up, up, up. Andy and Nader were both strong that day and we all reached the summit together around 8:00 a.m., gaining access to the spectacular view into Cotopaxi's massive summit crater. The girls we were trying to fix Nader up with

Me on Cotopaxi's summit.

the night before were on the summit with us, so we made sure to talk to them and get some photos of Nader with them. Despite our unwelcome match-making efforts, Nader was all grins from ear to ear. He was on the summit of Cotopaxi and he was just so proud of himself! It was great to share that with him. It was also a new personal altitude record for me, a whopping seven feet higher than my previous high on top of Kilimanjaro.

As is usually the case, the descent is harder for three reasons: 1) it is downhill and gravity is pulling you down a little bit faster than you might otherwise be comfortable going, 2) you are tired from climbing up, and 3) you can actually *see* some of the scary parts that you climbed in the dark on the way up. I clearly remember one corner entering the Khumbupaxi ice fall where Andy and I both had to turn to face into the mountain and front-point down something that looked like an Olympic bobsled run, the picks of our axes firmly placed in the near vertical snow chute. The consequences of a fall were severe. Jose-Luis had us on belay from above, but I was still very happy to get down that chute and around the corner. The rest of the descent was straightforward and we were back on our shuttle bus in no time.

Bruce congratulated us, but he was clearly disappointed that he had not gotten to the summit of either mountain. He had planned to go home that night, as he had not signed up to join Nader, Andy, and me for the final climb of Chimborazo, so this was the end of his trip. Bruce told me on the shuttle that he was really struggling with the realization that he was getting older and that maybe his body was not going to be able to get him up big glaci-ated mountains any longer. Even though he was in amazing shape for his age and had the right attitude and mental toughness, his body just couldn't move quickly enough up the slopes any longer for him to safely climb them. At least not on this trip. I sincerely hope Bruce is able to get back on top of a high peak again and not have Antisana and Cotopaxi as his last attempts at climbing bigger mountains. I knew that someday I would have to retire from climbing like my dad had, but I hoped it would not be for a long, long time. Bruce was certainly coming to terms with his retirement potentially being sooner than he wanted. It was difficult to watch him struggling with that.

After seeing Bruce off, Andy, Nader, and I headed with all three guides to the La Cienega Hostelry for the night where we enjoyed a celebratory dinner and tour of the historical site. The next day we moved on to the Abraspungo Hostelry about two and a half hours away. I located the massage therapist there for a tune-up before the final and highest climb on our trip.

Chimborazo is not only the tallest mountain in Ecuador at 20,702 feet, but also has the distinction of having its summit as the farthest point away from the center of the earth (the earth is about 27 miles thicker at the equator than at the poles). We moved up to Whymper Hut on Chimborazo's slopes in the afternoon and again tried to catch a few hours of rest after dinner. Trying to catch a glimpse of a fox hanging out by the hut provided entertainment each time we had to go outside to use the latrine.

On this climb, we would each have our own guide and I was paired with Jose-Luis. We began in the dark just after 1:00 a.m., not knowing how the day would go given it had snowed up high on the mountain quite a bit over the past week. Jose-Luis and I climbed at a consistent pace and were soon pulling ahead of the headlamps from the others in our group. At one point, I looked back and couldn't see any headlamps below us anymore. I asked Jose-Luis about it and he said that the other two ropes in our party had radioed him and said they were both spinning because Andy and Nader weren't feeling up to another climb that day.

I really wanted to get above 20,000 feet for the first time ever, so I was seriously motivated to get up Chimborazo. As we got higher on the slope however, the snow was getting softer and softer and I was beginning to get nervous about avalanche danger. I asked Jose-Luis about it and he agreed that we should dig a snow pit to check the condition of the snow. When Jose-Luis dug the snow pit, we both looked at each other when we saw the three-inch slab layer sitting on top of a one-inch layer of powdery, unconsolidated sugar snow. Jose-Luis reached his gloved hand underneath the top slab and easily brushed away the snow in the middle layer. Yikes! We were walking on a slab of steep snow sitting on top of a layer of ball bearings! We were at 19,300 feet, only 1,400 vertical feet below the summit—but this slope was not safe.

Jose-Luis said he didn't think it was safe to go on and I agreed. I got up and started heading downhill as fast as I could with Jose-Luis behind me. After twenty minutes of descending down the worst of it very quickly, Jose-Luis told me that we were in the clear now and I could stop running down the hill. Once we were back down at the hut, he pulled me aside and told me that I was a strong climber and that I would have easily made the summit had the conditions been safe. This made me feel good and I look forward to going back to Ecuador someday (hopefully with Melissa, at least for all of the beautiful lodges in the highlands, even if she doesn't climb) and getting to Chimborazo's summit with Jose-Luis. But better to descend than push a bad situation. The mountain will still be there someday when I go back.

CHAPTER 18

What Comes Around Goes Around

Having been on the end of requiring a rescue to get off of a mountain, I can certainly appreciate how easy it is to get oneself in trouble up there. While I am out in Colorado's mountains today, usually preparing for a bigger mountain climb elsewhere, I am always on the lookout for ways I can return the favor to others. I carry extra clothing in my pack on every climb I do now—usually three pairs of gloves/mittens of various degrees of warmth, an extra balaclava, one more insulating layer than I expect to need, etc.

I have loaned out many a pair of gloves over the years to people who have assumed that they wouldn't need them in the summer, including one young man I encountered on Longs Peak who was wearing wet tube socks over his hands to try to warm them. I have given up on the idea of having a "redo" that will make our accident go away and cause Melissa's toes to suddenly grow back, so being ready, willing, and able to help others seems like the next best thing. My survivor's guilt is still with me down deep, but I feel that thanks to my efforts to repay the favor, maybe the balance in my karma bank account is close to where it was before my mistakes cost Melissa her toes.

Over the course of a four-day period in July 2014, I returned the favor to others twice. The first was on a hike of 8,461-foot Bear Peak just outside of Boulder, Colorado, where I was hiking with my cousin, Emily, and my brother, Todd, who was in town from Phoenix. We reached the summit on this nice summer day and began our descent of the 7-mile round trip hike. We were nearly down when we found a group in need of help.

About half a mile from the trailhead, we encountered two teenage girls, their mother, and their teenage brother (who we later learned had just had some sort of chest surgery), along with their golden retriever named Aspen. Aspen had hurt her paw somehow and was refusing to move down the rest of the trail to their car. A half-mile doesn't sound like a lot, but with a seventy-pound dog that refuses to move, these folks were in a bit of a pickle. They asked if we would help, to which we gladly agreed.

We tried to coax Aspen to move down the trail, but the most she would do was stand up, walk two steps, and then lie back down again. We tried to put Aspen into my backpack to carry her down, but she was just a bit too big to fit, so Todd picked her up and began walking down a nearby dirt trail that exited the woods more quickly than our ascent trail. When Todd was ready for a break, he lifted Aspen up and set her on my back in between my neck and my backpack, which turned out to be the perfect saddle for her. I carried her the rest of the way down while the mother and Emily went to the trailhead to get the cars. They would meet us at the alternate descent spot. We got Aspen loaded into their SUV and called it a day. The mother asked if she could get a quick picture of us, but the teenage daughters told her that they had already taken some of us carrying the dog. There are pictures out there somewhere of us carrying Aspen—I just don't happen to have them.

Four days later, Emily, her boyfriend, Rick, and I were climbing 13,427-foot Grizzly Peak on the Continental Divide. I had stopped to talk to a descending climber who introduced himself as "Art from Ft. Collins, Colorado." Art was training for climbs of the Matterhorn and Eiger in Switzerland and we hit it off. I mentioned someday wanting to traverse the jagged ridge from Grizzly Peak over to nearby Lenawee Mountain. Art said, "How about next weekend? It's my last training weekend before I leave. I could go Friday, Saturday, or Sunday." We exchanged cell phone numbers and agreed that I would send him a text so we could firm up details if our schedules lined up. Art raced off. He was in great shape and he was solo, so he was moving pretty quickly as he traversed up and down the ridge back toward the trailhead at Loveland Pass. Emily and Rick caught the tail end of my conversation with Art as they arrived at the spot where we had been talking. Another descending climber passed us with his dog.

Emily, Rick, and I started climbing again, and after only a few minutes, Emily yelled, "Keys!" I had walked right past them somehow, but sure enough, Emily was holding a Jeep key fob on a keychain with a small flashlight. We looked back and saw that Art and the guy with the dog were gone, having dropped down below the previous bump in the ridge. But there were three people climbing up over the bump on their way up, and they were within earshot. We held up the keys and shouted to them to please ask whether someone behind them had dropped their car keys. They yelled behind them to check, but relayed back to us that the answer was no.

I told Emily to set the keys back down by the trail in plain sight so that the person who lost them would find them when they came back looking—they obviously weren't going to get out of the parking lot without them. We would pick them up on our way down if they were still there. She reluctantly started to set them down, but decided to have one last look at them. She studied the flashlight and saw that it was engraved with a name and address. The name was Arthur something and it was a Ft. Collins address. Emily got excited and said, "Wait, that guy said his name was Art and said he was from Ft. Collins. They have to be his keys!" We thought we had just asked him through our relay, but realized that our relay may have been asking the guy with the dog instead.

Emily excitedly said, "Call him! He gave you his number, remember?!?" Sure enough, I had just texted him about possibly climbing next weekend, so I called his cell. No answer. I left a message telling him exactly where the keys were in case they were his. We prepared to put the keys down and continue up to Grizzly's summit when I had second thoughts. It was really going to stink for Art if he got all the way back to his car, realized he didn't have his keys, then picked up my message and had to do a good chunk of the climb again scanning the ground looking for his lost keys. I decided to set my pack down and run back to see if I could catch Art before he got too far. Emily and her boyfriend are flatlanders from Ohio, so I told them to keep heading up the trail and that I would catch up with them in a bit.

I took off running up the bump on the ridge over which Art had disappeared. I quickly but carefully rock-hopped down the other side of the bump until I got to a point where I could see someone way off in the distance heading up another large bump in the ridge. I yelled, "Art!!!!!" but got no answer or reaction from the guy in the distance. I ran some more and yelled his name again. This time the guy appeared to stop and turn to look at me (he was a *long* ways away). I grabbed my phone and texted him, "Keys?" My phone rang and it was him. I asked if he was the same Arthur from Ft. Collins whose name I was reading from the flashlight keychain and sure enough, it was him. I offered to meet him halfway with his keys, so he turned and began to come back toward me and I continued along the ridge to meet him. When we did the handoff, he told me that he had had his keys and cell phone in a jacket pocket. When he pulled his cell phone out to stow the jacket, the keys must have fallen out. He was extremely grateful and we bid each other farewell. Art and I didn't end up climbing together before his trip to Europe, but I did manage to find him on the web. He is a dentist in Ft. Collins—if I ever need a root canal or some painful dental procedure, I think I'll look him up and remind him to be gentle.

In addition to these minor helping hands, I've had the privilege of assisting two people who were in real trouble. The first was on August 28, 2011. Through an unusual turn of events, I found myself at the start of the knife ridge on Torreys Peak's Kelso Ridge route at over 14,000 feet only to find a woman in her late forties who was paralyzed by fear and could not go across. The thing that made this odd was that I had already climbed this route once that day—this was my *second* time up the very same day! My mom is convinced that God sent me up the mountain for a second time to help this woman. But it was really a guy named Kaleb.

After climbing the rocky ridge solo earlier that morning, I found myself sharing the summit with a young man named Kaleb who had started out in the dark with a headlamp, first climbing the standard route up Grays and then coming over to Torreys via the easy saddle trail. Kaleb and I talked for a few minutes on the summit and he asked if I had been the person he had seen ascending the rugged ridge. I told him I was and he replied that he had always wanted to do it, but hadn't wanted to climb the more difficult ridge alone. He told me that he was thinking about descending via the ridge, then climbing it that day. It is generally much harder to descend Class 3 and 4 terrain than it is to climb it and also generally not a good idea to attempt to descend a route that you haven't climbed, so I talked him out of doing the ridge descent. But I did offer that if he was serious about wanting to climb it that day, I might be willing to climb the ridge with him a second time after descending the standard route.

We descended the easy standard trail and reached the 12,300-foot turn-off to the more difficult ridge route. I asked him how he was feeling and he said he wanted to go for it. We had both started so early that morning and climbed so quickly that it was only mid-morning at this point. We set off up the ridge and I led the way, having done this route more than fifty times over the years. When we reached the knife ridge, a smooth, solid stretch of rock that is only about 20 feet across, but drops steeply on both sides, we found the woman sitting on the ridge just before it got difficult. Her college-aged son was attempting to bypass the knife ridge on some treacherous, steep, loose slopes below and was quickly getting himself into trouble. I shouted to him that the crest of the knife ridge was really the easiest and safest way to go and that the summit was only 200 feet beyond once the knife ridge and a group of jagged white rocks on the west side were crossed. The woman told me that she didn't think she could get across the ridge—she was terribly afraid of heights and was stuck. She and her son were from Houston and had read that Grays and Torreys were easy 14ers and had set off to hike the standard trails. They had made a wrong turn and left the easy standard trail and climbed onto the more difficult ridge instead.

I remembered then that I had thrown my 30-meter half rope into the bottom of my pack that morning for some extra training weight. I told the woman that I had a rope and would be happy to give her a belay across. Her eyes lit up when she repeated back to me, "You have a rope???!!!" I got the rope out, quickly flaked it out to get kinks and knots out, then tied her in around her waist. I went across the knife ridge to the other side and set up a quick hip belay, sitting in a stable position and wrapping the rope around my hips to control the pace and provide friction if needed. Knowing she was on a rope made a *huge* difference to this poor scared mother. She gingerly, but consistently, crawled across the ridge crest on all fours, careful not to lean one way or the other. She was across in no time, then I sent her up and over the jagged white rocks that marked the last difficulty of the climb. I continued to belay her from above as she climbed down to the solid ground that marks the top of the Dead Dog Couloir.

Her son retreated and climbed back to the ridge crest then came across on his own. We all reached the summit together and I pointed out the standard descent trail on the south side of the mountain, wanting to make sure they didn't try to descend the same way they had just come up. I was exhausted from having climbed Kelso Ridge twice in one day! Maybe God told me to grab my rope that morning and sent me back up the second time to help the woman, or maybe I'm just dumb enough to think it's fun to do a

A look at the knife ridge section of the Kelso Ridge route in winter (top right climber visible is me in January 2014). Photo courtesy of Jeff Shafer.

Melissa looking out over the sunrise from halfway up Dead Dog Couloir in 2009.

tough climb twice in the same day. Either way, the woman and her son got down safely while I got the satisfaction of having helped someone in need.

The next year, I would have another opportunity to assist, again on Torreys Peak. Grays and Torreys are definitely my "home mountains," having climbed the two a combined eighty-eight times at this point. I have even gone as far as introducing myself as a Grays and Torreys search and rescue volunteer in gently asking someone to move off of the fragile tundra and back onto the well-worn trail.

On May 9, 2012, I climbed the steep snow Dead Dog Couloir on Torreys Peak solo. I started at 4:00 a.m. from the trailhead and reached the summit at 7:15 a.m. It was a nice crampon climb in ideal spring snow conditions. I was dreaming of my Main Street Restaurant sausage, eggs, and hash browns down in Idaho Springs as I walked back down the standard descent trail. At around 12,000 feet, there were three guys sitting down on one of Kelso Mountain's snowfields. One guy saw me and ran over and asked me if I had medical training.

I said, "No, but I do have a first aid kit. What happened?" The leader of their party, Robert, had apparently been trying to show the other guys how to self-arrest on the easy snow slope and somehow grabbed the wrong end of his ice axe and ended up with the sharp pick going about an inch into the inside of his left foot, just behind the ball of his foot around the instep. They wisely had not removed the axe in case he had hit an artery, so they splinted the long handle of the axe to his leg to prevent it from moving the pick and making things worse.

Robert was in a lot of pain and couldn't walk or even hop (not even with support from his friends). I gave Robert some Tylenol from my small medical kit and then the three of us tried to carry him out by making a seat for him out of two of our ice axes. Two of us held the ice axes horizontally about eight inches apart, then had Robert sit on them so that we could carry him like a king on a throne. The third guy walked behind Robert to support him from the back. It was very slow going. They had a fourth in their party who had gone down to the trailhead for help and had found an emergency medical technician preparing to hike up the mountain. The EMT and Robert's other friend reached us fifteen to twenty minutes later and the EMT concluded that there was likely no serious damage to the foot, but concurred on keeping the axe in to prevent bleeding.

Now we had five people trying to carry Robert out. We put a couple more ice axes across his bottom and tried to continue carrying him down. It was still extremely slow going; we were over a mile away from, and a thousand vertical feet above, the trailhead. Two more people arrived and offered to help and pretty soon we were going even slower, tripping over each other with every step. We asked Robert on a number of occasions whether he wanted us to call in a helicopter to get him, but he was a poor college kid, embarrassed by his mistake, and not wanting to have to be taken by helicopter off the mountain, so we kept trying to carry him down.

The lower trail was mostly snow given that it was early May, so I offered to run down to my car and get my Thermarest sleeping pad on which I had slept in the back of my car the night before. I despise running, but I ran down the mountain to my car, got my Thermarest, and hiked back up to them huffing and puffing. (I was the only volunteer rescuer who was on their way down the mountain that day—the others were still fresh having just left their cars forty-five minutes before.) Much to my dismay, the others had not moved him a single inch by the time I got back. I was frustrated and took charge. I put the Thermarest down on the snowy trail and had them carry Robert over to me. Time for a bobsled run, Robert!!

I pulled on the Thermarest while the others steadied Robert; the mat slid down the snow with ease and it was clear we had a way to make great progress now. Another group of volunteer rescuers had a hammock in their car that was retrieved and eventually went under the Thermarest so we could lift him and carry him when we got to the few rocky patches and for the final quarter mile of dirt trail.

After five hours of this, we got Robert into the back of his buddy's station wagon. I pulled my Thermarest out from underneath him and off to the Summit County emergency room they went. My arms and back were very sore the next day, but it was well worth the effort to help get an injured party off the mountain. I didn't take any photos during our rescue work and I don't know anything about Robert—where he lives, what he was studying in college, or what happened when they got to the ER that afternoon. Robert is out there somewhere though, with a big scar on the inside of his left foot and a great story that he has told often (likely laughing with friends over a beer). I just hope he hasn't tried to demonstrate self-arrest with an ice axe to anyone else!

CHAPTER 19

Denali's Lower Glacier

In the summer of 2013, I decided to step down as the head of EKS&H's audit practice and began to train for a May 2014 climb of North America's highest point, 20,320-foot Mt. McKinley, or as most climbers refer to it, Denali. The change in job responsibilities freed up lots of time to train, which was good because the Alpine Ascents' suggested Denali training program is just plain scary looking. I also started writing this book in the fall of 2013 on a day when I was scheduled to go for a training climb, but opted not to go due to a blizzard outside. I wrote a lot between Thanksgiving and New Years, but ultimately, the training time commitment took a commanding lead over my desire to finish writing this book and I had to set aside my writing efforts until my return from Alaska.

I set three goals for myself when I signed up to do the Denali trip: 1) train hard and be in the best shape of my life, 2) return safely, and 3) have fun and enjoy the experience on the mountain. Noticeably absent from my goals was to reach the summit. I deliberately refused to set this as a goal because I was concerned that it could be in conflict with the most important goal—returning safely to Melissa and the kids. If I accomplished all three of my goals, but did not reach the summit, I was okay with that. If, however, I reached the summit but did not achieve goal number two or number three, it would not be worth it.

I pursued goal number one rigorously immediately upon signing up for the trip in July 2013. During my ten months of training to prepare for Denali, I generally did some form of workout at least six days per week. Some days it was road biking (including some mighty cold early morning rides in December!), some days it was lifting for upper body strength, some days it was a cruel and unusual self-punishment called "leg blasters" (consisting of four consecutive sets of ten lunges, squats, jump lunges, and squat jumps). Other

My "icicle beard" after a crisp morning bike ride in December 2013.

days were fun days of hiking or climbing, while countless others started with sixty minutes on the stair machine in my office gym with fifty pounds of water-filled orange juice bottles in my backpack. I also did fifty pushups and a hundred and twenty sit-ups each and every day during this training period.

I would also set small goals for myself along the way, such as reaching twenty-five 14er summits in the time span from when I signed on to the Denali trip to the time I departed in May 2014. I ended up with thirty-four 14er summits during that time period:

Month	Jul	Aug	Sep	Oct	Nov	Dec	Jan	Feb	Mar	Apr	May
14er Summits	4	4	5	6	2	2	3	1	4	2	1

Melissa and I also climbed Camelback Mountain in Phoenix together over her Christmas break from school while visiting my brother's family there. Another goal that I set prior to my departure was to finish off the "monthly cycle" on two of my most frequent climbs—completing them in every month of the year—climbing Mt. Bierstadt and Kelso Ridge on Torreys Peak. I finished the Mt. Bierstadt cycle in March 2014 with an overnight trip on the mountain where I also pulled a sled attached to my pack for the first time.

I needed to climb Kelso Ridge on Torreys Peak in the tough months of November, December, January, February, and April to complete the cycle on Kelso Ridge. During the course of my Denali training, I found willing friends to accompany me on these attempts (these are good friends—winter mountaineering in Colorado is not for the faint of heart). We were able to climb the steep, snowy ridge and summit the peak in four of the five months,

Melissa on Camelback Mountain in Arizona in December 2013.

Me on the summit of Mt. Bierstadt in November 2013.

leaving only February remaining on my Kelso Ridge "cycle." February proved to be a tough month for a few reasons. First of all, I am an accountant by trade and February tends to be a busy time in my profession. Second, it is a shorter month with fewer days, and finally, we found ourselves in a very windy weather pattern that prevented attempts the couple of days when the stars of our busy calendars aligned. Maybe next year.

Other "training" for Denali happened in unusual places and at unusual times. For example, one afternoon in late April, I was running from meeting to meeting for work and realized as soon as I got into my car in downtown Denver that I really should have used the restroom after my last meeting. Sure, I could have gotten back out of my car and wandered a block or two to find a Starbucks, all the while hoping not to return to find a parking ticket on my car, but I thought, "Bummer, I guess I'll try my Denali nighttime camping skills and use a 'pee bottle' instead." So I downed the last of the water in my Nalgene water bottle and decided that it was now my pee bottle.

Peeing into a thirty-two-ounce plastic bottle is not actually as easy as it would seem. Especially in a car. While driving. I unzipped my slacks and readied myself, careful to make sure that I was "tucked" inside the rim of the bottle. I then tilted the bottle as much as I could, wanting to maximize the downhill slope in the bottle away from my body and my slacks. Once I was fully in position, I tried to convince myself that despite not having a urinal or toilet anywhere in sight, it was okay to urinate. It took quite a bit of coaxing, but finally I felt the relief begin. The relief kept going, however, and much

Winter shots of the upper part of Kelso Ridge.

to my dismay, I was rapidly becoming in danger of overflowing the heavily
tilted bottle. In a panic, I squeezed closed the internal valve to cut off the flow
of urine to the bottle. I still needed to pee more, but first I had to get rid of
the liquid already in the bottle. Feeling bad about doing so, I put my window
down and poured it out the window, telling myself that at least I wasn't leaving trash on the street like cigarette butts that are so frequently expelled from
car windows. I finished urinating into the empty bottle and continued on to
my next meeting. What great training for the upcoming three-week trip! It
really makes a huge difference if you can use a pee bottle while lying horizontally in a minus 40-degree sleeping bag versus having to get dressed and
leave the tent to pee.

Melissa recalls:
Through the years I have been happy to play the support role to
Brad's quests. At times this has meant being basecamp manager
while he summits: filtering water, planning and cooking meals, etc.
Other times I have supported his trip by calming another spouse
whose husband was with Brad. On several occasions, when Brad
and his friends were late coming back and non-responsive to calls
and texts, I have been the calm voice explaining that everything
was going to be okay. It's not that I don't get anxious during these
times, it's just that I understand that getting upset at home won't
help him out on the mountain. There have been a few times when
I vented my frustration via an angry text that he received when he
was back in cell service. But, I never share these concerns with our
children or the worried women who have reached out to me.
    The biggest support role, however, comes with a big expedi-
tion like Denali. For the ten months of training, my role was to
encourage him through the grueling exercise to prepare physically
and watch the kids while he was out hiking, riding his bike, etc.
This was also training for me in a way. Brad was going to be gone,
with no communication, for three weeks. The longest he had been
gone previously was two weeks for Ecuador, and he had been able
to Skype with us on and off during that trip. During the three weeks
in Alaska, the children and I were going to be finishing the school
year. This is always a hard time for me since I need to close out my
grades and write end of the year report card comments. It's also
emotionally difficult as I prepare to say goodbye to a class of students who I have come to love. The end of the year is difficult for
Connor and Megan because by May, they are exhausted from nine

months of school. Adding Brad's absence to this was just going to make everything that much more difficult.

The first week was the hardest; we all missed him so much. But after that week, it got a bit easier. We settled into a routine and worked together to get through the last two weeks. Each night we would check the Alpine Ascents website for an update. I had printed Brad's itinerary and a map of his route for the kids so that they could track his progress and feel connected while he was away. I also mapped his route in Google Earth from the GPS coordinates that I received from Brad's SPOT beacon each night when he arrived at camp. During these three weeks, I got a glimpse into what life is like for military spouses during a deployment. I have tremendous respect for these men and women who keep things going back home.

The Denali trip was a nine client, three guide trip through Alpine Ascents. I knew two of the other clients—my friend Ryan Chase from Colorado and my friend Rob Miller from California (who I met and ended up summiting Mt. Rainier with in 2012). Rob, Ryan, and I arrived in Talkeetna, Alaska, a day early to have some time to explore the town a bit before leaving for the glacier. We stayed at a wonderful bed and breakfast that tailors to climbers called the Fireweed Station, which would also serve as our meeting point with the rest of our party. It was May 17 and in Alaska, the land of the midnight sun, it does not get dark at this time of the year—only twilight. That night, I sent Melissa an "all okay" message using my new SPOT personal locator beacon. I wanted to test it out since the SPOT would be my only means of communicating with her (albeit in a one-way fashion) once we departed for the mountain. Exhausted from the long travel day, I managed to fall asleep pretty easily despite the lack of darkness. But just as I was drifting off to sleep, a train came ripping through the woods not 100 yards away from the Fireweed, startling me awake, sure that a 747 must be about to land in my bedroom!

I awoke early the next morning, still being on Denver time two hours later than the local time, and enjoyed coffee, solitude, and one of my last days reading my *Denver Post* newspaper on my iPad. After breakfast, Rob, Ryan, and I took our hosts up on their offer to let us use bikes to ride the 12 to 15 miles into town to explore Talkeetna, which one bumper sticker describes as, "A quaint little drinking town with a climbing problem." We enjoyed a burger and beer at the West Rib, then got homemade blueberry ice cream at a small stand across the street before walking over to the airport to watch some of the small planes take off for sightseeing tours or to drop off climbers like us on the glacier at Denali base camp. That afternoon, the three of us also walked to the other end of town to the banks of the Talkeetna River. From there, we got our first glimpse of Denali, the massive tower of snow and ice off in the distance. The daunting sight reminded us why we had come and served as a concurrent dose of humility.

Ryan and Rob would each be doing Ironman triathlons during the summer of 2014 upon returning from Denali. On the bike ride back to the Fireweed, they demonstrated their level of physical conditioning and biking skills as they blew me away riding up the first big hill on the return journey. Once I had given up on keeping up with them, figuring that maybe my body was getting too much oxygen given Talkeetna sits at just 300 feet above sea level, I set my sights on a husband and wife riding up the next hill, one of them with a toddler buckled into the seat on the back of the bike. I felt better after easily passing them up the hill and told myself that surely this meant that my ten months of training had been successful and I would have what it took to climb Denali!

We took some time to arrange our gear back at the Fireweed later that afternoon and waited for the rest of our group to arrive around dinner time. Around 8:30 p.m. (everything seems to happen later in Alaska), dinner was served and we met the other six clients. We had a geologist from Calgary, two Irish pilots who were currently based out of Dubai, two attorneys (one from New York and one from Washington, D.C.), and a Russian guy who quickly established himself as the official trip photographer, having taken something like eight hundred photos with his $10,000, ten-pound camera by the time he arrived in Talkeetna to begin the trip! The eldest of the clients led off with a statement, "I'm the oldest one here, so you guys better be able to keep up with me." I thought, "Yikes! Maybe he's doing an Ironman when he gets home, too. I could be in trouble here!"

We also met our three wonderful guides over dinner at the Fireweed: our leader, Seth, who was from Montana and who dropped out of a physics PhD program to focus on guiding and climbing; our second in command, Micah, an intense but funny guy from Utah who's girlfriend was in the process of moving them to Colorado while he was on the trip; and finally a British guide named Tom who had a dry sense of humor and had moved to Texas and developed a passion for spicy food while raising the four cows that he had purchased (an odd combination all around!).

The guides briefed us on the plan for the following morning—the first official day of the expedition. Breakfast was at 7:00 a.m. (I was up at 5:00

a.m. again), then to the Alpine Ascents hangar for gear check, then lunch in town followed by our check-in and briefing at the National Park Service office at 1:30 p.m., with a target of being at the airport by 2:30 p.m. The small planes used by the air taxi companies can only land at the Denali base camp, on a glacier at 7,200 feet, in fair weather (and it was breezy that day), so there was a big question mark as to whether we would be able to get onto the glacier.

Luckily, at 4:00 p.m. we got the green light to go and quickly loaded onto two different planes our masses of duffel bags, sleds, and grain sacks filled with group food. The forty-minute flight to base camp was filled with amazing views of Denali and the rest of the Alaska Range, but also with enough bumps to make me airsick. I alternated between taking photos out the window and focusing on a single spot on the horizon while breathing deeply in an effort to avoid being the one person on the flight who needed to take advantage of the air sick bag in the seat pocket in front of me. I was successful—barely—and we landed at base camp at 4:40 p.m. on May 19.

After digging out and leveling our tent platforms in the snow, we enjoyed veggie stir-fry for dinner and settled in for the night, all of us anxious to get started on the adventure of moving up the mountain. Rob, Ryan, and I were thankful to have been given a four-man tent to share during our time on the lower mountain (the standard tents used are three-man, which means you can fit two comfortably and three if you *really* have to). The other six clients were divided up into three of the standard tents—the attorneys bunked together as did the Irish pilots, leaving the geologist and the Russian in the final tent. Our three guides shared another of the larger four-man tents, which they pitched next to our "cook tent," which was just the vestibule of another four-man tent pitched above a trenched-out cooking area with seating benches on the sides.

The inside of the cook tent with snow benches.

Day two of the expedition consisted of packing up our gear at base camp and moving to our camp at about 7,500 feet in a "single carry." When we arrived on the glacier, each of us had about 110–120 pounds of gear (including our share of the "group gear"—food, fuel, tents, shovels, pickets, etc.). A "single carry" meant that we carried everything we had with us to our next destination as opposed to carrying only a portion of it, then "caching" it (meaning digging a hole in the snow, burying it, and marking it for later retrieval) and returning to our prior camp in order to move the rest of our stuff the following day.

Moving from 7,200 to 7,500 feet in a single carry doesn't seem as if it would be that hard. It's only 300 vertical feet after all. The complication is that we first had to *descend* about 700 vertical feet down "Heartbreak Hill" (I would learn to fully appreciate its name upon our return to base camp three weeks later!), then climb up 1,000 vertical feet over miles of glacier, all the while carrying a fifty-five–pound backpack and pulling a sled with at least that much weight.

I was initially assigned the last spot on one of the three rope teams because I was one of the bigger guys, which was apparently going to help me better control the sled that would be behind me. Rob was in front of me and Ryan in front of him, with our guide Micah leading the rope team. Rob, Ryan, and I were each instructed that our primary job in descending Heartbreak Hill was to keep the sled of the guy in front of us tight on the rope so that it didn't bang him in the ankles and knock him down. Piece of cake I thought. "Wait! Who's behind me controlling my sled?" No one. Micah simply told me that I was free to cuss as much as I wanted or needed to as we descended the hill. That didn't make me feel more confident about it.

Even though the path was well packed, we were all wearing snowshoes on the lower glacier. As I might have mentioned, I hate snowshoes. I find it difficult to get them to stay on my size fourteen mountaineering boots, and I often find my boot toe catching against the plastic at the front of the toe bed with each step. It's safe to say that I was not excited about pulling an uncontrolled, fifty-five–pound, loaded sled downhill while wearing my snowshoes. Sure enough, the sled went rogue on me three different times on the way down that first hill, twice zipping past my right side, wrapping the rope around the back of my calves and nearly taking me off my feet. On the third occasion, it crashed into the back of my foot and caused my snowshoe to pop off. Not wanting to stop the whole rope team for a break to put my snowshoe back on, I just grabbed the silly thing and carried it as inconspicuously as I could until Micah called for a break at the bottom of the hill. Since misery loves company, I was glad to hear that one of the other guys assigned the last spot on his rope team *was* knocked off his feet by his sled twice versus my near misses.

Mt. Foraker, the Alaska Range's second highest peak at 17,400 feet, had dominated our views thus far as we descended Heartbreak Hill. Its 10,000-foot east face is one of the largest continuous mountain faces in the world. Although the views of Mt. Foraker were spectacular, it was a relief when we turned right at the junction of the southeast fork and main Kahiltna glacier and began our slow ascent up to the 7,500-foot camp. The main Kahiltna glacier is a 44-mile long river of snow and ice descending from Kahiltna Pass at just above 10,000 feet. Thank heavens the airplane lands on the southeast fork, a long ways from the snout of the glacier.

For this first leg of our long journey up Denali, I wore just a baseball cap, a white polypropylene shirt (to reflect the sun's intense heat), light gloves, and my soft shell climbing pants. My massive orange boots (rated warm enough for climbing 8,000 meter peaks like Mt. Everest) were definitely overkill on the lower glacier, which serves almost like a microwave oven, reflecting the sun's rays into a pocket of warmth near the surface. I liberally applied sunscreen to my face and ears at each of our breaks, wanting to avoid getting sunburned my first day on the mountain. Five hours after leaving base camp, we arrived at our first camp, with several of us (including me) finding minor hot spots on our feet once we had a chance to take our boots off in the comfort of our tents. I hoped those hot spots would not be an issue later.

We take small things for granted at home—things like beds, pillows, running water, and indoor plumbing. My two Thermarest sleeping pads made for a fine bed in my tent and I treated myself to my travel-sized Temperpedic pillow up until 11,000 feet on the mountain, but there was not much I could do about the lack of indoor plumbing. Each camp has a few designated "pee holes," which you can imagine start out small, but grow quickly as people urinate in the same spot over and over. Since the problem of running water is solved by the abundance of snow available for melting, it makes sense for everyone to consolidate their pee into a designated pee hole rather than risk tainting the "water supply" with yellow patches everywhere in the snow. Our guides told us that one pee hole at the 14,000-foot camp got so big that one of the National Park Service climbing rangers actually slipped and fell into it and had to be rescued a few years ago—yuck! Luckily, we didn't have any of these man-eating pee holes at any of our camps on the mountain.

When nature calls for "number two," the National Park Service mandates the use of something called a "Clean Mountain Canister" or "CMC" for short. The guides told us to make sure not to pee in our CMC, instead using the pee hole before taking care of number two (it was a bit awkward to have to make this a two-step process). Our group had two CMC's that we were responsible for returning to Talkeetna at the end of the expedition. A CMC is basically just a green or black bucket, about 12 inches in diameter and about knee height. You place a compostable plastic bag inside the bucket that serves as your toilet until it is full, and then the bag is discarded deep into one of the designated crevasses near camp where it dwells for thousands of years as it eventually dissolves and becomes part of the glacier.

Privacy on the glacier is pretty hard to come by. Some pee holes are smack dab in the middle of camp at surface level of the glacier. Others can be almost luxurious if someone has taken the time to dig a four-foot deep hole in the snow and carve steps down into it, creating not only a semi-private area for CMC use, but also a bit of a shelter from the wind while doing one's business. I had a strong preference immediately for these combination CMC pits with built-in pee holes, but one was not always available. Sometimes it would take me a couple of different tries to coax my urine out while standing in the center of camp with a constant flow of people around me. Even if I got one of my preferred CMC pits, things did not always go smoothly. On day three of our expedition, my diary reads, "Morning disaster on the CMC! Frozen toilet paper & wipes + full CMC bag = BIG MESS!"

At Melissa's urging, I had brought a large sixty-four pack of baby wipes on the climb and initially had stored them in a large ziplock bag with one of my two rolls of toilet paper. I had the ziplock bag in an outer pocket of my backpack for easy access. Unfortunately, at each break we took on that initial move up to the 7,500-foot camp, I would sit on my backpack to rest—right on top of that outer pocket. This had made my baby wipes ooze out some of their moisture onto my roll of toilet paper. This wasn't a problem until I left my backpack in the vestibule of the tent at the 7,500-foot camp and everything froze overnight. When I went to use the CMC after breakfast the next morning, I could see that the CMC bag was definitely nearing capacity, but I honestly thought I could squeeze one more load in.

I pulled down my pants, beginning the start of the refreshing spindrift on bare butt experience that would become routine over the next three weeks, sat down on the nearly full CMC and was proud to produce my morning poop. That's when I realized that my baby wipes and saturated toilet paper were frozen. I did my best to tear hunks of toilet paper off the roll fully aware, however, that I only had two rolls of toilet paper to get me through three weeks and I could not afford to be wasteful on day three. It wasn't pretty. By the time I was done wiping myself and trying to push my newly made deposit down into the now full CMC bag, I was definitely going to need to fully bathe my hands in hand sanitizer. But I had learned my lesson. From that point on, the toilet paper was in a separate bag from the baby wipes and I began sleeping with both bags in my minus 40-degree sleeping bag at night to prevent them from freezing.

Thankfully, that day got better after the morning CMC disaster. We packed up our sleds with a bunch of food and fuel and did our double carry/cache day by carrying loads up Ski Hill to 9,700 feet, the site of our next camp. On three different occasions, we heard loud booms on the peaks far off to our left and saw small avalanches raining down from cornices high on the walls. When we returned to the 7,500-foot camp that afternoon, I taught Rob, Ryan, and one of the attorneys, Curt, how to play Hearts (cards were another luxury item I had brought). I was thrilled when I was able to "shoot the moon" (basically taking all of the possible points) twice in a row, but my new playing partners didn't seem to think it was as much fun. Curt tagged out with another client, Pat, and I again shot the moon (three times in one day!) before they all caught on and began to try to team up on me. I was really happy to be a part of this team of climbers. All nine of the clients on our team were in great physical condition and we were bonding nicely. After all, they say you don't climb Denali—you camp up it. If you are going to be on a three-week winter camping trip, it's going to be a heck of a lot more fun if you like the other people.

After a very windy night, we woke the next morning to find a ground blizzard blowing snow around and severely limiting visibility. Despite this, we were all happy to get the call from our lead guide Seth that we were going to go ahead and pack up to move to the 9,700-foot camp. Rob got traded to another rope team for the day, joining a guide and a client from the Alpine Ascents team scheduled to be two days ahead of us. The client had been ill at the 7,500-foot camp and had not been able to move to the 9,700-foot camp when the rest of her team did. She eventually caught up with her team at the 11,000-foot camp, but again struggled with the altitude and was sent back to base camp. This was also the day that we heard the story about two clients who were on the first Alpine Ascents trip of the year who had both summited Mt. Everest, but who refused to set up their own tents at Denali base camp and decided instead to get on a plane and return to Talkeetna. Our group thought it was amusing that two people who had previously summited Mt. Everest arrived on Denali, looked at how big the surrounding mountains were, learned that they had to set up their own tents (versus having sherpas or porters do it) and opted to just go home, forfeiting the more than $10,000 dollars they were already out.

The next morning was beautiful and we decided to single carry up to the 11,000-foot camp, where we would begin our acclimatization in earnest.

Rob was back with our group and everyone did well on the three and a half hour journey up the hill with our full packs and loaded sleds. We passed a group of three on the hill going up to the 11,000-foot camp, with the last guy struggling badly to walk five steps before needing his next break. I personally wouldn't have been wearing my Goretex shell layers from head to toe on the warm hike up that hill and thought this was probably part of his problem, but I didn't figure it was any of my business or my place to give him pointers. He did make me feel pretty good about my own fitness level, though. I wondered whether he noticed me passing him and whether he noticed that I was not even breathing hard in contrast to his incessant huffing and puffing. I was quite optimistic that if we got a good weather window up high on the mountain that our team would all be able to summit.

My spirits increased even more when the guides pulled out Boboli pizza crusts and the fixings for dinner that night! I used to love Boboli pizza—it was my weekly Sunday football season lunch for many years before my wife (who doesn't care for them) put a stop to it. I proudly took a picture of the Boboli pizzas in our cook tent to show Melissa that normal people really do eat them and think they taste good (it turns out that Melissa doesn't believe that people who try to climb Denali qualify as "normal people"). Maybe I'll frame that picture for our dining room someday.

Rob, Ryan, and Curt enjoying the Boboli pizza inside the cook tent.

We took a rest day at 11,000 feet the next day with a quick snow school refresher from Micah. We would be caching our snowshoes at this camp and transitioning over to our crampons from here on out, which was fine with me. The first Alpine Ascents team of the year came down through the 11,000-foot camp that afternoon and I was able to visit with one of the guides on that trip who lives in Colorado and who I've climbed with a couple of times. Their team did not get a suitable summit window, so their high point was the 17,200-foot camp. He also told me that no guided parties had summited Denali yet in 2014. I sure hoped that our team would change that if and when we got our chance.

The following day we carried a load of food and fuel up out of the 11,000-foot camp, climbing Motorcycle Hill and Squirrel Hill, through the Polo Field, and around Windy Corner to a cache site at 13,500 feet. I had retained my spot as the caboose of my rope team, so I was a bit worried about controlling my sled coming around Windy Corner where there is a short traverse of a steep snow slope. I did much better controlling my sled this time and never felt off balance. At the cache site, we were instructed to stay tied into the ropes even though we were stopped. Curt learned why when he went hip deep into a small crevasse venturing just a few feet away to pee. On the descent, we kept our same positions on the rope but reversed directions back to the 11,000-foot camp. This meant that I was now in the front leading the way down. As we approached the top of Squirrel Hill, I could see a mass of avalanche debris off to our left, sitting at the crest of a slope that dropped down into the 11,000-foot camp. The previous evening when we heard the avalanche, I was horrified for a few seconds when I thought the avalanche might just be headed for us. It was sobering to see the huge debris field.

Rob and Ryan at our 13,500-foot cache site with Denali's summit in the background.

We had finished dinner and a few of us were socializing in the cook tent when we heard a loud "BOOM!" above us. We all dashed out of the cook tent to see what was going on. We looked up the slope to the right of Motorcycle Hill and saw that a large chunk of snow and ice had cleaved off of the serac above the slope. The cloud of powdered snow rumbled downhill for a few seconds toward the edge of the slope. I quickly looked down at the base of the hill trying to decide whether the slight downward slope off to the right would be enough to funnel the avalanche down the hill away from camp or whether it would come right across into the camp that was then the home of roughly a hundred to a hundred-fifty climbers.

Everyone in camp was standing and looking upward as the avalanche unfolded before our eyes. Instinctively, I started walking quickly backward and slightly uphill trying to put as much distance and elevation between myself and the avalanche that I thought was heading my way. Others in camp began to outright sprint toward the far edge of the camp. "Please stop, please stop, please stop" I willed the snow above me. And somehow it did stop just short, right at the edge of the basin above us, just before gravity would have taken it down the slope toward us. I don't know whether or not it would have hit the 11,000-foot camp had it crested that lip, but I was extremely grateful not to find out. Even if gravity had pulled it downhill to the right of our camp, it might have taken out any climbers that were climbing the final hill up to the camp, as they would have been right in its fearful line.

Having the near miss with this avalanche and seeing the debris perched above camp the next day on our descent from our 13,500-foot cache site had me thinking a lot about Melissa and the kids. Was I crazy to be here at all? Was I putting myself in grave danger? Was it responsible at all to have mountain climbing as a hobby being the father of two young kids? We were seven days into the expedition now with still two weeks to go. Despite having a wonderful group of climbers and guides around me, I was missing Melissa and the kids and also missing my quiet time alone in the mornings, reading my newspaper and drinking my coffee. It is not uncommon for me to miss my "regular" life and feel a touch lonely when I am in the mountains for more than a day hike, but it was unusual for me to feel that way and still have two weeks and another 9,000 feet left to climb before going home.

The next day was Memorial Day, May 26, 2014. Seth decided we would take a rest day at the 11,000-foot camp and it was probably good that we did. One of our nine clients, Pat, was showing signs of altitude sickness, complaining of shortness of breath during the night and a loss of appetite. He had something called Chain Stokes breathing, which is a form of sleep apnea where the respiratory rate slows so much during sleep that the brain suddenly sends a signal to the lungs to gasp for air. Pat described it to us as feeling as if he was being suffocated every time he fell asleep—not a restful way to spend the evening. He broached the subject with Seth of whether he

The 11,000-foot camp perched below the serac that avalanched. Photo courtesy of Roman Reutov.

Avalanche debris at the crest of the hill above the 11,000-foot camp. Photo courtesy of Roman Reutov.

should continue up the mountain and they spent the day discussing the pros and cons of continuing, along with the options should he need to descend. With three guides, it was certainly possible for two of them to escort Pat back down to base camp 4,000 feet below us and return the next day, but we were all hoping there would be a better option.

I knew that if only a single guide escorted Pat down, per National Park Service regulations, the guide would not be permitted to climb back up the glacier unless he could find another guide or party to join. This rule is in place due to the risk of crevasse falls and the fact that self-rescue is nearly impossible in those cases of solo travel. I have described to friends the logistical challenges of guides getting sick clients down the mountain and returning back to their teams as similar to the brain teaser in which there is a fox, a chicken, a handful of people, a river, and a small canoe. Everyone must get across the river, but the fox must never be left alone with the chicken or else the chicken will turn into the fox's lunch. Seth spent the better part of that day on the radio and in other guides' tents talking with other professionals on the mountain, trying to figure out his own fox and chicken problem.

Meanwhile, the other eight of us made preparations for our planned move up to the 14,000-foot camp the next day, weather permitting. We dug a large cache hole near our tent at the 11,000-foot camp in preparation for leaving most of our "luxury" items behind, as well as a few days of food and fuel that we would need for our return journey. I decided that this was the point in the trip when I would switch over to my other pair of clean underwear and my other clean base layer shirt (yes, that's right—two pair of underwear and two base layer shirts for twenty-one days on the mountain). I also changed my socks for the first time on the trip—but I had brought three pair of those per the pack list, so I still had one more clean pair as a treat for later. I would leave the dirties behind in the cache along with my Temperpedic pillow.

We were all anxious to move to the 14,000-foot camp as it is more sheltered from the weather, and I was still a bit spooked looking up at the serac that had avalanched a couple of days before. Unfortunately the weather didn't cooperate Monday night and Tuesday. It stormed all night, rattling our tent incessantly while we did our best to sleep. Pat didn't sleep a wink again on Monday night, still struggling with the Chain Stokes breathing, so he and Seth made the decision that he would head down and our team would take a weather rest day. We kept hearing that the weather had been a big issue on the upper mountain as well, and that only twenty people had summited so far this year (on May 27, four weeks into the climbing season).

All the guide services operating on Denali work together out of professional courtesy and necessity. Inevitably, they are going to need a favor from another guided team at some point, so they are eager to help out other guides if and when asked. On Tuesday morning, a battered-looking guided team descended Motorcycle Hill in the bad weather, having given up on their summit aspirations, and were headed for base camp. Seth negotiated Pat's joining of that team for the descent to base camp and within minutes, Pat was packing up his stuff, tying onto a rope with his new team, and heading down the mountain. We took a quick group photo of our whole team before we lost our first member, and then he was gone.

We hoped that he would sleep better that night at lower elevation and that he would be able to get a flight off the glacier the next morning rather than being stranded at base camp. Unfortunately for Pat and the rest of his new team, base camp was socked in with bad weather for the next four days, so they were forced to wait and wait and wait some more. How frustrating that must have been for them! To be done with the mountain climb and be anxious to go home and see family and sleep in a bed, but be forced by the weather to continue to sleep in a sleeping bag in a tent on top of the snow and ice for another four days. We desperately hoped that would not be our fate. And we hoped that we would move to the 14,000-foot camp the next day.

Our other attorney, Dan, inquired that night as to whether Seth would mention Pat's departure in his nightly cybercast. We weren't all that surprised when Seth replied that, no, he wouldn't mention it. But we were a bit surprised by the reason. Apparently a few years ago, a client decided to leave a guided group on the first day of a Denali climb. The guide mentioned on the cybercast that evening that the client had descended and would be missed. Three days later, the client's wife called the office, telling them that she had not yet heard from her husband even though he had apparently left the climb on the first day. It turned out that the guy was having an affair and used the three-week climb as an elaborate (and expensive) way to go see his girlfriend for a few weeks.

CHAPTER 20

Denali's Upper Mountain

On Wednesday, May 28, we finally got our wish and moved to the 14,000-foot camp, but it was one of the worst weather days we had on the entire trip. The weather was far from perfect as we were packing up camp at 11,000 feet and filling our cache hole, but it was nothing compared to what we found at the top of Motorcycle Hill.

Motorcycle Hill is the first steep hill of the whole climb and is the first one done with crampons instead of snowshoes. I much prefer crampons to snowshoes, especially on firm steep snow such as this, but the duck walking crampon technique takes its toll on my body. In this technique, used for moderately steep snow slopes, you face uphill and point your feet out (like a duck, as you might guess from the name). You then waddle uphill with your ice axe centered above you. I find that this technique puts pressure on my Achilles tendons, making them feel as if they are stretching two inches beyond their comfort zone. When I couldn't duck walk any more, I would switch over to the "French technique," where you face sideways and do crossover steps up the mountain. The top of Motorcycle Hill is also the home of at least one crevasse, which one of our Irish teammates fell into up to his waist.

At the top of Motorcycle Hill, the wind's velocity increased dramatically. It was an all out blizzard with gale force winds. I had started the day with long johns, soft shell pants, a base layer on top, an insulating hoody, and my soft shell jacket. I also wore goggles instead of sunglasses and had placed one half of my Buff (a thin tubular layer that is quite versatile as a balaclava, face mask, neck gaiter or cap and which I had cut in half in Talkeetna at Seth's recommendation) in a strip covering my nose and the other half in a strip covering my neck. I was ready for the wind and the bad weather and I desperately wanted to get to the 14,000-foot camp and get out from under that avalanching serac above the 11,000-foot camp.

No matter how bad the weather is, your body can stay reasonably warm in the right clothing as long as you are moving. As soon as you stop moving, however, it is extremely easy to get bitter cold, regardless of your clothing layers. When Micah decided to stop for a break right at the top of Motorcycle Hill, with all of us in this vortex of malevolent wind and blowing snow, I was perplexed. Sure, I could have used a drink and a snack, but this didn't seem the time or place for it. But I couldn't talk to him about it or plead my case because I was still at the back of the rope and he was at the front of the rope (and you maintain extended ropes at all times, even during breaks, in case someone falls in a crevasse and the others have to self-arrest to stop the fall and rescue the fallen climber). Later at camp I learned that Micah had needed to switch from sunglasses to goggles. I felt much better about the freezing cold break once I knew there was a good reason for it.

After what seemed an eternity of growing colder and colder in the wind, vigorously shaking my arms and legs to try to keep my hands and feet warm, Micah's goggles were on and we got moving again. We climbed up Squirrel Hill and into the Polo Field, a large, relatively flat area with Denali's West Buttress looming thousands of feet overhead and a smattering of recently fallen rocks between the size of a softball and the size of a picnic cooler constantly reminding us of the dangers looming above. This area is actually the one spot on the entire climb where the National Park Service mandates that guided climbers wear helmets. We continued up to Windy Corner, which lived up to its name, and negotiated the steep traverse on the other side along with a few precarious snow bridges over crevasses, which didn't seem likely to stay in place for very many more weeks.

We took a break at our 13,500-foot cache site (much to the relief of one of our Irish teammates, Shane, who had gotten an intestinal bug and was in dire need of the CMC!), but didn't dig it up yet (that would be tomorrow's project on a "back carry" day). We continued on up the remaining distance to the 14,000-foot camp, which is tucked in a massive basin below Denali's West Buttress. It had taken us seven hours to do the move from the 11,000-foot camp to the 14,000-foot camp, by far our longest, hardest day yet on the mountain. Macaroni and cheese with tuna never tasted so good as it did that night for dinner. They say hunger is the best spice ...

For the first time on the expedition, I felt the altitude when we got to the 14,000-foot camp. Although I had been up to 14,000 feet almost weekly during my training in Colorado, I hadn't actually spent that many hours at this elevation (generally I eat a quick snack on the summit, take a couple of photos, and then start my descent). Everything was just a little bit harder living at that elevation, from shoveling out flat platforms in the snow and setting up our tents to simply walking up the tiny hill back to our camp spot after using the pee hole.

On Thursday, May 29, we had an easy back carry day, retrieving our cached food and fuel from the 13,500-foot cache site. We were done with our sleds now until the trip back down the mountain. From here on out, everything we carried went into our packs. In the afternoon, we set up a snow quarry and began working as a great team, cutting snow blocks and assembling them into wind walls to protect our tents. Our technique was raw and unpolished at the 11,000-foot camp when we had first been tasked with building these snow walls, but today we were a vision of efficiency and quality, each of us having established our highest and best use in the assembly line. My job was to shovel horizontally into the snow slope to create a flat top edge of the slab from which Rob, our designated cutter, would expertly slice blocks of just the right size.

We also prepared our summit food bags hoping that we would cache those at 16,500 feet on Friday. Summit day food is basically a ton of simple carbohydrates such as candy bars, hard candies, Gu gel, and other easily digestible foods. I recall standing in the checkout line at the grocery store back home in Denver after doing my summit food shopping. I was in line in front of a mother with her grade school child and watched the horror in her eyes

Our team building wind walls for our tents at the 14,000-foot camp.

as I unpacked my shopping cart and placed my items on the conveyor belt. Three six-packs of Snickers, some Baby Ruth, Almond Joy, Twix, Milky Way candy bars, and last, but not least, some Oreo and Nutter Butter cookies. The kid looked at me like, "I wish you were *my* Dad!" The mom looked at me like, "You should be ashamed of yourself!" all the while wondering in the back of her mind, "How is he so skinny when he eats all of this junk???"

The Alpine Ascents team in front of us on the mountain was also at the 14,000-foot camp, so our guides conferred often. Our official team name was "Alp 3" since we were the third Alpine Ascents team of the season, making the one before us "Alp 2." We learned that Alp 2 was sending two more clients down that day, which would reduce their numbers down to five clients (still with three guides—a great ratio).

On Friday, May 30, we had hoped to cache our summit snacks along with some food and fuel for the 17,000-foot high camp up at the top of the fixed lines at 16,500 feet on the ridge. The weather once again interfered with our plans and we were stuck at the 14,000-foot camp. For the first time, I began to be concerned that we were running out of time. I was booked on a flight out of Anchorage a week from Monday, just ten days away. We killed time at the 14,000-foot camp by playing cards (Believe or Don't Believe was the favorite game by this point with our Russian teammate leading the charge) and by talking with other expeditions. We heard a lot of interesting stories and met a lot of interesting people. There was a one-legged climber from Columbia making his second attempt to climb Denali, a solo Chinese climber that we nicknamed "Mr. China," and attractive female twins from India attempting to climb all of the seven summits (the highest point on each continent). Since there was far from an abundance of women on the mountain, the twins were quite popular.

The two main stories floating around camp involved a group of Korean climbers who had attacked another expedition, and a solo climber (not Mr. China) who had fallen on the fixed lines and been saved only by crashing into nine other climbers on the fixed lines one after the other, eventually slowing his fall to a stop. The Korean team had left their campsite at 14,000 feet and moved to high camp. Protocol on the mountain is that once you leave a camp spot, it is fair game for another expedition, with it being considered poor form to attempt to mark or reserve your former campsite for your return journey. This team, however, was still quite attached to their former 14,000-foot campsite upon their return from high camp. When they found it occupied, a confrontation ensued that could not be solved with words due to the language barrier. The Koreans took to throwing blocks of ice and snow at the people who were occupying their former camp and the National Park

Service rangers had to come intervene. Since we had created our tent platforms from scratch, thankfully no one came back down and tried to reclaim
them with violence. We were a bit surprised one night by a climber coming
over to our newly constructed wind wall and stealing a single snow block
from it. Odd, we thought.

I found my thoughts drifting more and more toward going home, seeing
Melissa and the kids, and riding my bike down a sunny, warm bike path with
green grass and trees all around. That day, I also finished reading the book
I had carried up the mountain with me, ending my mental dilemma as to
whether or not I was going to carry it up to the 17,000-foot camp. We had
given the Irishman with the intestinal bug his own private CMC bag to try to
limit any risk of the rest of us getting the bug and he seemed to be working
the bug through his system over the past couple of days. We were optimistic
that the eight of us would get to the summit with our three guides if a weather
window opened soon.

On Saturday, May 31, we got the green light to make our cache at 16,500
feet, which meant our first trip up the headwall and the fixed lines. It was
snowing when we left camp, but we quickly climbed out of the clouds and
the weather proved decent the rest of the day. We climbed up two moderate snow slopes, breaking once on the small shelf in between them, before
arriving at the base of the fixed lines. We took one more break there as we
waited for the line of climbers going up to shrink. There are two parallel lines
of rope (the one on climber's right is the "up line" and the one on climber's
left is the "down line") fixed into the mountain periodically with three-foot
snow pickets.

The fixed lines protect climbers from falls from the headwall which is a
50–55-degree pitch that rises about 1,500 feet to the crest of the West Buttress's ridge. Generally, the headwall is firm snow, but this year it was a sheet
of hard, blue ice with just a smattering of snow where climbers' footsteps up
the fixed lines had caused the snow to stick. Technically the fixed lines are
illegal on Denali, in violation of the National Park Service's rule of no fixed
protection or anchors (to maintain a wilderness feel). The ropes are infor-
mally maintained by the various guiding companies (Alp 1's guides having
dug them out from inside the blue ice and replaced many suspect old ropes at
the start of this climbing season), with the NPS climbing rangers looking the
other way since there would be significantly more rescues (and even worse,
recoveries) without them.

To ascend the fixed lines, most climbers use a device called an ascender
that attaches to the rope and slides effortlessly uphill, but will not slide backward downhill on the rope due to directional teeth that bite into the rope in

Teams of climbers ascend Denali's icy headwall.

the case of a fall. When it was our turn to get on the fixed lines, we clipped our ascenders onto the rope along with our safety carabiners (which allows you to always have something attached to the rope when transferring your ascender to the next strand of rope above each snow picket anchor you come to) and began climbing. It was incredibly slow going that day! The line of climbers only moves as fast as the slowest climber and there were *a lot* of climbers going up the fixed lines. There were also some people coming down the down line, returning from high camp, most of them exhausted and defeated without a summit attempt to their credit, having finally run out of food and fuel to wait any longer for good weather.

Not long after I clipped into the fixed lines, I looked up and saw one such exhausted climber descending hundreds of feet above me. That's when the junk show started. This guy was *really* struggling, with his climbing partner attempting to assist him down. First, his goggles came rolling down the icy slope toward me, plunging into the large crevasse below us. Next came what initially looked to me like some sort of a small animal. It turned out to be his raccoon hat, tumbling down to join the goggles, forever part of the glacier now. Next came some carabiners, rattling down on a sling. The guy couldn't even stand up and didn't appear to actually be clipped into the fixed lines at all—he was just holding on with his bare hands. I sure hoped he didn't fall.

I climbed on, then heard Micah yell from above me, "Brad! Backpack!!!" I had elected to wear my climbing helmet for the fixed lines even though it was not required by the park service or my guides, but I really don't think it would have helped me all that much had this fifty-pound backpack, sliding freely down the ice, hit me directly. I looked up when Micah yelled and did my best to side-step my cramponed feet to the right to get out of the way. The guy's backpack zipped past me on my left, missing me by about three feet, going on to join the rest of his stuff in the crevasse. Yikes! This was serious stuff and the people coming down were not making the upper part of the mountain look as if it was much fun.

We climbed the rest of the fixed lines without any more falling objects, although one of the clients of an RMI-guided team ahead of us on the fixed lines got tired of carrying his backpack on the way up and simply took it off, clipping it to an anchor and leaving it sitting there blocking the up line. His guide asked Seth whether it was okay there and whether our team could just please navigate around it. Seth thankfully told the other guide that he wasn't going to have us all try to work around it, so Seth picked up the pack and strapped it to his chest (now doing double backpack duty with one on his back and one on his chest). Seth carried the pack a ways up the fixed lines before RMI's lead guide, Brent, responsibly descended to get his client's abandoned pack.

Once on the ridge and off of the fixed lines, we took a break for water and snacks while the guides dug a hole and cached our summit food and fuel along with a shovel or two. One of the attorneys, Curt, had aggravated an old tendon injury by duck walking up the fixed lines and told Seth that he thought his expedition was most likely done. Seth told him to stay focused on the descent and we quickly got ready to go back down the fixed lines.

Seth told us that the headwall was as icy as he had ever seen it and informed us that he wanted us to descend facing downhill using a combination of an arm rappel and our ascenders used in reverse. I was a bit freaked out by the thought of going face out on the descent, having expected that we would be rappelling down them facing into the mountain like normal. The arm rappel consisted of taking my left arm and putting it over the top of the rope (which was on my left as I faced downhill) and wrapping it beneath and around the rope before gripping the rope with my gloved hand. This arm rappel was our speed control. I then reached across my body with my right arm and hooked the ascender to the rope, with the ascender facing uphill just as it had been on the way up. Since the ascender is designed not to move downhill when facing in this direction, we would need to "feather" the trigger open with our right hands while controlling our descent speed with the left arm rappel. If we started to fall, we would stop feathering open the trigger on the ascender and it would close on the rope with its teeth biting in, preventing any further downward movement.

This would have been a slight challenge for all of us at sea level, in 70-degree weather without gloves on. Above 16,000 feet with bulky clothes and thick gloves on, it was downright tricky. With the eleven of us descending together and each rope team needing to stop when any member of that rope team reached an anchor that required them to move the ascender to the next rope strand lower, then redo the arm rappel on the lower rope, the pace was excruciatingly slow. I certainly appreciated Seth's addition of the ascender, in addition to the arm rappel and safety carabiner that was the original plan, since the slope was so icy and I knew my ice axe would do me no good in a self-arrest attempt on such hard, blue ice (our axes were stowed on our packs for the whole descent). I slipped once on the way down, but immediately stopped thanks to my ascender. Once we were down and off the fixed lines, we cruised back down to the 14,000-foot camp using my beloved "heel plunge step" into the softer, more moderately sloped snow below the fixed lines.

That afternoon we were all exhausted but happy that we had been able to get our cache in above 16,000 feet on the ridge. The guides started the daily ritual of melting snow for water so that we could have a hot drink before dinner. I and a few others were sitting in the cook tent waiting for hot drinks when one of the National Park Service rangers came over and "knocked" on the tent door, saying, "Seth? It's Chris from the NPS. Can I have a word with you out here?" I wondered what was going on, but figured it was some kind of problem. Maybe there was an accident up higher or maybe Chris wanted details on the falling backpack guy or the abandoned backpack guy. Or maybe, I joked with Roman (our Russian teammate), there had been some sort of international incident involving him, the Indian twins, and the one-legged Columbian.

The guides were gone for quite a long time and the water was finally hot and ready for drinks. Since I was sitting closest to the stoves and the pot, I stood up and assumed the role of chef for a moment, pumping the stoves to keep the fuel pressurized and began offering hot water to the others for their cider, cocoa, or tea. I was caught in the act of playing guide when Tom, the British guide, came back in the tent. He took over the cooking duty, and then Seth and Micah came back into the tent. I made a stupid joke about the international incident briefing and Seth replied that no, this was not what the meeting was about. I felt my foot go rapidly into my mouth a moment later as Micah started to leave the tent and Seth asked him to stay for a moment.

Seth then told us the news and it was far worse than an accident above us or wanting information on missing backpacks.

There had been an avalanche on Mt. Rainier's hardest route, Liberty Ridge, which had swept another team of Alpine Ascents' clients and guides off the mountain, killing all six of them (the two guides and their four clients). Just a month before, Alpine Ascents had lost five of their Sherpa guides in an avalanche above the Khumbu Ice Fall on Mt. Everest (which took the lives of sixteen Sherpa guides in total) and now this. Details were (and still are) sparse on exactly what happened to these six climbers on Mt. Rainer, but what was for certain is that a helicopter had picked up the signal from their avalanche beacons in a debris field many, many thousand feet below the Liberty Ridge route. The bodies will likely never be recovered due to the danger involved for the recovery team in such an operation.

We asked Seth, Micah, and Tom whether they personally knew the two guides and learned that yes, each of the three of them knew the two deceased guides very well. One of the deceased was Seth's frequent climbing partner around the world and this same guide was scheduled to be Micah's number two in command on the Denali expedition Micah was to lead in June 2014. Rob had actually just done his Denali preparation course on Mt. Rainier with these same two deceased guides in March and had gone out for beers with them afterward, remembering them both as great guys and very safe guides.

This tragic event changed the environment in our cook tent dramatically from then on. The laughter and joking that had been frequent and loud became rare and reserved. Our guides were understandably in shock and saddened by the loss of their close friends, but maintained the utmost in professionalism with us. They knew that we were depending on them and their expertise on Denali, so they didn't allow themselves to lose focus during their grieving. The Mt. Rainier avalanche also got me thinking about Melissa and the kids again. I had finished reading Ed Viesturs' book, *No Shortcuts to the Top*, on the flight to Anchorage two weeks before. One of the most haunting parts of that story was when Ed's wife, Paula, went to bed one evening with Ed unaccounted for on Annapurna, his final (and the most deadly of all based on the ratio of deaths to climbers attempting) of the fourteen peaks in the world above 8,000 meters (26,240 feet). Thinking he was probably dead, she had silently screamed out at him during the night he was missing, "Screw you! How am I going to tell the kids?"

In my diary that night on Denali, I wrote, "Very mixed feelings tonight. Never want Melissa to get that phone call [and certainly never want my mom to have to go through a second night not knowing whether or not I'm alive and safe], but I love climbing and can't imagine life without." I resolved to myself again that night to be careful and prudent, but in the back of my mind I knew full well that those two Alpine Ascents guides, Matt Hegeman and Eitan Green, were qualified and consummate professionals, guiding clients who had spent years accumulating enough experience and skill to accompany them on such a challenging climb and that all six were simply in the wrong place at the wrong time. It was not the lack of care and prudence; avalanches are an objective hazard in the climbing world and the risk can only be managed, not eliminated.

Spirits around our camp were understandably still down the next morning at breakfast on this first day of June. Curt informed us that he was as high as he was going since he didn't think his foot and injured tendon could safely ascend and descend the fixed lines a second time. After spending our fourth night at the 14,000-foot camp, I felt that my acclimatization was in good shape. I had slept as well as I ever sleep in a tent the night before a climb and had no headache at all. My appetite continued to be voracious and I followed our guides' advice of "eat your way to the top"—another good sign. Back in Talkeetna after the expedition, I would be voted by the guides as "best eater" on our trip, narrowly beating out a disappointed Rob; he thought his climber-leading requests for "thirds" would put him on top, but the guides broke the news to him that he could be a bit picky from time to time whereas I would eat "seconds" of anything they put in front of me.

After lunch on Sunday, Shane, our Irish teammate who had been working to fight off the last of the intestinal bug, informed us that he also didn't feel he had the strength to safely go higher. It wasn't immediately clear how Curt and Shane would get down, but we suspected that Tom would probably end up taking them down and not returning to join us. That would reduce the size of our team to six clients and two guides from the original nine and three, respectively.

Things continued to get worse later that afternoon when Ryan, my good friend from Denver, complained of a headache and asked me for two Excedrin. I gave them to him, and then we worked on making sure our crampons were still fitting as tightly on our boots as we needed them to be for our planned move to the 17,000-foot camp the following morning. At dinner, Ryan looked across the cook tent at me and said that the Excedrin were really messing him up. He complained of feeling "buzzed" (understandable given Excedrin contain caffeine) and nauseated. He managed to down two full burritos, knowing how important it is to eat at high altitude even if you don't feel like it. We hoped that the food in his stomach would absorb the Excedrin from his system and get him feeling normal again.

Like me, Ryan had the advantage of having trained at altitude, so I didn't think it was likely that this was acute mountain sickness (AMS). After dinner, Ryan abruptly left the cook tent and Seth asked me if anything was wrong. I told him about Ryan's headache and nausea and the two of them discussed how Ryan was feeling later that evening. Ryan had been a strong member of the team to this point and we were all hopeful that he would feel his normal self again the next morning.

It turned out that he didn't. On Monday at 7:00 a.m. (very early in Denali mountain time where breakfast was usually served around 10:00 a.m.), Seth made the call that we were going to attempt to move up to the 17,000-foot camp along with Alp 2 and two RMI teams. While the weather forecasts on Denali make trying to pick the winning lottery numbers look like pretty good odds, there was no denying that Wednesday, June 4, was looking like the best weather day we were going to get. That meant that if we could move to the 17,000-foot camp on Monday, we could have a rest day on Tuesday and take advantage of the forecasted great weather on Wednesday. Rob and I sprang into action at Seth's announcement and began getting dressed, stuffing our sleeping bags and getting our boots on. Ryan didn't move. I thought maybe he was listening to music and hadn't heard Seth, so I shook his shoulder a bit and said, "Ryan—did you hear Seth? We're moving! Time to get up buddy."

He stuck his head out of his sleeping bag, looked at me with stunned defeat in his eyes, and said, "Dude, I'm sick." He had thrown up small amounts a couple of times during the night and was fighting a splitting headache. I went and got Seth so that he could come over and talk to Ryan (and hopefully figure out what was wrong along with the right remedy). Seth convinced Ryan to get up and try to move around a little bit (which triggered another bout of minor nausea) to see if getting some deeper breaths in him could fight off the AMS that he thought had struck Ryan.

Seth got Ryan into the cook tent and tested his blood oxygen saturation, which came back at an extremely solid 94 percent (you wouldn't expect much better at sea level). Seth told Ryan that he had been rock solid up to this point and with the 94 percent oxygen level, he was willing to have Ryan come with us up to the 17,000-foot camp. Ryan needed to understand, however, that he might have a couple of pretty miserable nights at 17,000 feet and there was a chance he wouldn't feel well enough to try for the summit, even if he made it up the fixed lines again.

We encouraged Ryan to get his stuff packed up as though he was going up with us and not to make the go/no go call until he absolutely had to. Ultimately the time came for the call and Ryan didn't feel as if he could go. He opted to stay at 14,000 feet with Curt, Shane, and Tom and the other seven of us (now five clients and two guides) headed out toward the fixed lines. I'm still astonished at how quickly it all happened with my best friend on the trip suddenly falling ill with AMS and staying behind as the rest of us went up. I didn't have much time to think about it that day because we were back at the base of the fixed lines within two hours after leaving the 14,000-foot camp. One RMI team had gone up ahead of us that morning, but Alp 2 and the other RMI team were right with us when we got to the bottom of the fixed lines. Alp 2 got on them first, then my team with me last on the second of two rope teams, followed by the other RMI team. This time, our technique was much more refined and efficient ascending the fixed lines and we didn't have any slow climbers on the lines in front of us. The result was cutting a full hour off of our time up to our cache on the ridge.

We knew the wind would pick up as soon as we reached the top of the fixed lines and got onto what the guides referred to as 16 Ridge. We would need to dig up our cached summit food and supplies, get it into our already overflowing backpacks (which contained our tents, bulky down sleeping bags, sleeping pads, our huge summit parkas, and other extra clothing); then we would have about three hours of climbing left to get to the 17,000-foot camp. Seth and Micah went to work immediately on digging up our cache when we got to the ridge and began divvying up the summit food and group gear. They estimated that the wind was blowing around 20 miles per hour, which is not terrible, but when combined with air temperatures that they estimated at minus 20 degrees, it was downright cold. I had no skin exposed on my body, again opting for the goggles, Buff strip covering my nose and lower buff covering my neck (my beard was fairly burly by this point on the trip, covering and well insulating my cheeks, upper lip, and chin). Even sitting still waiting for everyone to get their cached gear stowed in their packs, I was not terribly cold. The wind was annoying to say the least, but honestly I had fought through worse wind during my winter training back home in Colorado (actually getting mild frost nip on my nose on two separate occasions much to Melissa's chagrin).

To my left at our cache spot was the Alp 2 team, digging up their cache and making identical preparations to continue up 16 Ridge. I watched as one of the Alp 2 clients went to pull a green compression stuff sack out of his backpack. Just as he got it out of his pack, it slipped from his grip, dropped to the snow, and began rolling down the 40-degree slope toward Peters Glacier, thousands of feet below us. When Alp 2's leader, Stu, saw the compression sack falling down the slope, he wisely took charge and ordered his client, "Do NOT go after it! Do NOT go after it!" With the green sack now out of sight, Stu began to yell over the howling wind, "What was that??? What was in that sack???" His client feebly informed him that it was his big down summit parka. Stu was in disbelief and told the client, "You're going down. Your climb is over. You can't climb any farther without your parka." I felt bad for the guy for sure and vowed that I would use extreme care getting anything in or out of my pack so as not to suffer the same fate.

Just when everyone on our team had their cached gear packed up and ready to go, Seth looked at our two teammates closest to him and didn't like what he saw. Each of them had white, waxy spots on their faces in a couple of areas that were exposed to the elements. I had seen these once before on a December 2010 climb of Mt. Bierstadt with Ryan Chase, Mark Dunning, and another friend on a very windy, cold day. Seth knew these were the beginning of frostbite and he told all of us to make sure that no skin was exposed. Seth then walked over to talk to Stu and a guide powwow ensued. Rob was sitting next to me, trying to listen to what they were saying. He reported to me, "The RMI group is heading down and it sounds like Stu and Seth are trying to decide if we should go down, too." This was definitely not what I wanted to hear. I was still reasonably comfortable in all of my layers, desperately wanting to get to the 17,000-foot camp that afternoon. Seth told Stu about our two teammates with the beginnings of frostbite on their faces, and then noticed that Stu had a white spot on his nose, too.

After another few minutes of talking among themselves, our guides came back over to us and gave us the call—"We are going back down. It's another three hours to the 17,000 foot-camp and the wind is only going to get worse as we climb higher on the exposed ridge. It's not worth getting frostbite on our faces or fingers. Take your cached food and group gear back out and give it back to us. After we re-cache it, we'll head back down to the 14,000-foot camp." I was bummed, but respected the call. I gave my summit food and group gear to the guides to put back in our cache hole and got ready to descend the fixed lines for the second time.

We saw two more falling objects on our way down the fixed lines that second time, both of which plummeted into their new homes in the crevasse at the bottom—a helmet that someone took off for some reason and a water bottle from one of our own team members. Clearly, the 16,500-foot elevation was making everyone a touch sloppy. Once off the fixed lines, Rob, Micah, and I cruised down the moderate snow slopes back into the 14,000-foot camp where we would have to reassemble our tents. Our campsite was still unoccupied, so Rob and I quickly put up the smaller three-man tent that would be our new home for the rest of the trip. It was very strange being back at the 14,000-foot camp that night in a different tent and without our friend and tent mate Ryan. The cook tent felt different (and colder) as well—it was downright spacious with only five clients and two guides now, compared to our original nine clients and three guides.

Over dinner that Monday night, we had a serious conversation about what our plan should be from that point forward in the trip. All of us were tired from doing the 2,500 vertical foot climb that day, so we had to try to put that fatigue aside for the discussion. The weather forecast (albeit unreliable to date) for Wednesday was still quite favorable and looked to be what Seth called a "summitable" day. The next storm front was predicted for Thursday, worsening into Friday. Tuesday was looking like it could go either way—the high winds we had encountered Monday on the ridge might continue or it could be the beginning of Wednesday's nice weather window. The question before us that night was: do we pack up camp again tomorrow morning and try to move to the 17,000-foot high camp for a second day in a row or do we take a rest day and plan to move up in the good weather Wednesday? Neither Seth nor Micah had ever had a "false start" on one of their Denali trips before where they had attempted to move a team from 14,000 feet up to 17,000 feet and had to retreat. If we were to climb the fixed lines for a third time on our expedition, it would certainly be unique.

Seth and Micah expressed concern that if we moved Tuesday, summited Wednesday, and descended Thursday, that would mean four very big days all in a row (including the big day we had just had on Monday, ascending the fixed lines for the second time). They weren't sure we were strong enough for such an effort. They reminded us that it was critical that we had enough stamina left to safely descend the mountain after any summit attempt we made. The other concern Seth expressed was that two National Park Service climbing rangers had attempted to go up from 14,000 feet Monday to set thirty to forty more snow pickets on a dangerous traverse between the 17,000-foot camp and Denali Pass, morbidly named "The Autobahn" after the Germans who fell and died there in a very fast uncontrolled fall in the early days of climbing attempts, but who had to turn back (like we did) due to the weather. No one was exactly sure how many snow pickets were already in place to serve as anchors for running belays on this stretch, but everyone agreed that more would be better.

Our team at this point consisted of two guys roughly thirty years of age, two guys roughly fifty years of age, and me right in the middle at forty. The two fifty-year-olds seemed in favor of taking a rest day on Tuesday; the two thirty-year-olds were feeling strong and ready to push up again the next morning. I honestly could have gone either way. I was tired that night and felt a rest day Tuesday would sure be nice, but I also thought I was strong enough to do the move the next morning if that was our best chance to get to the summit. Ultimately, we expressed that we had confidence in Seth and Micah's judgment and would defer to what they thought was best. Seth then told us that he believed we could get to the 17,000-foot camp Tuesday, but that if we did, he honestly did not think that we would all make the summit on Wednesday. He didn't single anyone out as the person or people that he didn't think would make it, so I don't know whether he was talking specifics or was just giving general odds based on his years of experience.

His statement that he could easily see one rope team going for the summit and one rope team having to turn around and go back to the 17,000-foot camp got us thinking that maybe we were better off to take the Tuesday rest day. We felt we had five strong clients left and we really wanted to all summit together. The weather forecasts had certainly been wrong plenty of times before, so we hoped that maybe the good weather forecasted for Wednesday would last until Thursday instead. One thing we knew for sure was that we couldn't risk going up the fixed lines for a third time only to be turned around by weather again. If that happened, our trip was over. We didn't want to waste a perfect weather day either, however, so we agreed to plan to rest Tuesday, but change plans and move up if the weather was absolutely perfect when we woke up Tuesday morning.

Rob and I had a long night in our new tent, which it turned out was much shorter than the four-man tent we had been sharing with Ryan up until this point. My toes were terribly cold throughout the night as they pushed against the thin nylon wall of the tent. I made fists with them all night long trying to keep them moving and warm them up, but to no avail. My cold toes made me think of Melissa and the accident. Seth got up at 6:00 a.m. Tuesday and had a look outside to check for signs of wind on 16 Ridge and the rest of the upper mountain. Sure enough, it was still blowing up there, so he went back to bed and Tuesday was now officially a rest day. After a leisurely breakfast, we agreed to take a field trip over to a rocky outcropping on the far edge of camp called "The Edge of the World." It is so named because from there, the mountain simply falls away some 6,000 vertical feet to the glacier below. Our luck with the weather wasn't much better from The Edge of World. We found plenty of clouds moving in and out, obscuring what would otherwise have been spectacular views looking down toward base camp.

We learned that the first RMI team that had gone up the fixed lines ahead of the other three guided groups the previous day had only made it about another twenty minutes up the exposed ridge before they decided to set up tents and hunker down for the night. Looking up at the ridge Tuesday morning and seeing the snow blowing off of it, we thought a lot about that RMI group and what it must have been like up there on Monday afternoon and evening. That had to be one miserable night getting pounded by the wind all night long at over 16,500 feet. But then again, they were up there and we were down here. The views were clear all around us Tuesday, so if the winds died down just a bit, that RMI group up high would be able to have a nice leisurely hike the rest of the way along 16 Ridge up to the 17,000-foot camp and be in perfect position to summit in the good weather on Wednesday. The lead guide on that RMI team seemed to have something of a reputation among the other guides on the mountain as being highly driven to get his teams to the top, perhaps by taking a few risks with frostbite that the other guides would not. His nicknames included "Frosty" and "Frost-Brent" because of this, yet all of our guides indicated that Brent was just such a nice guy that they couldn't fault him for pushing things just a little bit.

A topic of conversation among the clients on that Tuesday rest day was whether each of us would come back and try again if we were unable to reach the summit. For me the answer was that I honestly didn't know. I was feeling helpless and as if more of this climb was outside of my control than I was used to. The weather was so unpredictable and it was so cold that the margin for error was pretty slim. I felt great about the ten months of training that I had done to get ready for the climb, knowing that I could physically get to the summit if and when the weather allowed, but three weeks was sure a long time to be away from Melissa and the kids. I hoped that I didn't have to make that decision about whether or not I'd try again. Hopefully we would be able to move to 17,000 feet on Wednesday and summit on Thursday.

Tuesday night at dinner, Seth and Micah talked to us about our planned move the following morning. They wanted us to go as light as we possibly could, leaving any remaining luxury items behind. They went as far as telling our trip photographer Roman that either he or his huge camera could come tomorrow, but not both. If he wanted to go for the summit, the big camera was staying behind at this camp. Roman agreed and brought his smaller camera instead (which was still at least as good as my small camera). They also told us they were a bit concerned about our footwork on the upper ridge and needed us to be 100 percent sure of our foot placements and balance, especially as we were clipping and unclipping from the snow picket anchors that we would encounter along the way. It was somewhat awkward in the cook tent that night; I felt all five of us were being addressed when perhaps the intended audience was a specific person for different concerns.

I tend to not like broad feedback such as this as I'm never sure if someone is talking to me or talking to someone else. I expressed to Seth that if there was specific feedback or concerns that he or Micah had with any of my techniques that I would definitely want to know so I could address them. The other guys quickly echoed my request for one-on-one feedback, too, if it was necessary. Micah assured me after the group broke up that he is not shy about providing specific feedback—if he had a concern with me, I already would have known about it. That was good to hear.

Wednesday, June 4, dawned as glorious as could be. There was absolutely no wind visible on 16 Ridge above us, so we excitedly packed up camp again and headed toward the fixed lines for the third time. The ascent up the head-wall was even easier the third time and we were quickly back at the cache site on 16 Ridge. We packed up our gear and began to climb the steep narrow ridge, clipping into the fixed anchors along the way. Since I was last on the second of two rope teams, my job was to "clean" the anchors, meaning unclipping the rope from the carabiner and removing the carabiner from the sling attached to the anchor. By the time we got to our next break at the base of a large rock formation called "Washburn's Thumb," I was jingling like Santa's sleigh with all of the carabiners rattling around on my harness gear loop.

Me ascending Denali's West Buttress at nearly 17,000 feet.
Photo courtesy of Roman Reutov.

There was another short stretch of fixed lines going up to Washburn's Thumb, but we were old pros with our ascenders by now and easily climbed the pitch. After a delicate traverse around a large rock at the top, we were off of the fixed lines yet again and back to using our running belays off of the snow picket anchors. As we climbed with our fifty-five to sixty-pound packs up the ridge, we enjoyed the stunning views all around us. To our right, we could look down and clearly see the 14,000-foot camp, with its paths in the snow making it look like a small city. We could see the trail coming into camp from near Windy Corner, the trail going out of camp over to The Edge of the World, and even the trail to the poop crevasse on the outskirts of camp. Still lower in the distance was the Kahiltna Glacier, including small specks that were the camps at 7,500 and 9,700 feet. How long ago it now seemed that we were calling those lower camps home. To our left was Denali's north summit and next to it was a striking black pyramid of rock separating the north summit from the true summit to the south.

I caught my first look at the 17,000-foot camp from a stretch of 16 Ridge just past a very narrow knife-edged portion of the route. The camp actually looked slightly lower than our current elevation, which proved to be correct as we continued to climb, then got a better look at the camp, now clearly below us. We descended the last little hill into our high camp and removed our packs and crampons. Seth and Micah leveled a few platforms for us, and then we set up our three tents. We had left the cook tent behind at the 14,000-foot camp, so the vestibule of the guides' four-man tent would serve as their cooking area and we would eat either outside or in our own tents. Rob and I had done the work of carrying a three-man tent for the two of us, so we were able to spread out a little bit that afternoon. The other three clients shared the other three-man tent, feeling cramped I'm sure.

After our tents were set up, I started to study the upper part of the mountain for the first time. The Autobahn was clearly visible, an indented line in the snow rising from the plateau where we were camped up to 18,200-foot Denali Pass, the low point in between the north and south summits. I could see quite a few climbers still descending the Autobahn even though it was past 10:00 p.m. at this point (it was odd in the land of the never-setting sun to be able to see clearly at 10:00 p.m.). Rob's and my tent was set up next to the cooking area of Frosty's RMI team that had camped on 16 Ridge the previous day. The word was that lots of people (maybe as many as one hundred) had summited that day, including the RMI team. We were very happy for the climbers who had reached the summit that day, even giving a warm round of applause to welcome back to the 17,000-foot camp the one-legged Columbian who was among those who summited during the day. Dinner that night was Ramen noodles with a coconut milk sauce, which still tasted good to me (a good sign at high altitude) after our hard day's work moving up to our high camp. After dinner we tucked into our sleeping bags for the night and prepared our much smaller summit packs for Thursday morning, just hoping to have a chance to go for the top.

I was really feeling the altitude at high camp. I began to develop a head-ache late that evening, but I was determined to follow Seth's advice to "breathe it off" by sitting up in my sleeping bag and focusing on my breathing for two minutes each time I felt the headache. I didn't sleep much that night due to nerves about Thursday's summit attempt, my persistent headache, and the cold that I couldn't shake from my toes despite more fist-making with them. I went to the pee hole just before calling it a night, but had to pee again (this time in my pee bottle inside the tent) within an hour of getting in my sleeping bag. When I needed to go yet again during the night, I had lost confidence that there would be enough capacity in my pee bottle, so I begrudgingly got dressed, put my boots on and left the tent to pee once again into the nearby pee hole. I also emptied my pee bottle so that this would be my last time leav-ing the tent for the night. It was starting to snow lightly in the odd twilight Alaskan sky and I desperately hoped the snow would blow over by morning.

My iPod had made the cut to come to the 17,000-foot camp with me, so at least I was able to listen to some nice, soft music while I did my best to rest that night. As the night progressed, it gradually became more and more windy and I could hear snow blowing against the tent walls. There had been several other windy, snowy nights on the trip that had dawned into fine days, so I tried to remain hopeful that Thursday would be a "summitable" day, as Seth liked to call them. I frequently checked my watch, curious as to the time and whether maybe I had slept a little bit since the last time I had checked my watch. When I saw that it was 7:00 a.m., I began to try to listen for Seth over the rattling of the wind. If today was to be a summit day, we would need to get up and get moving before long.

Then 7:30 a.m. passed with no word, then 8:00 a.m., then 8:30 and 9:00. When it turned 9:00 a.m., I had pretty well given up on it being a day on which we would try for the summit. We really needed to be walking by 10:00 a.m. at the latest to give ourselves a reasonable chance at the twelve-plus hour round trip summit day. I figured there wasn't much of a chance of us eating our breakfast and getting suited up to go in anything less than an hour. Seth confirmed this a short time later when he came to our tent vestibule, told us that it wasn't a summitable day, and said they were working on oatmeal for breakfast. The forecast for Friday wasn't any better; the storm was just sup-posed to get worse, so we needed to start packing up our things and getting

The 17,000-foot camp on the morning of our planned summit attempt.

ready to head down after breakfast. Our trip was to end with a high point of 17,200 feet, one day's climb short of reaching the top of North America.

I still had a pretty sharp headache that morning and really had to choke down my oatmeal. It took me a full forty-five minutes to get that bowl of oatmeal down. I took a bite or two, then worked on stuffing my sleeping bag and sleeping pads, and then took another bite. By the time I finished the oatmeal, it was ice cold and I was done packing my pack. Definitely no "seconds" for me that morning! Rob and I were both pretty bummed as we prepared to take down our tent as the last step before we were ready to descend.

Outside, the wind was blowing moderately and it was snowing. The upper part of the mountain that had been so clear the day before was entirely obscured by the clouds. I took a picture of where the summit would have been; there was zero visibility up high that day. As I looked around the entire camp, everyone seemed to be packing up and preparing to head down. Our understanding was that no one even attempted to summit on that Thursday.

A few minutes after 10:00 a.m., we were packed up and ready to head down. The guides assumed their positions at the rear ends of their ropes for the way down and Micah instructed me to lead us all out of camp. I breathed hard as I climbed the small hill out of camp, still trying to fight off the altitude headache and reestablish a rhythm. We were all tired as we descended the narrow ridge back toward the fixed lines that would take us back down to 14,000 feet and thicker air. I concentrated on each and every step, making sure to keep my feet far enough apart to avoid catching a crampon on my pant leg. Soon we were back at our cache site at the top of the fixed lines where a bad traffic jam had developed.

Most of the groups that had summited on Wednesday had stayed the night at the 17,000-foot camp Wednesday night, planning to descend Thursday morning. The teams that had summited were understandably much happier and more jovial than our team, which had missed the weather window by a mere twenty-four hours. With so many people descending Thursday morning though, the fixed lines became a bottleneck. At first, we were just taking a leisurely break at our cache site and thinking that the other twenty or so people there were also just taking breaks. Then we realized that there was actually a queue to get on the fixed lines, but no one was moving. We moved slightly closer to the fixed lines to establish our position in queue, and then continued to wait for our turn. Twice, Seth and Micah descended to the top of the fixed lines to see if they could identify the hold-up. It appeared that some climbers lower on the ropes were struggling, so we were pretty well stuck with nowhere to go until the down line began to move again.

I put on my massive summit parka for only the third time on the expedition to keep warm while I sat there waiting for my turn to descend. I found myself as frustrated by the logjam as I get on a freeway in the city in my normal life. I've often asked myself while sitting in heavy traffic, "Why can't everyone just move a little? If everyone moved just a little and kept moving just a little, we would all be moving, right?" Looking at the mass of tired climbers waiting to descend, I wondered the same thing. Surely there must be someone not moving at all downward on the fixed lines; otherwise, everyone would be moving and new people would be able to get onto the start of the fixed lines to head down. Who wasn't moving and why not?

After a full hour, whatever or whoever the bottleneck was cleared off the lines and the queue began to steadily move, one after the other, clipping into the top of the lines and beginning the descent. I was relieved when it was finally my turn to clip in. "Pay attention," I told myself. This is not the time to make a mistake and fall. Nearly all accidents happen on the way down mountains because climbers are tired and get sloppy, eventually making a mistake. I was determined not to add to that statistic. Slowly, but surely, we descended without any difficulty. When we got back to the 14,000-foot camp, it was nearly 7:00 p.m. We made a quick soup dinner, loaded up our remaining group gear that we had left there, transferred as much as we could into our sleds, and continued down out of camp.

Micah, Rob, and I made a pit stop at the poop crevasse to dispose of our used CMC bags, and then we continued down toward the 11,000-foot camp. Our plan was to stop at 11,000 feet, dig up our remaining cached items there, switch back over to snowshoes and continue our descent through the night all the way back to base camp. Aware of how Pat had been forced to spend four nights at base camp waiting for his flight off the glacier, our motto was that we wanted to get to base camp as quickly as possible to maximize our chances of getting a flight out on Friday before the weather worsened. The Alp 4 team that was camped at 11,000 feet kindly filled up our water bottles and offered us snacks. Our team was now the "battered looking" team on their way down, just like the team with which we sent Pat down. There was a brief discussion of us taking two of Alp 4's clients who could go no farther down with us, but they ended up deciding to send one of their guides down the following morning with the two climbers instead.

It was about 11:00 p.m. when we left Alp 4 and our former camp behind. I was still in the lead, but was beginning to find the route finding slightly more difficult since the mountain was socked in with clouds and the Alaskan twilight was just enough to play tricks on my eyes. It was surreal leading downhill with nothing in front of me except gray clouds and white snow. I looked down most of the time to make sure I was still on the firm snow path that was created by climbers before me. I glanced up now and then and scanned the horizon searching for the next route-marking wand. I would find it, and then aim in that direction, careful to stay on the firm path while doing so. Below Ski Hill, the wands started to get harder to see through the fog and the path was becoming less obvious, so Micah took over the lead to our next break, where we had one more cache to dig up at our 9,700-foot camp. After that Seth took over the lead and used his GPS to navigate us through the thick fog back to the southeast fork of the Kahiltna Glacier. There, we took a left hand turn and began to climb the aptly named Heartbreak Hill to return to base camp, where we hoped to be retrieved by an airplane in a few hours.

I had been at the front of the rope team for so long that it was actually quite odd to be following again at this point. I was wearing my baseball cap and just looking down now, the bill of the ball cap creating black areas on both sides of my peripheral vision. We began climbing Heartbreak Hill at about 4:45 a.m., almost nineteen hours after leaving the 17,000-foot camp the previous morning. It had been forty-six hours since I had slept (since I hadn't really slept during our night at high camp). I began to hallucinate as we climbed Heartbreak Hill, convinced that I was walking on some sort of a snowy suspension bridge. With the blackness in my peripheral vision caused by my baseball cap and seeing a strange orange stripe below me, separating the two never-ending planks of the snow bridge, I really started to wonder where I was. The orange stripe in front of me appeared to be moving, but it looked to me as if I was looking down through the two planks of the snow bridge at a valley floor far below the bridge. I was so confused. How could it be that I was on a bridge high above a valley floor, and why would that valley floor be orange? Was it lava? Was I inside a volcano like in *Lord of the Rings*? If I was, why hadn't the snow bridge melted from the heat? I tried my best to come up with a logical explanation and then it finally hit me. The rope! That's what the orange thing was! Sure enough, I looked up for the first time in quite a while and saw Rob and Micah with the rope stretched out between us. "Wow, I need sleep," I thought.

Heartbreak Hill went on and on. I was in despair. My heavy backpack and my heavy sled tied to it were tugging at my shoulders and neck. I tried to grab the shoulder straps with my hands for a while to change the pressure, but this was only a short-term fix. We needed to get the rest of the way up the hill and into base camp. I was elated when finally I saw one of the runway markers on the glacier and thought we must be almost there. Unfortunately, the scale of everything is different on Denali, and no matter how much farther we went up the hill, the runway marker looked exactly the same. Finally on the verge of collapse, I saw tents up ahead and knew we were just about there.

We rolled into camp at last at 6:00 a.m. after our herculean twenty-hour push down the mountain from 17,200 feet all the way down to 7,200 feet. We unroped and staggered to set up our tents so we could catch a couple of hours of sleep before we could check in with the base camp manager at 8:00 a.m. to see about a flight out. Rob and I saw a pretty flat looking area and set our tent up without doing the little bit of extra flattening that can make all the difference when you'll be at a camp for a while. I got in my sleeping bag and was out almost instantly.

The sound of a plane coming in for a landing on the glacier at 8:30 a.m. woke me and I felt my heart leap, knowing this meant that they were flying in and out that day, at least for the time being. Micah had checked us in immediately at 8:00 a.m. when the base camp manager (who also served as air traffic controller) was up. We hurriedly broke down our hastily put up camp and got all of our backpacks, sleds, and duffels in a neat pile, ready to go as soon as we got the word that it was our turn. With our overnight push, we ended up beating the vast majority of descending climbers, so we were fairly early in the queue for a plane. By 10:00 a.m. we were boarding two different planes and heading back to Talkeetna and civilization.

In Talkeetna, we unloaded our gear from the plane, then ate a huge brunch before heading to the Alpine Ascents headquarters to unload all of the group gear. After an amazing shower, my first in almost three weeks, we caught a Friday night outdoor concert at the park in Talkeetna, then went out for dinner and beers afterward. It would have been more fun if Ryan, Shane, Curt, and Tom had been there with us for sure. Unfortunately, they were all long gone by then, back home getting readjusted into their normal lives. Rumor had it that they had been asked to leave the famous Fairview Inn during their post-mountain celebratory beers, so we were pretty sure they had a decent time without us. We resolved to do the same without them. Ryan has since told me that he vaguely remembers being asked to leave. They went outside and hung out for a few minutes, then went back in and had another beer.

The next morning Rob and I went off in search of souvenirs. After seeing way too much of the same old thing at a number of gift shops along the main street in Talkeetna, I remembered that Roman (our Russian friend) had found some cool stuff in the National Park Service Ranger Station. We headed there and two good things happened: 1) I successfully purchased gifts for my wife and kids so as not to go home empty-handed, and 2) I saw the Denali summit statistics board on the wall behind the counter. This statistics board is an old-style grooved board with the sliding magnetic letters and numbers, which the National Park Service updates daily as climbers check in and check out. I took a picture of the board that morning so I wouldn't feel so bad that our team had not reached the summit.

As it turned out, of the 352 climbers who had completed their climbs as of that morning, only 74 (21 percent) had reached the summit. Rob and I were at least in the good company of the other 276 climbers who had also not reached the summit. The NPS maintains these statistics throughout the climbing season, and then posts season totals to its website, adding the newest season to its running tally of *every climbing season since 1903!* The 2014 season ended in mid-July with a dismal summit percentage of only 36 percent, compared with 2013's 68 percent summit rate and the cumulative average of 53 percent (from 1903 to 2013). The 2014 summit rate of 36 percent was the lowest since 1998. I suppose I should have attempted Denali in 2013 instead of 2014 and maybe I would have stood on the summit. Yet again, Mother Nature showed her power over the will of men.

All in all, Denali was a wonderful trip with an amazing group of climbers and guides. We didn't reach the summit, but I felt good about accomplishing my three stated goals. My training was successful—truly I was in the best shape of my life when I left for Alaska. Most importantly, I had returned safely to my wife and kids. Finally, I had fun and enjoyed the experience. I know I will go back to Alaska someday as there is so much more to see there. I still don't know whether I'll try for the summit again. I'm thinking probably yes, but most likely with a smaller group of Colorado guys, where we can hopefully move up the lower glacier a little more quickly to give ourselves more time at the 14,000-foot and 17,000-foot camps to catch what will hopefully be a better weather window next time. Only time will tell.

CHAPTER 21

Lessons Learned

It was awesome to see Melissa and the kids upon my return home from Alaska. The feeling of hugging her in the airport was amazing and seeing the kids the next morning was a breath of fresh air. But I had unfinished business in the mountains.

After sleeping in my own bed for two nights upon returning from Alaska, I was ready to get up high again, oddly enough. Melissa said, "Are you serious? You just spent three weeks in a tent and you're going up again already???" I explained that during my various training climbs on Grays Peak during my Denali training, I had realized that somehow I had done this peak in every month except June. It was definitely odd that I had not done one of Colorado's easiest and most accessible peaks in the month of June (a month with spring conditions early on, but still considered the first of the "summer months"), so I was determined to remedy that when I got home from Alaska.

It seemed anti-climactic to finish the monthly cycle on Grays by climbing it via the easy standard route, so I had decided to solo the toughest route on the peak when I got home from Denali, climbing it via the Lost Rat Couloir. A mid-May conditions report on 14ers.com had discussed a "school bus-sized cornice" at the top of the couloir that looked poised to release, along with a recommendation to wait until it had cleaved off before climbing the route. I was a full three weeks later in my attempt and was hoping to not find the same ominous hunk of snow above me as I climbed.

I set off the afternoon of June 10 and packed into the snowy basin beneath the north face of Grays Peak, having to stop and hunker down once lower on the mountain due to rain and thunder. I set up my small two-man tent on a shelf below the Lost Rat Couloir, which would be my target for the next morning. Once I had settled into my tent, a wave of loneliness hit me and actually brought me to tears. What the heck was I doing lying by myself

My tent with the Lost Rat Couloir up Grays Peak in the background.

in a tent at 12,800 feet two days after coming home from spending three weeks in a tent (versus sleeping in my king-sized bed with my lovely wife next to me)? I thought about packing up and going back home, but I needed to climb Grays in June and was in position.

Once I was crying, other emotions came out too. I had just spent ten months of my life training harder than I had ever trained for a climb, and I didn't quite know what to do with myself now. In my head, I knew that we had made the right decisions on Denali, but it was still disappointing not to have had a chance to summit. Once I pulled myself back together, I spent a sleepless night with the wind howling outside, pummeling my tent with ice crystals about every ten minutes. One of my climbing friends told me the next day that I was way tougher than him. My reply was, "No, I'm just not that bright."

After what seemed forever, I fired up my stove at 3:00 a.m., heated water for my Starbucks Via coffee and dehydrated bacon and eggs, then donned my crampons and made my way over to the base of the 40-degree Lost Rat Couloir that led to Grays' summit ridge. I moved slowly but steadily up the lower part of the couloir, enjoying the gorgeous oranges, reds, and yellows of the sunrise to the east. I looked up frequently, hoping to catch a glimpse of the top to see if the cornice was still there. I suspected it was not based on the debris field in the apron of the couloir, but still I checked often. Not thirty minutes into the climb, a rock just smaller than a baseball came hurling down from above and glanced off of my right hand. Oh good—rock fall; that's what this day needs! I had worn my helmet, for which I was glad, but I still didn't want to chance it. I moved to the left side of the couloir where I was sheltered from above by a large rock buttress around which the couloir turned above me.

After climbing around the buttress, I could see the summit ridge above me and could see that while there was still a cornice, it was considerably smaller and less ominous looking. I also saw some loose rocks in the middle of the couloir, just waiting for the sun's warming rays to get them on the move again. I quickly climbed up and around them to avoid the danger and soon was topping out beneath the meringue-like cornice where the couloir met the summit ridge. Once on the summit ridge, I climbed the easy last 700 feet to the summit to complete the monthly cycle of another Front Range 14er. My trip to Alaska and this first summer 2014 climb, complete with tears in my tent the night before, have given me plenty of opportunity to think. What lessons have I learned over the years and what knowledge do I have that might be helpful to others?

Today I stand as a moderately experienced amateur mountaineer. I still have lots to learn about the more technical aspects of climbing, assessing objective hazards such as avalanche conditions, as well as rope and rescue techniques. I learn something new every time I climb with a guide. I continue to climb mountains in my home state of Colorado as often as I can. I feel fortunate to have discovered the mountains and to have had so many experiences in those mountains that I love (including the good fortune of being able to afford wonderful guides and travel to remote places). Most of my Colorado climbs these days represent a part of a larger training program for my next big adventure, but I always feel the sense of peace and appreciation of the beauty around me, even while climbing a mountain that I have climbed sixty-plus times before.

My current count of Colorado 14er summits stands at 209, a count that is nearly equal to an average of four summits of each of the fifty-four Colorado 14ers. In reality, my six "home" mountains in the Front Range nearest Denver (Pikes Peak, Mt. Evans, Mt. Bierstadt, Grays Peak, Torreys Peak, and Longs Peak) comprise 133 of those summits. Included in my 209 14er summits are 55 solo summit climbs. I welcome hiking partners whenever I find a willing and able set of legs to join me, but still I find myself solo a lot of the time since I prefer to go during the less-crowded times of the work week whenever possible (which often means working at night or on the weekend). I usually climb routes solo only after I have previously climbed them with others. My solo climbs serve the purpose of giving me time to think. It is during these times that I most frequently reflect on the lessons I have learned as an amateur mountaineer.

Dealing with Adversity

The first lesson I have learned is that adversity is something we all face as we go through our lives, but how we deal with adversity is the key. To boil it down to simple terms, dealing with adversity will go one of two directions—it will either be used as an excuse for why things can't be done or it will serve as a motivator that redoubles our courage and resolve to accomplish a goal. Melissa and I (especially Melissa) could easily have used the accident on Mt. Evans as a reason not to climb again. She could have used the loss of her toes as an excuse to not stay physically fit, arguing that it is too hard to run, bike, hike, climb, or do yoga with only two toes. Instead, she chose to use the accident as a springboard to show others how much can be done with a physical disability. Melissa jokes every time she accomplishes something that she now holds the world record for fastest, highest, or longest effort for a two-toed person.

Melissa shares her story each year with her fifth grade class, and every year, at least one fifth-grader approaches her afterward and thanks her for providing such a great perspective on dealing with physical disabilities. These kids have included ones with birth defects such as webbed toes, skin disorders, and even an arm that didn't form properly. They have struggled with adversity and how to react to it since they can remember, but seeing a grown woman that they all love and respect that is "different, just like them" helps them realize that their disability does not need to define who they are or what they can or cannot do. Hearing Melissa's story also helps kids without disabilities realize how lucky they are and learn to treat other kids who are different with the same level of respect that they treat their favorite fifth-grade teacher.

Richard Bach wrote in his book *Illusions,* "Argue for your limitations and sure enough, they're yours." This has been my favorite quote since I first read it as a college student, serving as a constant reminder of the dangers of using the words, "I can't." Bach's statement is quite simple really—if you talk yourself out of something by telling yourself that you can't do it because of this or that, it will surely be a self-fulfilling prophecy. It would be easy for Melissa to utter the words "I can't" frequently and blame it on her lack of toes, but she has chosen to be strong and use the adversity to her advantage instead, accomplishing things that most ten-toed people don't believe that they can do. I tell people frequently what a tough person my wife is; she is physically tough and she is mentally tough (all the while being a loving wife and mother). I strive to deal with adversity in my life as well as she has. In Melissa's words:

I learned many lessons during my recovery. The biggest change has been how I respond to adversity. I now know the importance of personal responsibility. Responsibility to me means taking ownership of your life. I was not a responsible person when I was younger. I had an excuse for everything that happened "to" me; nothing was ever my fault. I had to learn the hard way the importance of this value. I can't pinpoint an exact moment of change, but I believe it started when we had our hiking accident.

During my recovery, people kept telling me how "strong" I was and how proud they were of how I was handling the loss of my toes. I liked being seen as someone who is strong. I think it was the first time in my life that I was seen that way. Something started to change within me. I started taking more and more responsibility for my life. I noticed that when I took ownership when things went wrong and explained what I was thinking to people, things worked out better than when I would finger point. I have had the fortune of meeting Chris Waddell who as a paraplegic was the first person to climb Mount Kilimanjaro in a wheelchair. His philosophy is that, "It's not what happens to you. It's what you do with what happens to you."

My father and I could have used the adversity of the accident as an excuse not to hike or enjoy the outdoors anymore. We could have justified that it was our punishment for coming out of the accident physically unharmed while Melissa suffered so much. Instead, we chose to use that adversity and our mistakes to make us stronger, better, and safer hikers. Another favorite saying of mine is "Good judgment comes from experience. Experience comes from bad judgment." I have definitely made mistakes during my times in the mountains, the most significant of which cost my dear wife her toes. But I have chosen to learn from my mistakes rather than dwell on them and gradually over the past seventeen years, bad judgments that I have made in the mountains have jelled into something called experience. I still make mistakes for sure, but I believe that using my experience at this point causes me to make far more good decisions in the mountains than bad ones and my experience has enabled me to assist numerous others in the mountains in making better decisions themselves.

I have a very good memory, which can be a good thing and a bad thing. Forgive and forget is a great saying, but if one lacks the ability to forget, it can be tough to forgive. Maybe enough time has passed now since our bad night out in 2001 that I've finally been able to forgive myself for what happened to

Melissa. I rarely think of myself as even having had a traumatic experience personally—it is all about Melissa in my head. I think writing this book and getting the opportunity to work with Melissa on it will only help heal.

Relationships

Another positive aspect of our accident on Mt. Evans has been the effect it has had on two key relationships in my life—with my dad and with my wife. My dad's and my time together in the mountains has been far and away the best time we have spent together. Working two jobs when I was a young boy, Dad wasn't around much. When he was home, he always had some sort of home improvement or maintenance project he was working on and I would be thrilled to get the chance to make a lumberyard run with him or help pound in a nail or something. I don't know how he made time for it, but he was always willing to throw the football with me when I asked or help me with a puzzle. I definitely enjoyed the time we spent together, but like most kids, I didn't really appreciate it until I was much older.

During my college years, Dad definitely had more free time than he'd had when I was younger, but I was much too busy with school and work to spend much time with him at that stage of my life. Wanting to give back, Dad volunteered in the Big Brothers Big Sisters program in Denver, one year even being named Big Brother of the Year in the wonderful program. Upon graduating from college and starting my career as an auditor with Arthur Andersen's Denver office, I worked my tail off those first several years and again didn't have much time to spend with my dad.

It really wasn't until that silly viral pinkeye struck that I slowed down enough to find time in my schedule to do anything with my dad again. I've described how we got into doing 14ers together previously of course. After the accident, we became our own support group, I think to deal with our feelings of guilt and regret for what Melissa had gone through. We initially talked more about the accident and the things that we wished we had done differently. We realized, though, that we couldn't go back in time and change things, so we didn't dwell on it. Instead, we tried to enjoy our time out in nature's beauty together and laughed and joked about good times. He provided fatherly advice on marriage and eventually fatherhood.

Somewhere along the way, Dad became much more to me than just my father—he became one of my very best friends. For him, going with me on so many of the 14ers was a role he could embrace as a worthy job of helping keep me safe. Dad developed keen mountain instincts that we would frequently listen to when we weren't sure about the weather, the route, or our safety. When we began climbing the more difficult peaks, I would always look at the crux pitch and turn to him with the same statement and question, "I know we can climb this. How do you feel about leading us back down?" since his comfort level with Class 3 and Class 4 terrain was initially considerably higher than my own. Each and every time he would descend the pitch first and then carefully talk me through where to put my feet and hands as I down climbed those pitches. I will always remember our climbs together as the high point (no pun intended) of our relationship. I hope to emulate my dad and the quality time he spent with me both as a child and as an adult, as I interact daily with my two children.

For Melissa and me, the accident was something that we decided early on was going to make our marriage stronger. It was certainly tough going early on after the accident—we had only been married for a year when it happened. The amazing support we got from our family and friends was instrumental in getting through the first couple of months that summer. I felt tremendous guilt whenever I saw her all bandaged up and I wanted so badly to make things better. Somehow in my head, this desire to make things better translated into wanting to buy her better hiking gear for every birthday and holiday. You can imagine Melissa's dismay when I showered her with new hiking boots, pants, shirts, and socks on her birthday in October 2001, just weeks after her toes had been amputated. She needed these things to replace her clothes that had been cut off of her in the hospital, but she was in no physical or mental condition to use any of them just yet. I remember the look of horror my mom gave me during Melissa's birthday party that year as Melissa opened her various hiking-related gifts and my mom turning to me and saying, "Surely you got her something other than this, right???" I think I did slightly better at Christmas that year, but only slightly. I was still looking for a "redo" and I was definitely ready to move on from the accident before Melissa was.

Once she was done with her physical healing, she still had a lot of emotional healing to do. Having a counselor through the University of Colorado at Denver to give her someone that she could talk to about her feelings was a huge help. I tried to be a good listener for her as well, but hearing her talk about the accident brought me to the verge of tears from guilt every time. She graciously told me that she wasn't trying to make me feel guilty and that she just needed me as her husband to understand how she was feeling. This gradually got easier and easier over the years, to the point where we can now talk about the accident freely and even with a slight sense of humor over various aspects of the story. As a result of having our young marriage survive such an ordeal only a year in, we know now that together we can get through anything that comes our way in the future.

Finally, because of our accident, there will always be a special bond between my dad and Melissa. After years of being in visual anguish just seeing her toeless feet, my dad can now sit and chat with Melissa with ease. He and Melissa laugh and joke more than I think any other father-in-law and daughter-in-law do—whether the topic is hiking, kids, or thinking back on their respective times on morphine drips. There is absolutely nothing that my dad would not do to help Melissa. Despite my dad's early feelings of being guilty of causing the accident, Melissa and I have always maintained that we were just as much at fault for the accident that cost Melissa her toes (honestly, I still believe that I was the most at fault for leading us astray that day) and it is really neat to see how strong the relationship has become between her and my dad.

Perseverance, Comfort Zones, and Inner Strength

My mountain adventures have also taught me the value of perseverance and using my inner strength when pushed outside of my comfort zone. Great things in life happen one small step at a time, not through a flash of light and sudden, blinding success. Until we invent teleportation, the summits of mountains will continue to be reached only through this same slow, steady progress, one foot after the other. I always know when I'm getting physically tired while climbing when I catch myself counting my steps in my head. Counting steps was an early trick I learned in the mountains in terms of setting small, attainable goals for myself. Initially, I would look up the mountain and pick a spot, and then try to climb to it before my next rest. But mountain landmarks are incredibly deceiving when looking uphill. They are always *much* farther away than they appear. Setting a small goal of doing another fifty or one hundred steps before stopping is a nice short tangible goal and keeps you moving gradually upward. I have also learned very well the even better lesson of the tortoise and the hare. Fifty or a hundred step bursts can be nice, but it is far more efficient to simply set a slow, steady pace that can be maintained for an hour or more between stops.

I demonstrated the power of the steady pace for three young college guys one summer morning on Grays Peak in 2012. I had just returned from my summit climb on Mt. Rainier a month before this particular Saturday, which happened to be the day we and two other families had scheduled a hike to give our then seven-year-olds the chance to climb their first 14er. My then five-year-old daughter, Megan, had done our shorter hikes building up to the 14er attempt and had actually been the strongest kid on our ascent of 13,200-foot Mt. Sniktau near Loveland Pass, so we gave her the option to join us on the 14er attempt. She said she wanted to go, and given her recent performance, we thought she could probably do the summit climb. But this was a different day than Mt. Sniktau and she began asking to get on my shoulders starting at about 12,000 feet. I would walk a few steps with her on my shoulders and she would announce that she was now well rested and ready to get down and walk. After doing this up and down routine about five times, I grew tired of it and told her that if she got up on my shoulders again, she was going to need to stay there.

She asked to get on my shoulders again at about 12,500 feet, so I put her on my back and told her that I was carrying her to the summit. Off we went up the mountain, with the slow, steady "expedition pace" and rest steps that I had just used all the way up Mt. Rainier. Gradually we passed more and more people who had stopped for breaks along the side of the trail. I kept telling Megan that we were tortoises and they were hares. Tortoises may be slow, but they don't stop. And they eventually pass the hares. Above 13,000 feet we saw three college-aged "hares" hiking as fast as they could for as long as they could, then stopping to catch their breath. I noticed that they were looking down at us each time they took a break and I could imagine their dismay in realizing that we were slowly gaining on them. Each time they stopped for a break, they looked down and saw us still coming up the mountain below them. Their breaks got shorter as did their bursts of energy up the mountain. These guys did *not* want to get passed by the old guy with the kid on his shoulders! They pushed themselves as hard as hares can push themselves, huffing and puffing as we approached, me not even breathing hard thanks to our slow, steady tortoise pace (and my recent Mt. Rainier training and successful summit). Finally, they gave up and

Megan gets a ride up Grays Peak on my shoulders in August 2012.

pulled over for another much needed break and allowed us to pass them. One of the guys shook his head and said to me, "That's impressive, man!" as Megan and I continued our journey on up to the summit, without stopping once.

Determination and a tortoise pace can definitely get you up a mountain, but what goes up must come down. Going down is usually where I find myself outside my comfort zone and it is these times when the inner strength that I have developed is critical to moving beyond the immediate feeling of fear and overcoming the challenge at hand. My key lesson in dealing with situations when I am out of my comfort zone is to pause for just long enough to get my bearings, use my experience to decide the best course of action, then to begin taking action. Pausing for too long causes me to over-think my problem and dwell on all of the things that could go wrong, almost to the point of paralysis. Two great examples of this are arriving at the knife ridge on Capitol Peak (either on the ascent or descent) and my first rappelling experience.

The second time I climbed Capitol Peak, I was the most experienced and de facto leader of our group, the only one who had previously climbed the peak and crossed the infamous knife ridge. But I was terrified when I saw the knife ridge again. The sheer drop off on either side had not become less dramatic and scary since I was there last and it remained quite clear that a fall here held catastrophic consequences. I began to freak myself out and my legs started to shake. This wasn't good. The other guys were looking to me to lead them across this scary part. I decided that staring at the knife ridge was not going to make it less scary (actually quite the opposite). The weather looked good and we were a strong party with the right equipment—it was time to go. As soon as I committed and made the first move out onto the ridge, I felt so much more relaxed. I took my time, but did not stop to think about the exposure again. Sure enough, the hand- and footholds appeared when I needed them and soon I was across the knife ridge encouraging the others as they followed behind me. Moving along and making decisions is a wonderful way of dealing with being outside of one's comfort zone. Over-thinking things is a great way to get stuck and get yourself in trouble.

The other time fear just about got the best of me was the first time I ever rock climbed. An experienced rock climber friend, Jeff Shafer, offered to take me up the first flatiron near Boulder, Colorado. He gave me great pointers all the way up the climb and I was enjoying it quite a lot. When we reached the top of this great slab of rock, I asked how we descended. We had clipped into the large eyebolt drilled into the top of the rock and he just tapped the bolt and said we would rappel down the backside off of the bolt. I looked down over the edge to the west and saw the ground some 70 feet below. Yikes! He explained that he would "pre-rig" my rappelling device onto the rope, then he would rappel off the summit first and give me what is called a "fireman's belay" from below, meaning he would have a hold of the rope and put tension on the rope if he needed to stop me. I liked the plan, right up to the point where he left me on the summit all by myself.

There is a slight overhang near the top, so I couldn't actually see him once he reached the ground. He yelled up to me, "Off rappel!" meaning that he was down. He then told me I was "on belay" and could rappel whenever I was ready. I suddenly felt more alone than I had ever felt in my life and began looking around frantically for a different way down. I looked back at what we had climbed up and thought, "Maybe I could climb down that," but quickly realized how silly that was—no one down climbs rock routes rated 5.5 unprotected after their first day of rock climbing! Clearly, the smartest, safest way down was to rappel down the rope with my partner protecting me from below. But that required taking myself off the anchor and stepping backward over the edge of a cliff, against every instinct from deep in my brain. Again, more time thinking about it was just going to freak me out to the point of paralysis. Someday a helicopter ride might be fun—but I decided it wasn't going to be today, fetching me (the guy paralyzed with fear) off the summit of the flatiron.

I double-checked the rope going through the bolt and through my belay device, then unclipped my anchoring tether from the bolt. Time to move! Gingerly, I stepped backward off the cliff, my mouth parched from fear. I

knew in my head that Jeff had me, but it was still incredibly difficult to get myself to trust the rope. Thankfully, the first step backward over the edge of the cliff is the hardest one by far, then gravity takes over and the rappel is actually almost fun. When my feet hit the ground and I knew I was safe, I thought—that was fun (Type 2 fun—fun when it was over!). Inner strength and perseverance win out against fear yet again.

Me topping out on the first flatiron with Boulder, Colorado, in the background. Photo courtesy of Jeff Shafer.

Stewardship and Beauty

My appreciation for the beauty of our natural world has also increased tenfold since I began hiking and climbing. Whether it is Colorado's Rocky Mountains, Mt. Rainier, the Grand Teton, Ecuador's volcanoes, the mass of Mt. Kilimanjaro, Denali, or even Phoenix's mountains in the middle of the city, there is beauty and peace in those hills. I am frequently astonished by the perspective that being up high offers. Looking off into the distance from the summit of a mountain, I consistently find myself tracing ridge lines, up and over the next mountain and down into the green valleys, just trying to understand how everything connects, wondering where I could go if I were to wander along all of those connecting ridges. From up high, nothing seems as far away or isolated.

A personal favorite of mine is hiking across fresh snow on a high ridge, windblown and free from any trace of human disturbance, the early morning sun at my back creating a long shadow across the crisp white snow. Similarly, I love the sound of my boots (especially if I'm wearing crampons) biting into late-spring hard-packed snow—the metallic crunch as I kick into the next step is such a pleasure to enjoy, knowing that I've got good traction as I climb higher. I also find the sight of the shadow of a mountain, stretching across the valley floor for dozens of miles, to be amazing. I first saw this while climbing El Pico de Orizaba in Mexico and have since seen it on a few other occasions including Kilimanjaro and Cotopaxi, with its nearly perfect pyramid creating a stunning view of a sharp triangle painted across the floor of the Ecuadorian highlands.

Some days, clouds obscure the views from the summits of mountains. I climbed 14,265-foot Quandary Peak on a December 2013 day, having promised a good friend that the view from the summit of his first winter 14er would be worth it. Unfortunately, when we reached the summit, we had climbed up into the clouds and could only enjoy the view of the gentle snowflakes falling around us rather than the vast expanse of snow-covered peaks that I had told him would be spectacular. Oh well—it was still a great day and beautiful in its own way as we descended back through the clouds.

I recall another day climbing into the clouds on a crisp, early spring day. When I reached the summit on that day, however, I was greeted by one of the most spectacular views I've ever had from the summit of a peak. I had actually climbed *above* the clouds and was looking down on them. The layer of white clouds hovered just below the summit all around me, leaving me on a small island in a massive ocean of clouds that obscured the valleys. Wow!

Enjoying this natural beauty from high places in our world requires more

A beautiful ocean of clouds covers Boulder as seen from high on Bear Peak.

than the physical effort exerted to reach the summits, though. If we want to continue to enjoy it and have those lands maintain their beauty for our children and grandchildren, we have to take care of them. Merriam-Webster defines stewardship as "the careful and responsible management of something entrusted to one's care." Some may not view stewardship of our public lands as being entrusted to each of our care, but I would argue that it is absolutely incumbent on each and every one of us. This is not just the job of the forest service or the national parks. It is not just the job of the Department of the Interior or Bureau of Land Management. These are *our* public lands, meaning we all have the right to enjoy them, and with that right comes a responsibility to steward them, for ourselves and for generations to follow.

It might seem too large of a task for one person to undertake—certainly it can be an overwhelming thought that each of us is responsible for areas so vast. Just like climbing mountains though, this must be done one small step at a time. Small individual actions such as picking up a piece of trash on a trail multiply when we have an army of stewards using our network of trails through our public lands. My personal goal is small and simple when I hike—leave the trail better than I found it. I have employed this small goal on each of my hikes whether at home or abroad. On Kilimanjaro, my fellow climbers began to eagerly await my daily "take" each night when we reached camp. It seemed I had a keen eye for the small hard candy wrappers that were a favorite of previous climbers on Kilimanjaro, and each day I would pick up each one I saw along the trail. By the end of the day, I had a whole pocket full of them and deposited them into our trash bags that we would pack out with us. By the end of the trip, others in our group were coming up to me at the end of the day to show me the wrappers that they had picked up. My small, simple action of picking up candy wrappers was multiplying without me asking anything of anyone else.

On other occasions, I have gone perhaps a bit overboard with my simple goal of leaving the trail a little better than I found it. In September 2013, I was walking down the Grays Peak trail as I have done so many times be-

One of my daily trash "takes" on Kilimanjaro.

fore. But on this day something new caught my eye lower on the trail. I had just walked the same stretch of trail two weeks before and this object was definitely new since then. I anxiously descended to see what this new thing was. When I got to its location, I stared at an old rusted metal object lying within a foot of the trail. I still don't know exactly what it was—it looked a bit like an old sink or an old toilet tank, with part of it broken off. I was somewhat dismayed to see that it already contained a used Kleenex and a banana peel. Perhaps hikers in the previous couple of weeks assumed that this old rusted metal object was a newly installed garbage can conveniently placed along the side of the trail and decided to make their deposits. I could see where this was going to go and I didn't want a garbage heap next to my trail, knowing full well that there is no weekly trash service at 12,800 feet. Yes sir, this object needed to come down the mountain to prevent it from becoming an eyesore on the trail. It looked awfully heavy though, but what the heck, I was beginning my Denali training and needed to get used to carrying heavy loads!

I took my backpack off just as an uphill hiker arrived at the spot. He and I talked for a moment, speculating that this must be an old piece of debris from an old mine (many of which are around in Colorado's mountains). Some well-meaning hiker must have seen it and thought about carrying it out, realizing at some point that he or she had signed up for more than they bargained for, deciding instead to set the object down by the side of the trail. The gentleman I was talking to agreed that a trash receptacle at this location was not a good idea and I asked him to help me lift it so I could strap it onto the top of my backpack. "You're going to carry it down????" he asked incredulously, being in his sixties and knowing he surely was not going to carry this thing down 2 miles to the trailhead!

"Yes" I told him, and he steadied it while I lashed it onto the top of my pack. He then helped me lift my backpack onto my back so I could head down the mountain. I got some very strange looks that day as I descended with the large wrought iron tank-looking thing strapped to the top of my backpack; I also got many "thank you's" from others who were glad I was disposing of the object. My knees were screaming at me by the time I reached my car (I weighed the pack with my fish scale upon arriving home—sixty-five pounds), but I'm happy to say that this object is now an antique flower planter in my backyard (thanks to Melissa's eye for such things). From candy wrappers to wrought iron tanks—stewardship is conducted one person at a time, one action at a time. And everyone can do it—my small children point out trash to me when we hike and they help me to leave things better than we found them.

The iron tank I carried down from Grays Peak in September 2013.

I would be remiss if I didn't also mention the principles of "Leave No Trace," an outdoor ethic that I follow. Whenever I agree to take someone for a hike or climb, I always provide them with a brief overview of the Leave No Trace principles and explain why I choose to follow this outdoor ethic myself. "Leave only footprints and take only pictures" is Leave No Trace in a nutshell. Leave No Trace has seven principles:

Plan Ahead and Prepare
Travel and Camp on Durable Surfaces
Dispose of Waste Properly
Leave What You Find
Minimize Campfire Impacts
Respect Wildlife
Be Considerate of Other Visitors

The plan and prepare principle is near and dear to my heart thanks to my desire to never again find myself unprepared in an emergency bivouac in a blizzard. I'll discuss planning and preparation more later. First, I'll expand briefly on the travel and camp on durable surfaces principle—something that each of us can and should do in our role as stewards of our natural beauty. The camping aspect is fairly straightforward—good campsites are found rather than made and they are generally not above timberline, nor are they located too close to water that could be contaminated by human waste. Traveling on durable surfaces really just refers to staying on established trails. Other "durable" surfaces include snow and rock, which can be traveled upon without negative impact on the fragile alpine tundra that grows incredibly slowly above treeline.

When we fail to stay on the established trail and instead choose to walk on the tundra, we do damage that takes decades to repair. Some people rationalize it, saying, "I'm just one person, so I won't have a big impact." The problem with that thinking is that hundreds of people are on each trail during a summer day—gradually newly braided trails appear as the tundra dies and the rare topsoil that it previously held in place erodes down the mountain. People seeking the softer footing of the tundra then go farther out in search of it and the trail widens and widens until the entire hillside is devoid of vegetation, becoming ugly and unsustainable. Groups such as the Colorado Fourteeners Initiative and Volunteers for Outdoor Colorado diligently work to build high quality sustainable trails so that we can enjoy access to our natural beauty—our job as stewards is to use the sustainable trails that these groups and countless volunteer hours have constructed rather than creating our own "social" trails. Our children and grandchildren will thank us someday when they can walk along the same trail, through a beautiful alpine meadow, with flowers blooming all around them.

Respect and Preparation

When I first started climbing, I thought about mountains in much the same way I've heard other beginners refer to them—as something to be "conquered." When I reached the summits of my early 14ers, I came home and told people that I had bested this mountain or that mountain through my superior skill and physical fitness. Spending the night stranded in a whiteout, helpless to do anything about it, and watching my wife lose eight of her toes as a result was a humbling experience, as you would imagine. Arrogance kills in the mountains. It is not that the mountains are cruel by any stretch of the imagination. The mountains don't care. Lou Whittaker of RMI was once quoted as saying, "Just because you love the mountains doesn't mean they love you." They are just what and where they are—piles of dirt and rock that have so far withstood the gradual grinding down of time and weather. They magnificently rise above the valleys and rivers below, their sheer girth dwarfing all life around them, especially life as small as a human venturing onto their slopes.

The key to co-existing on mountains that don't particularly care whether we climb them or even whether we live or die on their slopes is respect. Since the accident, I have never again used the word "conquered" to describe a climb. My view now after a successful summit climb is that I was fortunate to reach the summit and more importantly, descend safely. The weather is entirely out of my control and that weather has the ability to severely punish those who venture high into the mountains. The mountains are constantly changing due to the continuous effects of freezing and thawing. Water seeps into tiny cracks in the rock and then freezes, expanding the crack ever so slightly until one day, the crack will be so large that the rock can no longer maintain its perch balanced on the steep mountain slope. Unlucky is the hiker or climber who dislodges the rock, or even worse, is simply in the line of fire below it when it releases naturally.

Similarly, snow accumulates in the mountains and eventually comes down. It can come down the mountain when it melts or as part of a glacier, moving incredibly slowly in the form of a frozen river, or it can come down with a massive, lightning quick force in the form of an avalanche. These occur both naturally and from humans traveling across unstable snow slopes. The point is that there are objective hazards everywhere around us when we venture into the mountains. Showing the appropriate respect for the terrain we plan to enter, planning ahead, and exercising good judgment are our best defenses if we wish to come back and enjoy the mountains another day.

Turning back when conditions are not right can be a tough decision for sure. Countless mountaineering books over the years tell the stories of those who perished or barely survived on days when perhaps retreat would have been in order. Our story mirrors those—many things could be different had we chosen to retreat from the summit of Mt. Spalding or even postpone to a different day our hike of Mt. Evans that May 2001 day. My wife very well might be heading out to get a pedicure today! We unfortunately learned our respect for the mountains, the value of turning around when conditions are not right, and the value of preparedness the hard way. We are blessed however, to have received a second chance in that our mistakes did not cost any of us our lives. Many others, including my friend Mark Golden, unfortunately did not receive this second chance. We cannot change the past, but we can choose how we use our past to adapt going forward. Since the accident in 2001, I have turned around short of the summit on many occasions, including my first attempt on each of the Maroon Bells, my first attempt on Mt. Rainier, Chimborazo, and most recently, on Denali. I was certainly disappointed to not reach those summits, but I am also proud to have made the decisions I made in order to have the opportunity to climb another day.

My dad, Melissa, and I did a lot of things right in May 2001 from a preparation perspective. Most importantly, we let someone know where we were going and when we expected to return. This enabled the authorities to find us far more quickly once things had gone wrong. We also started very early, which gave us a decent chance of getting down that day—perhaps an alpine start before sunrise would have provided enough extra time to beat the storm down. Seldom do you hear a story where something goes wrong because someone starts *too early*. We also carried a small amount of extra clothing in the long underwear and extra socks that likely saved my dad's life that night. Clearly we didn't have overnight gear that could have provided shelter and kept us warm until morning and a second spare pair of socks sure would have come in handy.

I now carry an emergency bivy sack and fire starters on every hike I do (in addition to plenty of extra clothing). Melissa's parents also gave me a "don't ever do this to my daughter again" present in the form of a new GPS unit when they returned from Italy shortly after the accident. Today, I mark my car with a waypoint before I start every hike and frequently mark other waypoints along the way. GPS units certainly aren't perfect and shouldn't be relied upon exclusively, but I do wonder whether having my car marked with a GPS waypoint as I do now would have allowed us to find it through the whiteout that night in May 2001. It certainly wouldn't have hurt!

Most importantly, my mindset has changed when I enter the mountains. I have a tremendous amount of respect for my surroundings and how quickly things can change. I also now understand just how isolated a human can be high up on a mountain and how difficult a rescue can be. It is critical to enter the mountains self-sufficiently and prepared for what could happen. By maintaining respect for the terrain and the objective hazards, decisions are more likely to be sound. Another trick I have learned in making decisions in the mountains came from my first guide on Mt. Rainier. In assessing the slopes for avalanche danger, our senior guide deferred the decision on whether or not we would continue climbing to the two junior guides, who had only a fraction of his experience. I thought this was odd and inquired about it. He explained to me that this is an experienced airline pilot strategy as well—basically we eventually develop calluses from having seen things too many times before, and we assume that if it worked the last time, it will work again every time.

I am at the point now that I have been in the mountains an awful lot. I have seen tons of clouds on the horizon and tried to gauge whether or not the storm will come. I have crossed many, many snow slopes and gripped many, many rocks as I climbed up a route. It is too easy to assume that since it didn't avalanche or break off the last time, it won't this time either. Asking a less experienced member of the party for their opinion or gut feeling is tremendously valuable in those circumstances, for they have not developed the same calluses and their instincts may be more in tune with the possible dangers. Using this tool, I have retreated from a number of situations that might have been too dangerous. It is far better to spin in retreat than to push a bad situation and climb yourself into danger. The mountain will still be there another day—the key is for you to be there another day, too, so you can try again.

In Closing

My adventures as an amateur mountaineer are some of my most cherished memories in life and I look forward to many more years of sharing those adventures with my friends and family, including my children. I sincerely hope that the only "near miss" I ever have cause to write about is our accident on Mt. Evans. My vision is that through that unfortunate accident and all of my other experiences, I will make sound decisions and be able to enjoy nature's beauty and challenge with only a scrape or bruise now and then.

Hiking and climbing is something that our bodies have the ability to do well into our prime years and there is tremendous value in this. Staying active keeps us physically fit and fends off many of life's natural ailments. It is also something that is easily shared across a wide group of friends and family of all ages. Perhaps someday one or both of my kids will want to be my regular hiking partner just as I was for my father. I still hold out some hope that my dad will come out of retirement someday and finish his last nine 14ers with me (he is just sixty-four as I write this). I will always cherish the time that I spent with him in the mountains along with the time that Melissa and I have spent with our children and our friends exploring the beauty that surrounds us everywhere we look. These experiences are far more valuable in life than any material thing and we still have lots of great years to look forward to with each other and the kids (now ten and seven).

I hope that sharing these experiences might be helpful to you as you develop your own judgment and decision-making skills. I also hope that it motivates some of my readers to get active and go explore, appreciate, and steward our public lands—even if that exploration occurs on everyday hiking trails below treeline rather than on the slopes of high peaks. Have fun and be safe.

Acknowledgments

I have many people to thank for making this book possible—without their faith, encouragement, companionship, and support, this book would still just be an idea in my head.

First, I want to thank my wife and best friend, Melissa. She was strong during our accident and continues to amaze me to this day with her perseverance, compassion, sense of humor, and support. She could have withdrawn from our accident, but instead chose to embrace it so that others might learn from it. Our accident caused her much physical and mental pain and yet she was the first person in support of me writing about what happened and what we have learned from it over the years.

Thank you to Paul "Woody" Woodward and the Alpine Rescue Team for coming to our aid when we needed it. Thanks also to all of the other volunteer rescue groups in Colorado for their amazing service to the mountaineering community, including the team that recovered Mark Golden's body and brought it down that steep slope and back to his parents. Their selflessness, knowledge of the terrain, and expert rescue skills are vital to both our community and to our visitors.

Thanks to Ryan Warner of Colorado Public Radio for his work on the "Here's What Happened" program and for recognizing the value in having Melissa tell her story. Thanks also to the staff at *Backpacker Magazine* for their interest in including Melissa in the 2012 Survival Edition of their fine magazine.

I want to thank all of my climbing partners and teammates over the years. My father, Rich, has always been my favorite climbing partner and I will forever cherish our times together in the mountains. I am also blessed to be able to enjoy the outdoors with Melissa, Connor, and Megan—I know we will have many more adventures together. To all my guides over the years, I want to express my thanks for their diligence in keeping me and my fellow climbers safe. They do amazing work. Frequent climbing partners I want to thank include my friend Mark Golden (who left us too soon), Ryan Gosney, Rob Norris, my brother Todd McQueen, Jeff Shafer, John Balciar, Jeff Watkins, Tony Jensen, Mark Dunning, Jim Nottingham, Rob Miller, and Ryan Chase. I appreciate their friendship, willingness to join me on these adven-

246

tures, and their commitment to doing so safely. I have trusted my life to each of them and I would do so again.

Thank you to each of my partners at the accounting firm of EKS&H for their understanding and support when I go off on my adventures. I am in their debt for their assistance in serving my clients and guiding my engagement teams while I am gone. The firm's commitment to allowing employees to have work/life balance means so much to Melissa and me. Also, thanks to both sets of grandparents, Chuck and Vonnee Pell and Rich and Susie McQueen, for being willing and excited to treat our kids to such special time with their grandparents while we are off on our adventures. Thanks to Dr. Will MacPhee for reading my description of frostbite to ensure it was accurate.

I also owe a big thank you to my mother, Susie McQueen, and my sister-in-law, Monica McQueen, for calling in the Alpine Rescue Team and coordinating our rescue. Thanks also for their support in the aftermath of the accident, both for me as well as for Melissa and my dad. Specifically for Mom, thank you for understanding that Dad, Melissa, and I were going to keep climbing after the accident. Your support and sage advice over the years is much appreciated.

To my early readers: Connor McQueen, Bernie Towne, Erin Brotherton, Jeff Watkins, Amy and Jake Calabrese, and Cynthia Cerny—thanks for taking the time out of their busy schedules to read the manuscript and provide me with feedback. It was instrumental.

Finally, thank you to Mira Perrizo and Julie Heins at Big Earth Publishing for their outstanding work in editing and publishing this book. I am a decent accountant and an amateur mountaineer, but I don't know the first thing about writing a book. Their guidance and support through this process were invaluable.

From Melissa

I would like to begin by thanking the people who matter most to me: Brad, Connor, Megan, and my mom and dad. Their love and support is what gets me through the bad days and I'm happy to share my life with them! I would also like to thank Alex and Will MacPhee. Alex has been there for me longer than anyone besides my parents and is still the type of friend who will gladly sit in the waiting room during surgery. Dr. MacPhee's words to me about racing so long ago have stuck with me and helped me navigate my feelings about the outdoors.

Thanks also to Dr. William Mangione, Todd Johnson, and Ed Webster. Dr. Mangione helped me recover physically and always believed that the accident wouldn't slow me down. Todd's help when I was struggling with my emotions related to the accident helped me find focus, clarity, and peace with everything. Thank you Ed for sharing in my frostbite pain and welcoming me to "the club." It made a huge difference talking to someone who had been there. Thanks to all of them for helping me recover from my lowest point.

Thanks to the organizations who have supported my desire to get outside. Big City Mountaineers has given me a chance to find a new way to love the outdoors and share that with girls who did not already love backpacking and "Raul." Good Shepherd Catholic School took a risk and hired a teacher who was going to miss the first two weeks of school for a hike—thanks for that vote of confidence.

Finally, thanks to all of my friends and family. I am blessed that they are too numerous to mention here. All of them have helped me through my recovery, continued mountaineering quests, and crazy world of work and family. Each of them has listened to my fears and shared in my joys over the years. It does indeed take a village!

APPENDIX

Preparing to Go and Returning Safely

Melissa and I have learned a lot from our experiences and are always happy to share that knowledge in hopes that we can prevent others from repeating our mistakes. A safe return from your adventure is the most important objective, so let's look at some tips for proper preparation and returning safely.

Preparation
Good preparation starts with thoughtful planning and respect for the mountains. Be sure you understand the route, its difficulty, and the time commitment. Check the weather forecast and be prepared for sudden changes. Make sure to tell someone where you are going—both your planned starting point and your planned destination—and tell them what time you expect to be back. If you can get a friend or two to join you on your adventure, do it. Start early and follow the golden rule of being off the summit by noon.

The Ten Essential Pack Items
(For all outings, no matter how big or small)
1. Navigation (map and compass, GPS, etc.)
2. Sun protection (sunglasses, sunscreen, and lip balm)
3. Insulation (extra clothing)
4. Illumination (headlamp/flashlight)
5. First-aid supplies
6. Fire (waterproof matches/lighter/candles)
7. Repair kit and tools
8. Nutrition (extra food)
9. Hydration (extra water)
10. Emergency shelter

Melissa's standard pack list, with more details on these items, is included at the end of this section in case it is helpful.

During the Adventure

While out in the mountains, making good decisions on what seem like simple choices will help ensure a safe return:

- Stay on your planned route. If you get off the trail, backtrack to find it again. If the difficulty level seems more than it is supposed to be, you are probably off route. Backtrack until you find the easier way where you are supposed to be.
- Pay attention to your body. Make sure to stay hydrated and take in enough calories. Listen to your body for signs of acute mountain sickness like headache, nausea, dizziness/lightheadedness, etc. Descend if that is what your body is telling you it needs.
- Check in with your hiking companion(s). Make sure he or she is paying attention to his or her body as well.
- Stay together. When you start a hike or climb with someone, finish the hike or climb with them. If one of you needs or wants to turn around, you both should turn around. If you are in a larger group, it can be okay for part of the group to turn around and part to go on, as long as at least one person in each group is experienced. Never ever leave someone alone. Bad things can happen all too easily.
- Keep an eye on the weather. Turn around and descend if the weather looks like it is going to turn for the worse. Being the tallest thing on a mountain—which you often are above tree line—is a bad thing to be in a lightning storm.
- Keep things in perspective. Summiting is optional; returning is not. The mountain will be there another day, so if it's not feeling right that day, turn around and try again another day. Summit fever can be a deadly illness.
- Don't panic. If you do get stranded overnight, stay calm, stay together, stay dry, and try to make good decisions. Get your extra layers on and stay warm to fend off hypothermia as best you can (this will help you make better decisions). Take care of each other—make sure your companion(s) get their warmest clothes on. Find as much shelter as you can from the elements and trust that the sun will come up soon enough and you'll have another chance to find your way out (or have our wonderful search and rescue teams come to your aid because you told someone where you were going and when you could be expected back).

What Melissa Usually Takes
(Most of this stuff she just leaves in her pack at all times so that she doesn't have to worry about packing it. She pretty much just packs food and clothes each hike and leaves the rest in her pack.)
- Sunscreen and lip balm
- Sunglasses
- Skin-shielding hat and clothing (wind can be quite strong, so something that fits snug is best)
- Warm knit cap
- Gloves
- Light jacket or vest (synthetic)
- Heavy jacket to put on at breaks (preferably with a hood)
- Pants (non-cotton)
- Headlamp
- Extra batteries
- First-aid kit
- Matches
- Knife
- Duct tape strips wrapped around water bottle or trekking pole (handy for equipment repairs or blister prevention)
- Snacks (Fritos, nuts, energy bars, chips, peanut butter crackers, apple, etc.)
- Water bottle and/or hydration reservoir
- Reflective blanket (or tent, tarp, or bivy sack)

Beyond the Ten Essentials
(Some items can be shared and some are personal preference)
- Daypack
- Multifunction watch
- Camera
- iPod
- Trekking poles
- Toilet paper with baggies for packing out used paper
- Cell phone (beware—you might not have service)
- Powdered drink mix (like Nuun or Crystal Light)
- Water purification tablets
- Utensils

- Bag for collecting trash (try to pack out any trash you see in addition to your own)
- Trip itinerary left with a friend
- Personal locator beacon (like SPOT)
- Avalanche beacons, shovel, and probe (seasonal)
- Ice axe (seasonal)
- Snowshoes (seasonal)

Clothing Options
(Decide based on trip length and possible weather extremes)

Warm Weather
- Wicking T-shirt
- Quick-drying pants/shorts
- Long-sleeve shirt (for bugs, sun)
- Hat
- Insulating jacket or vest
- Bandana (like duct tape, great for a million uses)

Cool Weather
- Wicking long-sleeve T-shirt
- Wicking long underwear (good sleepwear)
- Hat, cap, or headband (synthetic or wool)
- Gloves or mittens (or both)
- Waterproof/breathable rain jacket with hood
- Waterproof/breathable rain pants
- Insulating jacket/vest/pants

Footwear
- Hiking boots or sturdy trail shoes
- Micro spikes or crampons if you'll need to cross any snow (good to have September through June)
- Socks (synthetic or wool)
- Gaiters

Glossary

Acute Mountain Sickness (AMS): Illness caused by high altitude, especially gaining altitude too quickly. Symptoms include headache, nausea, lightheadedness, tingling and swelling in the hands. AMS is generally "cured" by descending to a lower elevation, but being well-hydrated also helps.

Alpine start: A term used by mountaineers to describe getting an extremely early start on a climb. An alpine start generally means you are walking in the dark with the use of a headlamp. An alpine start could be as early as 11:00 p.m. or as late as an hour or so before sunrise.

Anchor: A point of attachment to a mountain slope or rock face. This can be done by clipping into bolts fixed into the rock or creating your own with an ice axe, snow picket, or rock gear such as cams and nuts.

Ascender: A small handheld device used to climb a fixed rope up a steep slope. Ascenders are designed to slide easily up a rope, but have small directional teeth that bite into the rope to prevent a climber from falling or sliding down the rope.

Belay: A technique used by climbers to keep their partners safe once they are anchored themselves. It consists of maintaining tension on the rope tied to the lower partner while he or she ascends to the anchored upper partner.

Bivouac (or bivy for short): Camping with little to no gear (such as tent and sleeping bag). Sometimes these are planned and climbers carry minimal gear to minimize weight; other times an unplanned emergency bivouac is required because a hiker or climber becomes stranded overnight.

Cache: Pronounced "cash," this is a supply of food, fuel, or other gear left on a mountain for later use and is often used on big climbs like Denali and Everest where climbers are using a series of camps and moving between them over weeks or even months on the mountain. They are generally buried so that birds and critters don't eat the food.

Cairn: A pile of rocks used to mark the trail above timberline when it might not otherwise be clear. Most are fairly small piles of rocks that can be difficult to spot. On crowded mountains near big cities, they can be eight feet tall in an effort to keep beginners from getting lost.

Carabiner: A coupling link with a safety closure, used by rock climbers and mountaineers.

Class 3, Class 4, and Class 5: Rating system for describing the difficulty of a climbing route. Class 3 generally indicates that you can expect to use both your hands and your feet. You might also find some exposure on a Class 3 climb. Class 4 is the start of "technical" climbing and often entails the use of a rope. Class 4 pitches will generally have significant exposure. Class 5 climbing is rock climbing that is almost always done with ropes and other rock climbing gear such as cams, nuts, slings, and quick draws (sewn slings with carabiners on both ends).

Couloir: A natural vertical break in a mountain's face. These natural weaknesses in the mountain make for excellent climbing when they are filled with well consolidated snow. If the snow is not well consolidated, they are prime avalanche territory. If there is no snow, they are generally filled with dangerous loose rock that comes tumbling down on a frequent basis (not a good place to be).

Crampons: Sharp metal spikes that are attached to climbing boots to provide traction on snow and ice.

Crux: The most difficult part of a climb. Generally the route is rated based upon the difficulty level of the crux.

Exposure: A term for being unprotected from the elements or describing the fall potential on a route. The bigger the fall that you could take from a section of a climb, the higher the exposure. Exposed pitches are also often referred to as "airy."

Glissade: A technique used to slide down snow, generally in a sitting position. This should always be done with an ice axe (and the training of how to use the ice axe to self-arrest) in order to control the speed of descent and to stop at the desired place.

Heel plunge step: A technique used to descend steep snow slopes when the snow is soft enough to absorb the firmly placed heel. With the right snow conditions, this technique can almost create a staircase back down the mountain while taking pressure off the knees on the descent.

Hypothermia: A potentially fatal illness where the body loses its ability to maintain its core body temperature due to long periods of exposure to the cold. It is accelerated by getting wet.

Ice axe: A mountaineering tool used to ascend or descend steep snow. The long handle is known as the "shaft." Atop the shaft is the "head," which consists of a sharp "pick" at one end for gripping snow and a step-cutting tool called the "adz" at the other end.

Pitch: A term used in rock climbing to describe a section of the climb. The length of the climbing rope generally limits the length of a pitch, but occasionally a good ledge or belay point will be the end of a pitch, even if there is still rope length remaining.

Post-holing: A miserable experience where a hiker or climber walking on snow punches through the top layer of snow into the softer lower layers. As they walk, they leave behind holes in the snow that are calf-, knee-, or even thigh-deep and look like they are ready for fence posts to be inserted.

Pressure breathing: A technique used by mountaineers at higher elevations that improves the oxygen exchange in the lungs. It can be a sudden, forceful breath out followed by a deep breath in or it can be a slow pressurized breath out (like blowing up a balloon) followed by a deep breath in.

Prussic knot: A special knot used by climbers that enables a climber to ascend a climbing rope in a self-rescue situation. The knot is tied with thin nylon cord and wraps around the climbing rope in a way that enables the knot to slide up the rope, but not down the rope. Prussic knots are also used for self-belay when rappelling.

Rappel: A technique used to descend a steep snow or rock slope using a device to lower oneself down a rope. Many accidents and deaths have occurred in the mountains due to incorrect rappelling setups.

Rest step: A technique used by mountaineers in which the rear leg is locked with each step and supports most of the climber's weight. Because the majority of the weight is on the skeletal system versus the muscular system, this is a great way to conserve energy on long, steep climbs.

Saddle: The low point on a ridge in between two mountains.

Scrambling: This is the point when hiking starts to merge with rock climbing. Class 3 climbs are often referred to as scrambles because you are using both your hands and feet to ascend a route.

Scree: Small loose rock on a mountain slope. It can be anything from pea-gravel-sized to softball-sized rocks that act like ball bearings and cause climbers to slide down the mountain a little bit with every step.

Self-arrest: A technique with an ice axe where a climber stops a fall or glissade using either the shaft or pick of the ice axe to dig into the snow. Failure to self-arrest in a fall or glissade often results in injury or death.

Serac: A pinnacle or ridge of ice on or above the surface of glacier.

Shoulder: Often used to describe the intermediate slopes on a mountain. There is often an initial steep hill after the approach that you have to hike up to reach the shoulder. Once on the shoulder, you continue to ascend, usually up another steeper section to attain the "summit ridge" and ultimately the summit.

Snow picket: A two- or three-foot aluminum shaft used to anchor climbers on steep snow slopes.

Talus: Technically the same as scree, but generally a field of larger broken rocks and debris than scree. Generally, the larger the rocks, the less chance of them moving when you step on them (but the larger the impact if one or more of them do move as you are navigating across, up, or down them).

Timberline (or tree line): The elevation above which no trees grow on mountain slopes. The elevation varies across the country based on a number of factors including temperature and moisture. In Colorado, it is usually around 11,000 feet. On Mt. Rainier in Washington, it is closer to 5,000 feet.

Wind chill: The term used to describe how cold it feels on exposed skin with the addition of the wind to the existing cold air temperature. On Denali in Alaska when the air temperatures are generally only 10 to 15-degrees Fahrenheit, the addition of even a light breeze can make it dangerously cold on exposed skin.

About the Authors

Brad McQueen is an avid hiker and climber and is a partner in the Denver-based CPA firm, EKS&H, where he audits public and private companies in a variety of industries. Brad is also an adjunct professor at the University of Denver where he teaches auditing. He has climbed all of Colorado's 14,000-foot peaks along with other mountains in the United States and abroad. He is a member of the American Alpine Club and currently serves on the Boards of Directors of Volunteers for Outdoor Colorado, a leading statewide stewardship organization, and Colorado Fourteeners Initiative, an organization working to protect and preserve Colorado's highest peaks.

Melissa McQueen is a passionate educator and outdoors person. She has climbed 11 of Colorado's 14,000-foot peaks and 19,330-foot Mt. Kilimanjaro, in addition to attempts on Mt. Rainier and the Grand Teton. Her frostbite story was first told on Colorado Public Radio's *Here's What Happened* program and she was featured in Backpacker Magazine's 2012 *Survivor Edition*. She unofficially holds large numbers of "firsts" and "speed records" for two-toed people. She is a member of the American Alpine Club and volunteers each summer with Big City Mountaineers, taking groups of inner city high school girls on their first backpacking trips.

Brad and Melissa live in Denver, Colorado, with their two children.